Debating Childhoods

Debating Childhoods

Critical Perspectives on Early Childhood

Edited by

Joe Brown & Timothy Clark

1 Oliver's Yard
55 City Road
London EC1Y 1SP

2455 Teller Road
Thousand Oaks
California 91320

Unit No 323-333, Third Floor, F-Block
International Trade Tower, Nehru Place
New Delhi 110 019

8 Marina View Suite 43-053
Asia Square Tower 1
Singapore 018960

Editor: Delayna Spencer

Editorial assistant: Harry Dixon

Production editor: Victoria Nicholas

Marketing manager: Maria Omena

Cover design: Wendy Scott

Typeset by: Lumina Datamatics

Printed and bound by CPI Group (UK) Ltd, Croydon, CR0 4YY

Library of Congress Control Number: 2024953025

British Library Cataloguing in Publication data

A catalogue record for this book is available from the British Library

ISBN 978-1-5296-8306-6

ISBN 978-1-5296-8305-9 (pbk)

Contents

List of Figures and Tables

Figures

Tables

Author Biographies

Jane Andrews

Jane is a Professor of Education at UWE with a passion for children's early language development and multilingualism. Recent research has explored how creative arts approaches can be used to celebrate children's languages, cultures and identities. At UWE Jane works with undergraduates and doctoral students on shared areas of interest including emerging languages and identities, supporting children developing English as an Additional Language, and multilingualism and learning. Jane is co-lead for the Children, Childhood and Young People strand of UWE's Education and Childhood Research Group (ECRG).

Melissa Arrowsmith

Melissa is a senior lecturer on Early Childhood and Education programmes at UWE. She is also the programme leader for the PGCE pathway to EYTS. Prior to this role, Melissa was a qualified primary school teacher (with Early Years specialism) who spent nearly ten years leading practice in Early Years settings before taking on an advisory role with Bristol local authority. She achieved a Master's degree in educational leadership, development and policy at Bristol university and having started her EdD this year, Melissa hopes to further contribute to early childhood research.

Joe Brown

Joe is the programme leader of the BA (Hons) Early Childhood programme at UWE Bristol. He has worked in the early childhood field for over 25 years, including 20 years teaching and leading a variety of higher education programmes in early childhood and playwork. Throughout this time, he has been motivated by the belief that children are confident and agentic social actors who can play an important role in their communities, as long as there are adults who are willing to advocate for them. Joe's professional interests include the impact of neoliberal policies on young children's lived experiences; personal interests include a perennial fascination with Neolithic standing stones.

Helen Butcher

Having jointly developed the BA (Hons) Early Childhood degree at UWE, Helen was its first programme leader. She spent 20 years as a senior lecturer in the Early Childhood Team in which time she worked with undergraduate and postgraduate students focusing particularly on Early Years policy and researching young children. Prior to joining UWE she spent 15 years working with young children in schools in London and Yorkshire. Her doctoral thesis examined Early Years leaders committed to the implementation of the UNCRC. Limits and threats to young children's rights to express themselves freely continue to concern her.

Timothy Clark

Timothy is the Director of Research and Enterprise for the School of Education and Childhood at UWE Bristol. Prior to moving into academia he gained 20 years' experience of working in early childhood settings, including 12 years leading and managing early education provision for a community organisation in Bristol. He has taught on the BA (Hons) Early Childhood at UWE for 5 years and conducted research into the experiences of early childhood graduates. He is a member of the Early Childhood Studies Degree Network (ECSDN) Research Strategy Group, and co-lead for the Children, Childhood and Young People strand of UWE's Education and Childhood Research Group (ECRG).

Katrina Diamond

Katrina is a senior lecturer at UWE on the Early Childhood and Education Degree programmes, teaching across a wide range of undergraduate modules. Prior to UWE, over the past 20 years as an educator, Katrina has worked in a variety of settings from post-16 and adult to secondary education and worked as a Head of School for Education and Training in a large Further Education college in the southwest of England. More recently her work has involved working with younger children and teaching assistants. Her research involves working with children living in challenging circumstances and with additional educational needs, using mindfulness and guided visualisation interventions to support children's self-regulation and school integration.

Sarah Gillie

Sarah is a senior lecturer on the BA (Hons) Early Childhood programme at UWE Bristol. After training in Early Years, she taught across primary key stages before specialising in learning support, working with and learning from children and families as well as early childhood professionals. Since 2016, she has lectured on undergraduate and postgraduate courses focused on early childhood and/or inclusive education. Sarah's research interests relate to inclusion in education across and beyond 'compulsory' schooling. She is a co-convenor for the British Educational Research Association (BERA) Special Interest Group for Alternative Education.

Kate Irvine

Kate is an Early Years Improvement Officer for Bristol City Council with over 25 years of experience in schools, inclusion, daycare, children's centres and local government. She is a qualified teacher and also has a MA in Early Years Educational Practice. With a responsibility for quality improvement across the Early Years sector in Bristol, Kate also leads on EYFS transition and assessment and has led on various government-funded and independent research programmes across the city. Kate has a strong interest in national Early Years policy development, and the role of systems leadership models to support educators with implementation through child development-informed and ethical pedagogies.

Eleri John

Eleri is a senior lecturer on the BA(Hons) Early Childhood programme and leads the PGCE International Early Years programme at UWE Bristol. After training as a primary school teacher, Eleri taught across the primary phase for several years with a focus on Early Years. Following her completion of her Master's in education, Eleri moved into higher education lecturing and has been teaching across a range of undergraduate and professional postgraduate programmes since 2016. Eleri is currently completing her EdD and her research interests include child agency, child voice, inclusion and children's emerging identities.

Rebecca Kingsley-Jones

Rebecca is an associate director in Education and Early Childhood at UWE Bristol. Having trained as a Primary School teacher she taught in the UK and Asia before managing her own 'Outstanding' Early Years setting. She worked for the LA as a SEN support across a range of Early Years provision and was one of the first EYPS trainer/assessors. For the last 15 years Rebecca has been teaching in HE across a range of Education programmes, including international delivery, with a particular focus on developing positive relationships and respecting the voice of the child.

Zoe Lewis

Zoe worked as a qualified Early Years teacher and leader before taking up her current post as a Senior Lecturer in Early Years at Birmingham City University. She also worked as a volunteer leader, trainer and outdoor activities adviser with Girlguiding UK for over 25 years. Zoe's doctoral research explored the relational nature of creativity in early childhood education. Her current research interests are mainly in the field of early childhood education with a focus on national policy, children's play and outdoor learning, and creativity as a characteristic of effective learning within the Early Years curriculum.

Alex Morfaki

Alexandra works as a senior lecturer in Early Years at Norland College. She initially trained as a Reception class teacher and worked in a range of Early Years settings in the capacity of teacher and manager prior to completing her Doctorate. Alexandra's research interests lie in inclusion in the Early Years for children with Special Educational Needs and Disabilities. Her doctoral thesis focused on Early Years educators' interpretation of inclusion in practice and explored interprofessional partnerships for inclusion and their influence on the formation of the role and identities of Early Years educators.

Jackie Musgrave

Jackie is part of the senior management team in the School of Education, Childhood, Youth and Sport; and a member of the Early Childhood at The Open University team. She was previously a Registered Sick Children's Nurse, moving into teaching NNEB students in Further Education. Jackie has taught Higher Education since 2003. Her research explores health in early childhood.

Joanne Munyard

Joanne is a senior lecturer in Education and Early Childhood at UWE. She has 25 years' experience working within education, including teaching within Early Years, Primary, Further Education and Higher Education. Her career began as a Primary Teacher of 10 years before she moved into Early Years teaching and lecturing. Her areas of expertise include leadership, professional identity and educational policy and she has a strong interest in the impact that Early Childhood graduates make to the educational experiences of children. Joanne is currently a Doctoral Student and her research 'Who am I? A Constructivist Grounded Theory exploration of the professional identity development of graduates within the Early Years workforce in England' explores these areas of interest.

Rhiannon Packer

Rhiannon is senior lecturer in Additional Learning Needs (ALN), programme director for the National MA (Wales) and ALN pathway lead at Cardiff Metropolitan University. She has taught on BA (Hons) Early Years programmes with a focus on inclusion and early childhood literacy. Rhiannon became interested in supporting children and young people with ALN while working as a Welsh second language teacher at a secondary school and she later undertook a PGDip in SEN specialising in Specific Learning Difficulties. Rhiannon's research interests include exploring the educational transition experiences of learners across a range of settings, supporting learners with ALN and bilingualism.

Vina Patel

Vina Patel has worked in early childhood for over 30 years. She has been a senior lecturer at Birmingham City University for 10 years. Vina led and area-managed provision for a large nursery chain. She then developed and led Early Years services, including a neighbourhood nursery, and Early Years outreach projects for a Sure Start local programme. Vina worked in a ward with high levels of child poverty. She is currently the UK Course Leader for DipHE in Preschool Education (Dual Award) in Guangdong, China. Vina has research interests in the early childhood workforce and is currently studying her PhD.

Jeanette Simson

Jeanette is a senior lecturer at UWE, working on the Early Childhood degree, the international Early Years PGCE and SHAPE partnership in Hong Kong. Prior to UWE, Jeanette worked in Early Years and primary practice and leadership, both in the UK and internationally. She holds a Master's degree in education, politics and society and is currently studying with the Froebel Trust. Jeanette's professional interests include the causes and effects of marginalisation on children and their families and in how a pedagogy of play can meet children's participatory rights throughout early childhood.

Sally Spruce

Sally is a senior lecturer at UWE and currently works on the BA (Hons) Early Childhood and Education degree programmes. She is the programme leader for the foundation year which feeds into both programmes. Before joining UWE in 2009, Sally worked for nearly 15 years as a primary school teacher within the Bristol area. During this time, she was an Early Years specialist and worked extensively with children with a wide range of learning needs including hearing impairment and autism. She also focused on developing outdoor learning provision within the Early Years Foundation Stage. Sally's professional interests include inclusive practice (Early Years and beyond) and the value of outdoor learning.

Acknowledgements

We would like to thank the students and staff from the Early Childhood programme at University of the West of England, Bristol for being invaluable sources of support and for inspiring the focus for this book through many animated discussions both in seminars and around the lunch table.

In particular we would like to thank the following students and staff who provided such useful feedback in the form of chapter reviews:

Nicola Bowden-Clissold
Sarah Chicken
Jessica Clinton
Tamsin Harcourt
Ella Mason
Emma Turner
Holly Vogt

Finally, we would like to thank Sage Publications, in particular Delayna Spencer and Harry Dixon, for acknowledging the value of this collection and providing support throughout the writing process. We hope to have the opportunity to work with you again in the future.

Chapter 1

Constructions of Childhood

Joe Brown and Timothy Clark

Debating Childhoods

Understandings of childhood in the 21st century are typically dominated by powerful adult voices including politicians, policy-makers and the media, who frequently frame children as under-developed, passive and in need of adult intervention (e.g. Ofsted, 2024). This creates a discourse within which some children as young as five can be labelled as failures. This discourse is significant, because it has the potential to influence the behaviours and actions of adults, including early childhood practitioners and graduates, who are, or will be, responsible for scholarship, policy and practice which directly influences the lives and experiences of young children. In response to this context, this book aims to illustrate, and critique, a range of competing perspectives, to offer its readers a critical and, potentially, provocative exploration of a collection of key contemporary debates relating to early childhood in the UK.

The concept for this book arises from long standing discussions, frustrations and aspirations within our BA (Hons) Early Childhood team at the University of the West of England (UWE). Here, our programme identity centres on a key principle which is that it is vitally important that the academic subject area of Early Childhood continues to encompass a focus on supporting students to think critically about, and aspire to positively influence, childhood in its broadest sense. By this we mean that, in the context of an increasingly narrow political and economic focus on 'training' a workforce to support early childhood education and care (Haux et al., 2022), we need to be cautious not to lose focus on the value of Early Childhood graduates who are equipped and motivated to engage with a much wider lens on childhood, which may include sociological, political, economic, philosophical, psychological viewpoints. One succinct take on this, which is often quoted in our team discussions, is that adults' influence on childhood does not just exist in schools and Early Years settings, but has impact across society in its broadest sense – in shopping centres, hospitals, community centres, online spaces, advertising, etc. With this in mind, early childhood experts (including graduates and professionals) have a role in understanding, contributing to and advocating for initiatives and practices in society which aim to enhance children's rights, well-being and experiences. In addition, this broader early childhood studies curriculum also creates a rich, interesting and multi-disciplinary focus, which in our experience is highly valued by students.

To achieve the aims for this book, we began by issuing a series of provocations, relating to ten key debates with the potential to shape childhood in contemporary society, to a group of early childhood experts. The authors are predominantly early childhood lecturers, many of whom are part of the team at UWE, but also include colleagues from other UK universities and several authors with current or recent involvement in local authority or early childhood settings. The authors' objective was to engage critically with the provocation, seeking to illuminate and respond to different viewpoints and consider the factors influencing these. In doing so, we hope that these chapters will provide a provocation to students and practitioners to enable deeper reflection about the key issues. Central to this, the book seeks to emphasise the importance of children's voices and advocates for a more inclusive and compassionate approach. By continually questioning prevailing assumptions, we hope it will support and scaffold readers' critical practice and writing.

As you navigate the chapters, you will note that one key aspect of their structure which aims to support this scaffolding is the inclusion of a set of consistent pedagogical features across the collection. These include reflective questions, which aim to encourage you to pause and reflect on key issues and viewpoints; case studies, which aim to illustrate and provide concrete examples in relation to the debates; and annotated reading which provides a list of useful sources at the end of each chapter, to encourage you to continue your research and thinking in relation to the specific topic. We hope that these features will support you to engage deeply, critically and proactively with the debates which are explored.

Constructions of Childhood

Central to the focus of this book is the notion of 'constructions of childhood' and how we individually and collectively shape our conceptions of childhood, including how we might define it, and what constitutes a 'good' childhood for children. Underpinning this is an understanding that childhood is not a fixed, naturally occurring phenomena, but instead a socially and culturally constructed concept, which is constantly evolving as it comes into contact with a complex set of inter-related factors (Blundell, 2011). These factors may include our own memories of childhood, the views of others we interact with, the legal, social and political frameworks we experience, and collective cultural practices. As a result, views about childhood are hugely varied, not only globally, but across and within communities. Indeed, even the most widely agreed notions of childhood such as the legal position – which defines children as anyone between the ages of birth to 18 – can be seen as a construction, something the social world has invented, albeit one which has been widely adopted.

Within this framing, it is easy to see how attitudes towards childhood are widely contested and debated, with no universal agreement about how to best support children to claim their childhoods, and certainly no single model of how children experience it. Our individual and collective views about childhood are therefore derived from the range of different lenses we use to view it – be they political, cultural, professional or personal. These lenses interact to build a personalised world view; our positionality, which itself is not fixed as it is mediated by external influences such as the media, governments and our own life experiences. However, we should be cautious about viewing our own positionality as an entirely rational response to the things we see and hear; in reality, particular constructions of childhood wield more influence than others, especially if they are created by powerful and dominant voices (Moss, 2018).

The Role of Power in Shaping Constructions of Childhood

As outlined at the start of this chapter, adult agendas can play a significant role in shaping early childhood experiences, and adults often wield considerable power over children. This is particularly true for political power which creates the social policy for and about children in fields such as education and health. Foucault refers to 'disciplinary power' which, he argues, utilises policy and surveillance as controlling 'technologies' in order to compel individuals to conform with societal norms (Foucault, 2020). This normalising process creates powerful, dominant discourses which construct particular views of childhood which can be difficult to challenge; not only are they presented as the 'common sense' majority view, but they are amplified by other powerful voices such as the media and government regulators. Moss (2018) cautions that these narratives, or 'stories', create such a powerful reality that it is easy to forget they are just stories, rather than a fundamental truth which cannot be questioned. These dominant discourses often frame the debates around children, not only in terms of the services we provide for them, but how they are positioned in society and the qualities and agency we ascribe to them. In practice, these discourses are created through the interaction of a number of influences and positions. Figure 1.1 proposes one way of examining how these narratives are created, amplified and maintained.

Figure 1.1 • Layers of Discourse

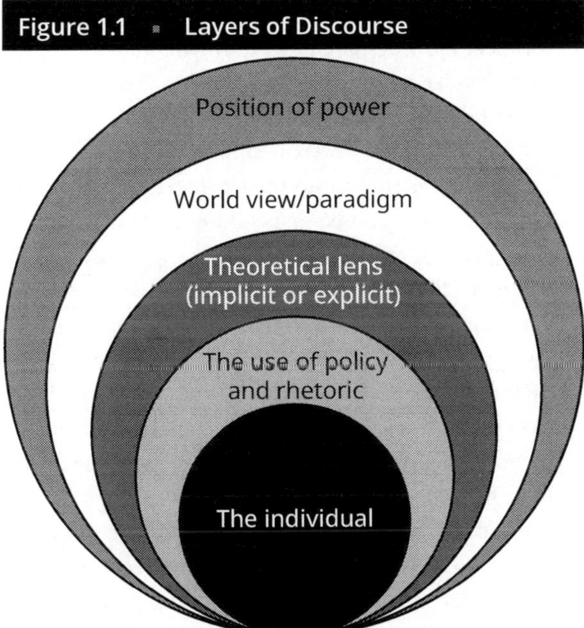

The layers shown in Figure 1.1 include:

- Position of power: dominant discourses are usually created, or amplified, by powerful actors, for example, politicians.
- World view/paradigm: these views are shaped by particular ways of understanding the world and how it operates, for example, neoliberalist perspectives.
- Theoretical lens: this underpins how particular groups should be viewed, and shapes the services which should be provided for them, for example, the constructivist learning theories of Piaget which often inform English education policy for young children.
- The use of policy and rhetoric: dominant views are amplified and 'sold' to society through social policy, the media, and more recently the internet.

The challenge, therefore, for anyone interested in childhood, is how to unpick these different layers to reveal the positions and perspectives and their impact on dominant constructions of childhood. It is this critical reflexivity which can illuminate the agendas at play and support the ongoing development, and perhaps revision, of our own positions and assumptions.

The 'New' Sociology of Childhood

Just as discourses about childhood are culturally, politically and socially mediated, they are also products of a specific time and place. Whilst this book does not focus on historical perspectives, but instead attempts to illuminate aspects of childhood as it is experienced now, it is nonetheless useful to reflect on changing constructions as a way of unpacking where we are today. Corsaro (2017) argues that until about 30 years ago children were all but ignored within the sociological field due to their marginalisation within societies. Theoretical framings of childhood therefore tended to focus on two key positions. Firstly, the deterministic model, where children were seen as passive empty vessels who required training to become competent and contributing members of society. These ideas can be seen in the behaviourist theories of Skinner and others, whereby children were socialised through a series of punishments and rewards with little thought given to their contexts or agency. Secondly, constructivist theories such as the work of Piaget who proposed that children's cognitive development passes through sequential stages as the child matures. Whilst constructivist ideas, and in particular the social constructivist position of Vygotsky, ascribe more agency to the child based on an understanding that they can shape their own development through interactions, the focus remains on the unilateral development of the individual. Furthermore, both these positions are limited by their focus on developmentalism; a view of the child as an incomplete adult and therefore only of interest in terms of what they are to become (Jenks, 2005).

In response to these perceived theoretical limitations, sociologists began searching for new ways of conceptualising childhood in the 1980s. The 'new' sociology of childhood proposes a view of children as competent social actors who are able to shape the societies and communities they belong to, if they are supported to do so (Matthews, 2007). Within this framing, children are not just socialised and encultured by the adults who care for them, but are able to actively construct their world and their place in it, making new meanings as they do so. Importantly, it also positions children as much more than simply the subjects of education systems, but as significant members of, and contributors to, wider society. It is this position which underpins this book. However, a word of caution – as you will read in subsequent chapters, traditional theoretical positions continue to have influence, particularly with powerful actors such as politicians and policy-makers, and adult agendas still exert considerable power over children. Furthermore, we are not suggesting other theoretical positions have nothing to commend them, but perhaps should be examined further in the light of other ideas.

A Note on Positionality

As previously highlighted, positionality is crucial in supporting us to make sense of the wide range of constructions and discourses which exist around childhood, and to support critical engagement with our own attitudes and beliefs. However, unpacking why we, and others, think the way we do is not easy, as we are all influenced by a wide range of social, cultural and historical factors. In its broadest sense, positionality can be seen as our own personal world view; how and why we think the world operates in the way it does, and what this means for our lives (Patton and Winter, 2023). Clearly this world view influences the attitudes we hold about any given topic, for example, children and childhood, and in turn, affects the information we engage with and the actions we take, in both personal and professional contexts.

We suggest this book has a clear positionality, typically centred around socio-cultural and 'new' sociology of childhood perspectives; however, we are not asking you to agree with the positions taken, just that you adopt a critical approach and be open to questioning the dominant discourses about children and childhood, just as the chapter authors have done. We have called this book *Debating Childhoods* because we hope the chapters provoke debate and discussion as a way of critically appraising the world which has been created for children in an honest and reflexive way. This mindset is particularly crucial for us to explore and create what Moss (2018) calls 'alternative narratives' which challenge the powerful and prevailing views about childhood; not only are these ideas crucial for a healthy democracy, they provide new ways for thinking about how to engage and support children to have a greater say in shaping their own lives.

Bronfenbrenner and the Bioecological Model

If we accept the position outlined by the new sociology of childhood that children are capable and confident social actors, then it is clear that the social and cultural context of the child is fundamental to the childhood each child experiences. As such, this book is strongly influenced by the work of Bronfenbrenner (1979), who views all humans as culture-creators, through interaction with a complex set of social and political systems. Initially, Bronfenbrenner suggested that human development is heavily impacted by the variability of the contexts and environments we experience; however he later adapted his work to also recognise the impact the individual themselves can have on these environments. This is significant, as it suggests that humans (including children) can influence their worlds at the same time as being shaped by them. This bi-directional aspect of Bronfenbrenner's model makes it especially pertinent if we accept the construction of children as agentic social beings as it suggests that they can affect change across all their environments, even if that change may initially feel quite insignificant. This is particularly important to recognise for young children who are able to impact their own lives but are often vulnerable and marginalised in the face of adult power. Bronfenbrenner's ecological model (as shown in Figure 1.2) consists of six systems:

- *Chronosystem* – changes over time which impact the child and their childhood
- *Macrosystem* – cultural values and societal norms related to childhood, e.g., laws and policy
- *Exosystem* – the indirect environment, e.g., wider community, parental employment
- *Mesosystem* – connections between systems on the child's behalf
- *Microsystem* – proximal processes, e.g., family and friends
- *The individual* – the child and their changing contexts over time

Figure 1.2 ▪ Bronfenbrenner's Ecological Systems Model

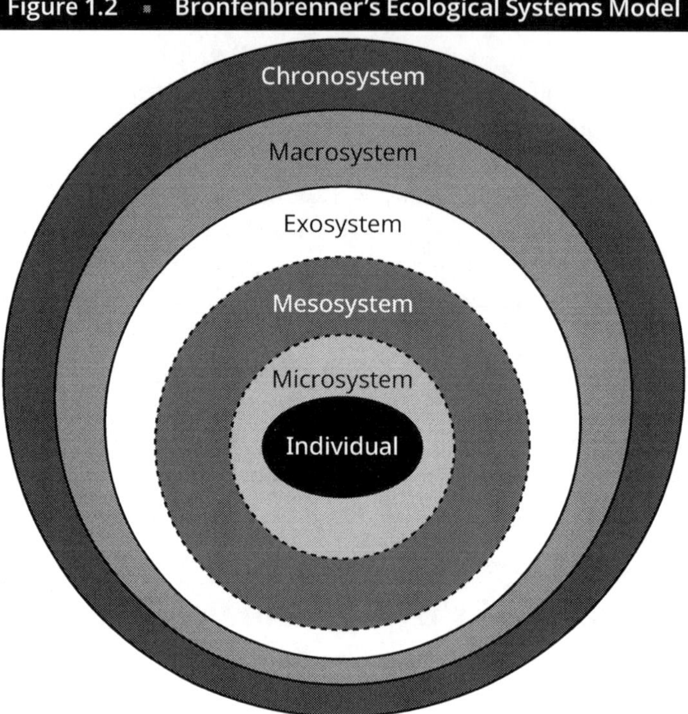

As the Figure 1.2 shows, Bronfenbrenner believed that an inter-related set of systems, all of which hold their own set of norms, rules and values, shape human development through our interactions with them. For example, within the macrosystem, the laws and policies which govern the education systems in specific countries clearly have a significant impact on children's experience of them, therefore it is easy to see how they may be shaped by these norms. However, key to Bronfenbrenner's ideas is how the different systems interact, meaning that children's experiences, and their reactions to them, will differ for each individual child. To illustrate this, we can draw on a widely discussed issue within early childhood – that of a child's access to outdoor play opportunities. Professionals and academics in the field have been expressing concerns about an apparent decline of children playing outdoors for some time, and suggesting various reasons for this (Louv, 2010). However, whilst the overall picture may point to children playing outdoors less often, Bronfenbrenner's model can illuminate how varied outdoor play experiences may be for individual children.

- Chronosystem – how has children's play changed over time? What are the drivers for these changes (e.g., safety fears or technology)? Have societal attitudes to play also changed?
- Macrosystem – which laws, policies and societal attitudes impact on children's outdoor play? For example, is access to outdoor play limited due to the time children now spend in settings, schools and out of school provision?
- Exosystem – how might the child's wider community affect their experiences of outdoor play? Does their community have safe spaces to play outdoors? Is there lots of traffic or anti-social behaviour?

- Mesosystem – What are the links between the child's family and the other systems which may support (or limit) outdoor play? For example, how might the family engage with the local community to provide outdoor play opportunities?
- Microsystem – how might the child's immediate environment support (or hamper) their opportunities for outdoor play? For example, do they have a garden? Does the child have any friends nearby to play with? Does the child's family support opportunities to access outdoor play?

This example has hopefully served to illustrate Bronfenbrenner's model and how complex and intertwined different aspects of children's lives are, and how dependent they are on social and cultural contexts. In particular, we would like to stress the crucial role played by the microsystem in the development of young children. As children in their earliest years typically spend much of their time with family, friends and their immediate community, these proximal processes not only form the site of most early interactions, they arguably exist in the space where the child has the most agency and ability to shape their own world, and the lives of those around them (Merçon-Vargas et al., 2020).

Overview of Chapters

The chapter order in this book was broadly informed by Bronfenbrenner's ideas which have been outlined above, the idea being that the text begins by engaging with issues relating more closely to broader macrosystems (e.g. politics, economy) and increasingly progresses to consider their impact within the microsystem (education, the unique child). As highlighted, inevitably these systems are part of a complex entanglement and can be difficult to separate; however the rationale for this approach was that an understanding of broader topics raised in the earlier chapters (e.g., neoliberalism in Chapter 2) will support reading of later chapters (e.g., commercialisation of childhood in Chapter 6).

In Chapter 2 – 'The Neoliberal Child: Current Consumers, Future Workers' – Joe Brown and Alex Morfaki confront neoliberal ideology, exploring how it shapes the lived experiences of young children in the 21st century. Focusing on the central tenets of neoliberalism – competition, choice and primacy of the market – the authors critically explore how neoliberalism has transformed pedagogy, giving prominence to notions of 'school readiness' and created a system of winners and losers within a dominant discourse of developmentalism.

Chapter 3 – 'The Successful Child: Forms of Capital and Childhood' – develops this focus. Here Jeanette Simson considers the concept of the successful child and how and where this is defined in society. Drawing on Bourdieu's (1986) concept of cultural capital, the chapter considers how this idea is embodied in current educational policy and aims to challenge the dominant idea that our education system offers everyone a 'fair' chance of success. To extend and illustrate this, placing focus on notions of social justice, consideration is given to the experiences of marginalised children, including examples of social exclusion and restricted rights.

Chapter 4 – 'Children as Rights Holders: Rhetoric or Reality?' – progresses the discussion to provoke reflection on the notion of children as rights holders and the alignment between what is agreed and what is experienced. In this chapter Helen Butcher and Jane Andrews introduce the United Convention on the Rights of the Child (UNCRC), focusing on Article 19 (protection from violence) and Article 30 (the right to learn and use the language, customs and religion of their family) to question the extent to which these are upheld with contemporary society in the UK.

Chapter 5 responds to the question 'Policy: For children or about children?' to re-evaluate the sociological tensions which exist in the development of early childhood policy. To do so, Eleri John and Joanne Munyard outline thinking relating to the development and construction of policy in early childhood, before using the work of Stephen Ball and other key thinkers to question the impact of shifting societal landscapes and constructions of childhood on key policies which affect the lives of young children. Returning to the earlier focus on the dominance of economic drivers, they question the disconnect between advancements in academic discussion about children's participatory rights and the absence of child's voice within political decision-making.

Chapter 6 then encourages readers to consider 'The Commercialisation of Childhood', analysing the extent to which children should be seen as vulnerable to corporate predation or empowered to make economic decisions. Katrina Diamond and Melissa Arrowsmith explore the role of parents and illustrate key considerations relating to technology, media and sexualisation, to highlight the complex ethical dilemmas associated with commercialisation and childhood in a contemporary, neoliberal society.

Chapter 7 shifts the focus to 'Children's Health and Well-being', outlining the significance of early childhood experiences on children's experiences throughout their lives. In this chapter Jackie Musgrave returns to Bronfenbrenner's ecological systems theory to frame some of the factors within society which influence children's health, addressing the diversity of socio-cultural and economic factors which may be significant. This chapter aims to highlight the role that all adults play in improving children's health.

Chapter 8 introduces a focus on children's play experiences to explore the question: 'Play: Investment or Pleasure?'. In this chapter Zoe Lewis and Vina Patel provide a historical view of children's play, tracing a shift from relative freedom in the early 20th century to increasing restriction and commodification. Using Foucault's ideas relating to power relations, the chapter engages with a debate regarding whether play is predominantly framed as a pleasurable activity for children themselves, or a developmental activity which acts as an investment for society.

With the focus increasingly shifting to practice and the role of adults within the 'micro' system, Chapter 9 takes a closer look at the role of assessment and measurement in children's lives. Framed by the title 'Measuring Childhood: The Good, the Bad and the Ugly', Kate Irvine navigates varying viewpoints on the impact of the increasing expectations in relation to the assessment of children, tracing its potential value and importance (the good), alongside the proliferation of a measurement culture across early childhood (the bad) and the dangers of its role in reproducing social inequalities and reinforcing discrimination (the ugly).

Sarah Gillie, Rhiannon Packer and Sally Spruce extend some of these themes into Chapter 10, where they address the topic of 'The Unique Child' through consideration of how inclusion may be reflected in policy and practice. This includes explorations of notions of inclusion versus integration, and equality versus equity. They aim to challenge deficit models of understanding, contemplating the potential of reflective practice and funds of knowledge in valuing and celebrating diversity.

The book concludes with the aim of critically exploring the role of the adult in relation to the issues and debates addressed throughout, aiming to provoke consideration regarding what all this might mean for adults who work with, and for, children. In Chapter 11 – 'Taking Childhood Seriously: Listening, Agency and Advocacy' – Timothy Clark and Rebecca Kingsley-Jones draw on John Wall's notion of 'Childism' to frame discussion about the significance of acts of genuine listening, the promotion of agency and the role of adults in advocating for young children. The chapter concludes with a series of reflective questions to support consideration of practice.

In illustrating, challenging and questioning dominant narratives which frame understandings of childhood in society, and through highlighting alternative narratives and opportunities for reflection, we hope that this book will act as a meaningful provocation for its readers. The topics addressed are complex and varied, and rarely lend themselves to one simple 'answer'; however what this book will argue, with conviction, is that adults with a critical understanding of key issues affecting young children's lives, and the ability to unpick and challenge dominant narratives, have a vitally important role in influencing and co-creating a fair and positive society for all children.

References

Blundell, D. (2011) *Education and Constructions of Childhood*. London: Continuum International Publishing Group.

Bourdieu, P. (1986) 'The forms of capital', in J. Richardson (eds), *Handbook of Theory and Research for the Sociology of Education* (pp. 241–258). New York: Greenwood.

Bronfenbrenner, U. (1979) *The Ecology of Human Development: Experiments by Nature and Design*. Cambridge, MA: Harvard University Press.

Corsaro, W. A. (2017) *The Sociology of Childhood*, 5th edn (international student edn). London: SAGE Publications.

Foucault, M. (2020) *Power: Essential Works 1954–84*. London: Penguin Random House.

Haux, T., Butt, S., Rezaian, M., Garwood, E., Woodbridge, H., Bhatti, S. and Woods, R. (2022) *The Early Years Workforce: Recruitment, Retention, and Business Planning*. London: Department for Education.

Jenks, C. (2005) *Childhood*, 2nd edn. London: Routledge.

Louv, R. (2010) *Last Child in the Woods: Saving our Children from Nature-Deficit Disorder*. London: Atlantic Books Ltd.

Matthews, S. H. (2007) 'A window on the 'new' sociology of childhood', *Sociology Compass*, 1 (1), 322–34.

Merçon-Vargas, E. A., Lima, R. F. F., Rosa, E. M. and Tudge, J. (2020) 'Processing proximal processes: What Bronfenbrenner meant, what he didn't mean, and what he should have meant', *Journal of Family Theory & Review*, 12 (3), 321–34. https://doi.org/10.1111/jftr.12373

Moss, P. (2018) *Alternative Narratives in Early Childhood: An Introduction for Students and Practitioners*. London: Routledge.

Ofsted (2024) *Early Years Inspection Handbook for Ofsted Registered Provision*. London: Crown Copyright.

Patton, K. and Winter, K. (2023) 'Researcher positionality in eliciting young children's perspectives', *Journal of Early Childhood Research*, 21 (3), 303–13.

Chapter 2

The Neoliberal Child: Current Consumers, Future Workers

Joe Brown and Alex Morfaki

Introduction

This chapter explores how neoliberal ideology has transformed the lives of young children and their families, reconceptualising what early childhood education and care (ECEC) is for, how it is practised and the role of the child within it. Firstly, neoliberalism will be defined, drawing on historical perspectives to uncover the key principles which underpin it. An analysis will be made of how neoliberalism has shaped education in England, exploring how successive governments have created a disparate childcare market which is designed to develop economically active citizens to service the needs of global capitalism. This in turn has created a dominant discourse which views children as passive knowledge-receivers who need to be moulded through instructional teaching to compete in the global marketplace. To illustrate this, we draw on the story of school readiness and how powerful state actors have utilised policy technologies to place this agenda at the heart of early childhood practice, reshaping the core purpose of settings and transforming pedagogy to suit neoliberal aims. Finally, the chapter concludes with some examples of how professionals can resist and challenge the neoliberal orthodoxy, developing alternate forms of practice and developing spaces to organise and debate.

Defining Neoliberalism

On the surface, neoliberalism is an economic and political philosophy, primarily concerned with the advancement of free market capitalism; a system whereby goods and services are traded with minimal government regulation. It has become such a powerful global force that it effects all aspects of our lives, shaping our behaviours, social relationships and even the way we think. Indeed, Davies and Bansel (2007) suggest it has become so pervasive that it is increasingly viewed as the only viable option for how the world can successfully operate. Despite this hegemony, it is a challenging concept to fully define, with a variety of contested ideas about its true nature jostling for position with those who deny it is even a coherent 'thing' at all, but instead an invention concocted by opponents of global capitalism (Mirowski, 2014). More recently, academics have begun to search for alternatives to the neoliberal term, arguing that it is too general an idea to adequately describe the different economic, social and political experiences found globally (Rowe et al., 2019). However, we would argue that neoliberalism's scale and reach is a key reason as to why it can be difficult to characterise; Monbiot (2017) argues it has become so central to public discourse that it operates almost invisibly as it adapts to diverse political and social contexts around the world. Within this framing, neoliberalism can be seen as an ideology which people experience differently, dependent on their cultural, economic and geographical contexts, albeit an ideology with common principles and aims irrespective of where it is found.

Whilst the ideas which underpin neoliberalism are certainly not new, the modern movement began to gather pace after a meeting of free market economists in 1947, called the Mont Pelerin Society (Mirowski, 2014). Sharing key aspirations, including the advancement of free markets, the deregulation of the economy and a smaller role for the state, they bolstered their numbers with like-minded thinkers from university departments across the world, in particular the University of Chicago and the London School of Economics. Harvey (2005) highlights how this group quickly developed a global network, funded by rich families and big business, who extended their influence through the development of think tanks, many of whom, like the Institute of Economic Affairs in the UK, still exert a considerable influence on government policy today. United by a desire to reshape the role of government to focus on economic growth and wealth creation at the expense of public services, their ideas finally had the opportunity to be tested in 1973, when a military coup in Chile overthrew the elected government and the country's new rulers exploited this crisis to adopt neoliberal ideas, creating a new economic orthodoxy focused on privatisation and individualism (Maisuria, 2014). However, the development of neoliberalism as a truly global movement came with the election of Margaret Thatcher in the UK (1979) and Ronald Reagan in the US (1980). These two leaders aggressively pursued neoliberal policy reforms in their respective countries, deregulating financial markets, privatising public services and extolling the virtues of self-interest, whilst backed by powerful international organisations such as the World Bank and World Trade Organisation, who themselves had become dominated by neoliberal thinkers. From here it was easy to 'persuade' other, especially poorer, countries to adopt similar policies through the conditions attached to large loans which imposed neoliberal ideas, often without any form of democratic consent from their populations (Roberts-Holmes and Moss, 2021).

Neoliberalism then, believes that the world is best organised along business lines, with competition and individualism at its core. However, to create the dominant global discourse highlighted by Monbiot, it is about much more than economic reform. Roberts-Holmes and Moss (2021) argue it has a specific set of values and beliefs, based on what they call the three Cs: competition, choice and calculation. Within these values, all human activity is viewed through a commercial lens, applying market principles to policy, public services and even inter-personal relationships. Therefore, it is about embedding these values beyond the economic sphere, by reshaping all human activity to ensure the aims of neoliberalism are met. Foucault (2008) argues that this has been undertaken by creating a new political rationality, or truth, underpinned by the political technology of governance, leading to economic practices being applied to previously non-economic areas such as education. Chomsky believes that neoliberalism is fundamentally about power and wealth – transferring public assets to the richest 1% in order for them to maintain their influence (Orelus and Chomsky, 2014). Others maintain it is profoundly undemocratic, ensuring these huge changes have been undertaken without public consent, through a side-lining of collectivism and democratic organisations such as trade unions via anti-union legislation (Maisuria, 2014). We argue neoliberalism is about reshaping the world, not only by seizing control of the state to ensure it is designed to support corporate, rather than societal interests, but about reconceptualising how humans behave, moving from engaged citizens to become self-interested consumers; reshaping an interconnected, social and collaborative world into one which is competitive, cut-throat and increasingly unequal.

Neoliberalism and Education

As neoliberalism established new ways of thinking and acting it infiltrated other sectors and reconfigured the way governments control and manage the welfare, health and education systems; instilling enterprise and 'businessification' (Costas Batlle, 2019) at the heart of the agenda. Within the education system, childhood has been reframed as politicians, economists and policy-makers have come to believe that children have roles to play, initially as consumers in the educational marketplace (Howlett, 2018) and ultimately as workers in the labour market (DfE, 2013; OECD, 2017). These beliefs align with Human Capital Theory, which focuses on improving economic productivity by providing 'improved' educational outcomes. Through this lens, education is viewed as an investment, where, through careful and suitable instruction, a range of desirable skills can be fostered that will result in the child eventually transforming themselves into a productive and economically successful individual (homo economicus) (Giroux, 2005). Parents are also expected to play their part, by exercising their consumer choices wisely in selecting an appropriate early childhood setting or school that will secure their child's educational future, and through the provision of a suitable home learning environment, designating them as children's first educators who should promote learning by offering specific didactic opportunities (HM Government, 2018).

However, government surveillance (Foucault, 1991) imposed through regulation is not restricted to the home but extends to schools and wider society. As schools and settings will transform children into future workers, their achievement must be monitored and measured to ensure they produce auditable progress outputs (Bradbury, 2019b) which place them on a trajectory that will equip them with the necessary skills to secure successful labour as adults. Equally, children's performance in formative and summative assessments instils a notion of accountability which is founded on their willingness to cooperate and conform with a value-laden system which prioritises certain skills and dispositions above others (Bradbury, 2019a). This creates a specific positioning of the child and parent; one of self-responsibility, adaptability and proactivity in adopting the mind-frame and attitudes that are considered compatible with neoliberal regimes. Whilst neoliberalism differs across different countries' early education sectors, dependent on structural, funding and curricular specificities, the direction of travel is amplified by a number of global organisations and educational conglomerates, such as the World Health Organisation and the Organisation for Economic Co-operation and Development (OECD) (Roberts-Holmes and Moss, 2021) who issue policy guidelines centred on 'effective education and care'. These organisations conduct comparisons between countries to measure children's academic progress in relation to specific subjects. Although these organisations adopt child-centred discourses that, at face value, aim at tackling inequality, reducing disadvantage and promoting social mobility for parents and children (OECD, 2017), they inadvertently establish ubiquitous educational standards and practices that are seen as universal and fail to acknowledge the cultural nuances of respective countries and individuals (Delaune, 2019). In doing so, they arguably do not address existing gaps in attainment between countries and individuals but perpetuate inequalities between advantaged and disadvantaged populations.

Reflective Questions 2.1

Neoliberalism and Education

- Can you identify any practices in schools or settings which reflect the neoliberal aims for education outlined above?
- How might international comparisons of education systems shape government policy and regulatory frameworks?
- How might children's rights be affected by the positioning of education and the role of parents under neoliberal education policy?

Structural Inequalities in the English ECEC Sector

Successive governments in England have come to adopt and embrace the neoliberal principles of building children's human capital through investing in their attendance at 'high quality' Early Years settings which align primary and preschool levels. However, this is heavily reliant upon young children's attendance in settings that are staffed by suitably qualified practitioners and provide a delicate balance of child initiated play and educator led learning opportunities that emphasise numeracy, literacy and self-regulation (OECD, 2017). Despite this, policy-makers have incentivised free market conditions which has led to the exponential growth of the private Early Years sector. Consequently, despite attempts at merging education and childcare in England, the two remain disparate and are offered across a range of private, voluntary and independent (PVI) settings, and to a lesser extent by maintained schools. Securing a place and sufficient hours of attendance is proving tricky for some families within this complex and competitive system and the ability to purchase early education and care has thus become contingent on parental circumstances and buying power (Vincent et al., 2010).

Funding is provided through supply-side subsidies in the form of funded hours offered to providers and demand-side subsidies offered to parents through the benefits system. This has firmly established parents as consumers (Lloyd and Penn, 2012) who are asked to make educational choices which have profound implications for their child's learning and well-being. While the universal aspect of education entitlement (15 hours) can be accessed by all eligible children, the childcare element (additional 15 hours) is currently being reserved for working parents. Recent research suggests that the provision of the 30 'free childcare hours', in their current form, has excluded a significant percentage of disadvantaged parents and families from attending settings, thus deterring children who stand to benefit the most from accessing services (Pascal et al., 2021). The provision of the additional entitlement to working parents could equally result in a deficit view of parents who may be unemployed or do not fulfil the eligibility criteria. By bestowing childcare to parents (and children) who are seen as worthy of investment, the state inadvertently discredits parents who are viewed as unwilling to transform themselves into productive workers and consumers. The problematisation of poverty and disadvantage associated with the targeting of funding towards working parent populations has given rise to a new 'politics of parenting' (Simpson and Envy, 2015) under neoliberalism. These politics have constructed binary discourses of parents and parenting which have resulted in the 'pathologising' of children living in poverty and disadvantage. Some children and families have thus become the targets of intense government focus to address their perceived shortcomings.

While parents are active consumers within this system, children remain passive; the age at which a child is removed from the familial environment and placed in an ECEC setting and the number of hours they attend are determined by a combination of parental specificities and arbitrary government regulations which transform their personal and family lives. At the time of writing, the newly-elected Labour government has pledged to continue to expand the free hours to include younger children. Given that the benefits of attending a setting at this early stage are inconclusive (Pascal et al., 2021), placing young children in settings appears to prioritise parental contributions to the labour market over the well-being of children. While governments' attempts to promote social mobility, through parental participation in employment, is seen as a remedy that combats poverty and enhances children's outcomes, voices from within the sector are raising concerns regarding the current funding structure's capacity to enhance maternal employment (Brewer et al., 2022) and tackle inequality (Pascal et al., 2021). Reported gaps in attainment between the most and least disadvantaged children also appear to be widening, thus questioning the role of the current system in perpetuating entrenched educational inequalities.

Reshaping Identities: The Discourse of Readiness

Neoliberalist attempts at shaping the child as a current consumer and future worker necessitate the regulation of educational programmes through curricula that focus on core subjects – such as literacy and numeracy, which have historically been linked to enhanced academic outcomes and productivity within a competitive working environment (Roberts-Holmes and Moss, 2021). Regulation alone, however, is not sufficient in preparing children for the jobs market. The current emphasis on the management of self requires the child to 'responsibilise' (Trnka and Trundle, 2014) themselves by demonstrating accountability and willingness to transform. The enactment of duties and responsibilities as learners could be seen to remove the child from the complex web of interdependency and care relationships that should govern Early Years practice and formulates a learner identity which prepares them for their civic duties and responsibilities in capitalist societies. This in turn, creates powerful discourses about the core purposes and practices which underpin early childhood provision.

One such discourse is the story of school readiness. Whilst how to effectively support young children through their early educational transitions has concerned educators and policy-makers for some time, international policy has more recently reconceptualised these transitions as 'school readiness'. In England there is now a concerted focus on readiness for the transition from the play-based pedagogy of the Early Years Foundation Stage to the formal curriculum demands of Year One (Brooks and Murray, 2018). Despite this attention, definitions of school readiness are contested, and tensions are particularly evident between policy-makers, who foreground cognitive and curriculum-centred conceptions of readiness (Ofsted, 2017), and early childhood professionals, who typically value social and emotional readiness, including independence and engagement (Niklas et al., 2018). Despite the lack of agreement, it is clear that school readiness has become a powerful global discourse which is shaping the lives of young children from the start of their educational journeys. In England, school readiness has been embedded through political technologies in an increasingly tightly governed sector, with the message amplified through the use of reports from the education regulator Ofsted (2014, 2017) which attempt to frame the debate both in terms of conceptions of school readiness and how it is best practised. It is clear that the EYFS now positions school readiness as a core function of the curriculum:

> The EYFS sets the standards that all early years providers must meet to ensure that children learn and develop well and are kept healthy and safe. It promotes teaching and learning to ensure children's 'school readiness' and gives children the right foundation for good future progress through school and life. (DfE, 2024: 7)

This focus on school readiness has led to a number of changes to ECEC provision, largely driven by the expectations which arise from standardised assessments. Whilst the Early Learning Goals (ELGs) arguably remain broad, there is an expectation that settings will focus on the core academic skills of literacy and mathematics both as key indicators of children's readiness and as a measure of setting quality. This is chiefly characterised by the 'schoolification' of ECEC provision where children are experiencing both curriculum content and pedagogical practice which mirrors that which takes place in later schooling (Brooks and Murray, 2018). This push-down is not only developmentally inappropriate, it simplifies the transition to school to that of assessed performance, and has embedded a culture of 'datafication', where pedagogic decisions are led by developmental indicators rather than the individual needs of children (Bradbury, 2019b). The establishment of three statutory assessments – the Progress Check at Two, the Reception Baseline Assessment and the Early Years Foundation Stage Profile – sets the tone for other high-stakes assessments that follow. Children's individuality and capacity to learn at their own pace is shunned in favour of approaches that focus on the children mastering developmental milestones (Bradbury, 2019b). Inevitably, this focus on data has led to a narrowing of the curriculum, with educators privileging aspects of the curriculum which are measurable, side-lining children's interests and their rich funds of knowledge. Pedagogy has also been transformed by the readiness agenda, where teacher-led instruction is viewed as the best way to 'teach' the skills and knowledge required to be ready; the formal teaching of phonics is now widespread in settings, and adult-led pedagogy is increasingly being positioned in policy documents as the optimum way to achieve readiness. The latest iteration of the EYFS (DfE, 2024) now uses the term 'teacher' throughout the framework, with the overarching principles not mentioning play once, and in *Teaching and Play in the Early Years*, Ofsted (2015) go so far as to argue that teaching and play are not to be seen as separate endeavours at all. As further explored in Chapter 8, this reframing not only leads to a slide-lining of playful pedagogies, but to an instrumentalisation of play; its use restricted to when it is deemed useful in supporting the development of the 'correct' forms of knowledge.

This discourse of readiness can be seen as fundamental to the neoliberal repackaging of education from a social good to an economic one, and has profound implications for the experiences and identities of children in ECEC settings. Despite the principle of the unique child continuing to appear in the EYFS (DfE, 2024), the normalising and standardising gaze of readiness has fatally undermined this in practice; socio-cultural constructions of children as confident meaning-makers have been relegated by a system which expects all children to reach pre-determined goals, irrespective of their personal histories and cultural knowledge. The psychosocial approach to children's development which borrows from Piagetian and developmentalist maturation theories is mirrored in the EYFS. This conceptualises children as autonomous knowledge-receivers who progress through sequential levels and reproduce simplistic and normative criteria for progress that are heavily based on chronological notions of development. It also reflects the neoliberal conceptions of individualism and self-interest in so far that it internalises readiness, making academic success (or failure) the responsibility of individual children and their families. This in turn exacerbates inequality; Podesta (2014) argues that it remains the middle class who have both the practices and resources to successfully support their children to be ready, with state-conceptions of readiness ignoring structural disadvantage and entrenching social reproduction. Readiness therefore positions children as incomplete, both in what they know, and are able to do; the construction of the child as a human becoming, ready (or not) to be filled with the 'right' forms of knowledge. Within this framing, children's agency and rights are relegated as readiness becomes a set of actions imposed on them without children having any say in how readiness is conceptualised or practised. But readiness also positions children as an investment, a view of the child as human capital who will support the state in gaining economic advantage in a competitive and globalised world. This is sold to children and adults as individualised success – developing the ability to become aspirational and entrepreneurial, to lead a fulfilling life. In reality, it is driven by governments and corporations co-opting education to ensure a steady supply of future labour to drive capitalist economies (Close, 2014).

Case Study 2.1

Creating and Amplifying Discourse: The Story of Bold Beginnings

As Foucault (2008) suggests, powerful actors such as governments and regulatory bodies create and amplify dominant discourses through the use of controlling technologies such as policy and official guidance to establish what Ng (2008) refers to as a 'hegemonic common sense', presenting opinion as objective fact which then becomes difficult to challenge. *Bold Beginnings: The Reception Curriculum in a Sample of Good and Outstanding Primary Schools* (Ofsted, 2017) is a review of what Ofsted term 'successful primary schools', specifically their Reception class provision, and how it readies children for later schooling. Ofsted visited 41 schools across England, spoke with staff and children, and observed taught sessions. Recommendations include making reading and phonics the 'core purpose' of Reception Year, further aligning the Early Learning Goals with Key Stage 1, and assigning time each day to the 'direct teaching' of mathematics.

Ofsted utilises a number of linguistic and rhetorical devices throughout the report in an attempt to embed and amplify the dominant narrative of school readiness.

- The use of emotive and rhetorical language to highlight the perceived problem and demand action: 'A good early education is the foundation for later success. For too many children, however, their Reception Year is a missed opportunity that can leave them exposed to all the painful and unnecessary consequences of falling behind their peers' (p. 4).
- The use of metaphor to position education as part of a global race in which schools and children must compete: 'false start' (p. 9), 'forging ahead' (p. 9), 'equipped to meet the challenges' (p. 4).
- Amplifying the voices of success, to present solutions derived from 'authentic experts' as unambiguous: 'Leaders and staff knew' (p. 17), 'While leaders believed' (p. 16), 'schools visited taught children to' (p. 21), 'successful primary schools' (p. 4).

Bold Beginnings can be seen as an example of a circular discourse, where policy-led evidence is derived from approved research which is then used to reinforce the prevailing political narrative (Wood, 2019). It normalises controversial practices such as instructional pedagogy, the foregrounding of academic knowledge and schoolification, to further embed the discourse that the core function of ECEC provision is preparation for future schooling and ultimately the labour market. This sits within wider neoliberal thinking which positions education as an economic concern, and ensures schools, and by extension, children and their families, are responsible for their own success within a compliance culture which is underpinned by developmentalist and interventionist narratives.

Reflective Questions 2.2

Neoliberalism and Policy

- Can you identify other policy or guidance documents which use language in this way to persuade others to share their position?
- How might reports of this kind, devised by powerful bodies such as Ofsted, impact on the professional identities of those who work with children?
- How might professionals and families challenge the orthodoxy of powerful organisations in a way which can lead to meaningful change?

Resistance and Hope

The effects of neoliberalism on the lives of children, particularly on their educational experiences, can appear to be all-pervading and unstoppable, a global discourse which is amplified and controlled by powerful state actors. However, Moss (2019) argues movements of resistance do exist and are creating alternative narratives which challenge the status quo and suggest new ways forward. Internationally, the most high-profile challenge to neoliberal orthodoxy arguably predates it; the early childhood education of Reggio Emilia. Literature exploring the Reggio experience is widespread and we don't aim to reproduce it here, but a key element of the Reggio model is the strong, progressive value-base which positions education as a community concern and a universal right, and children as confident meaning-makers who participate in shaping their own futures (Lindsay, 2015). This is delivered through forms of pedagogy which reject the developmentalist and readiness discourses of neoliberal education systems, and instead focus on child-centred play and creativity. Moss cautions against any attempt to export the Reggio model wholesale to other countries but argues it can act as a 'provocation to others to think about and construct their own cultural project … an example of possibility, not a model for replication' (Moss, 2015: 233). In the UK there are other signs of resistance, with the internet providing ways for people to come together, organise and debate, and forms of practice developing which are attempting to reclaim the progressive traditions of ECEC provision. The increasing popularity of forest school provision in UK settings and primary schools can be seen as one such example which challenges the academic notions of readiness found in the policy literature. Whilst there is rightly some debate on how UK forest school provision differs from its Scandinavian roots, it is clear that this form of provision can offer alternative forms of pedagogy from those espoused by the EYFS and Ofsted, in particular, a focus on playful interaction with natural environments which support well-being and confidence-building. Whincup et al. (2023) stress the tensions which exist between this nature-based approach and the demands of the formal curriculum, particularly with the challenges of measuring the benefits within a strict accountability culture. However, the popularity of this approach would indicate that professionals are increasingly challenging the prevailing orthodoxy of the neoliberal education system.

The story of *Birth to Five Matters* (Early Years Coalition, 2021) is another example of how academics and professionals have collaborated to try and navigate the tensions which exist between policy-makers and professionals about the direction of ECEC provision. Labelled as 'guidance by the sector for the sector' it was launched by the Early Years Coalition as a direct challenge to the Government's non-statutory guidance *Development Matters* (DfE, 2023). Whilst Birth to Five Matters is far from the disrupting and reconceptualising project that Reggio remains, there are important distinctions in its positioning compared to the prevailing government discourse, in particular the foregrounding of the holistic nature of children's development and the focus on children's participative rights. This has been widely supported by professionals including the National Education Union as an alternative to the academic developmentalism of the EYFS and Development Matters. Whilst these are localised responses to global issues, it is clear many professionals are questioning the direction of education and the impact it has on our children, and wider society.

Conclusion

This chapter has explored the ECEC sector as a way of illuminating how neoliberal discourse not only shapes young children's lived experiences, but also constructs dominant discourses of childhood which are difficult to counter. Successive neoliberal governments have, through the education system, primarily viewed children as unrealised human capital; incomplete workers who require moulding through engagement with standardised and normalising curriculum frameworks. However, we argue the current mixed-market configuration of the sector has also positioned children, alongside their families, as consumers of early education services, expected to make the 'correct' choices to secure their future success within a competitive system which idealises productivity and individual attainment, and reproduces inequalities. However, neoliberalism has a reach which extends far beyond education and care; subsequent chapters of this book will explore how neoliberal discourse is reframing childhood in other ways, including through narrow conceptions of success, the policy of measurement and as a market for consumer goods.

Within the ECEC sector, the relentless focus of neoliberalism prevents settings, educators and children from reclaiming a childhood which should be centred on meaningful interactions, care and the fostering of belonging within smaller and wider communities. We argue that the sector in its current form should be dismantled, and a new system constructed where early childhood education and care will no longer serve as a commodity bought by parents and traded through successful Ofsted inspections. This requires an overhaul which comprises several components including funding arrangements, existing infrastructure, attitudinal changes and workforce development. While these issues have been highlighted by prominent voices in the field, successive governments have been unable, or unwilling, to acknowledge these issues in the sector. Although the universalisation and homogenisation of education and care may be viewed as desirable, there should nonetheless be a concerted effort to cease the grip of neoliberalism upon it. Challenging this orthodoxy wherever it is found is vital in fostering a community-based approach to child-rearing which acknowledges early childhood as a stage in its own right, and to afford children opportunities to shape and determine their own lived experiences.

Further Reading

The Neoliberal Child

Monbiot, G. (undated) *George Monbiot*. Available at: www.monbiot.com/

George Monbiot is a columnist, author and campaigner who writes extensively on neoliberalism and its impact. This website features many of his columns and contains a section on education and childhood.

Roberts-Holmes, G. and Moss, P. (2021) *Neoliberalism and Early Childhood Education: Markets, Imaginaries and Governance*. New York: Routledge.

This book provides a full account of how neoliberalism has shaped the lives of young children and their early childhood provision, including the effects on parents and professionals.

References

Bradbury, A. (2019a) 'Making little neo-liberals: The production of ideal child/learner subjectivities in primary school through choice, self-improvement and "growth mindsets"', *Power and Education*, 11 (3), 309–26.

Bradbury, A. (2019b) 'Datafied at four: The role of data in the "schoolification" of early childhood education in England', *Learning, Media and Technology*, 44 (1), 7–21.

Brewer, M., Cattan, S., Crawford, C. and Rabe, B. (2022) *Does More Free Childcare Help Parents Work More?* London: Institute for Fiscal Studies.

Brooks, E. and Murray, J. (2018) 'Ready, steady, learn: School readiness and children's voices in English early childhood settings', *Education 3–13*, 46 (2), 143–56.

Close, P. (2014) 'Children's educational labour as slave labour', in *Child Labour in Global Society* (*Sociological Studies of Children and Youth*), 17, 107–47. Leeds: Emerald Group Publishing.

Costas Batlle, I. (2019) 'Non-formal education, personhood and the corrosive power of neoliberalism', *Cambridge Journal of Education*, 49 (4), 417–34.

Davies, B. and Bansel, P. (2007) 'Neoliberalism and education', *International Journal of Qualitative Studies in Education*, 20 (3), 247–59.

Delaune, A. (2019) 'Neoliberalism, neoconservativism, and globalisation: The OECD and new images of what is "best" in early childhood education', *Policy Futures in Education*, 17 (1), 59–70.

DfE (2013) *More Great Childcare: Raising Quality and Giving Parents More Choice*. London: Department for Education.

DfE (2023) *Development Matters. Non-Statutory Curriculum Guidance for the Early Years Foundation Stage*. London: Department for Education.

DfE (2024) *Statutory Guidance for the Early Years Foundation Stage*. London: Department for Education.

Early Years Coalition (2021) *Birth to Five Matters. Non-Statutory Guidance for the Early Years Foundation Stage*. London: Early Education.

Foucault, M. (1991) *Discipline and Punish: The Birth of the Prison*. London: Penguin.

Foucault, M. (2008) *The Birth of Biopolitics: Lectures at the Collège de France, 1978–1979*. New York: Palgrave Macmillan.

Giroux, H. A. (2005) 'The terror of neoliberalism: Rethinking the significance of cultural politics', *College Literature*, 32 (1), 1–19.

Harvey, D. (2005) *A Brief History of Neoliberalism*. Oxford: Oxford University Press.

HM Government (2018) *Improving the Home Learning Environment. A Behaviour Change Approach*. London: National Literacy Trust.

Howlett, M. (2018) 'Matching policy tools and their targets: beyond nudges and utility maximisation in policy design',. *Policy and Politics*, 46 (1), 101–124.

Lindsay, G. (2015) 'Reflections in the mirror of Reggio Emilia's soul: John Dewey's foundational influence on pedagogy in the Italian educational project', *Early Childhood Education Journal*, 43 (6), 447–57.

Lloyd, E. and Penn, H. (2014) 'Childcare markets in an age of austerity', *European Early Childhood Education Research Journal*, 22 (3), 386–96.

Maisuria, A. (2014) 'The neo-liberalisation policy agenda and its consequences for education in England: A focus on resistance now and possibilities for the future', *Policy Futures in Education*, 12 (2), 286–96.

Mirowski, P. (2014) *Never Let a Serious Crisis go to Waste: How Neoliberalism Survived the Financial Meltdown*. London: Verso.

Monbiot, G. (2017) *Out of the Wreckage: A New Politics for an Age of Crisis*. London: Verso.

Moss, P. (2015) 'There are alternatives! Contestation and hope in early childhood education', *Global Studies of Childhood*, 5 (3), 226–38.

Moss, P. (2019) *Alternative Narratives in Early Childhood: An Introduction for Students and Practitioners*. Abingdon, Oxon: Routledge.

Ng, P. T. (2008) 'Education policy rhetoric and reality gap: A reflection', *International Journal of Educational Management*, 22 (6), 595–602.

Niklas, F., Cohrssen, C., Vidmar, M., Segerer, R., Schmiedeler, S., Galpin, R., Klemm, V. V., Kandler, S. and Tayler, C. (2018) 'Early childhood professionals' perceptions of children's school readiness characteristics in six countries', *International Journal of Educational Research*, 90, 144-59.

Organisation for Economic Cooperation and Development (OECD) (2017) *Starting Strong: 2017 Key OECD Indicators on Early Childhood Education and Care*. Paris: OECD.

Ofsted (2014) *Are You Ready? Good Practice in School Readiness*. Manchester: Ofsted.

Ofsted (2015) *Teaching and Play in the Early Years: A Balancing Act*. London: Ofsted.

Ofsted (2017) *Bold Beginnings: The Reception Curriculum in a Sample of Good and Outstanding Primary Schools*. London: Ofsted.

Orelus, P. W. and Chomsky, N. (2014) 'Neoliberalism: The rich over the poor: Noam Chomsky and Pierre Orelus in dialogue', *Counterpoints*, 458, 65–76.

Pascal, C., Bertram, T. and Cole-Albäck, A. (2021) *A Fair Start? Equalising Access to Early Education*. London: Sutton Trust.

Podesta, J. (2014) 'Habitus and the accomplishment of natural growth : Maternal parenting practices and the achievement of "school-readiness"', *Australasian Journal of Early Childhood*, 39 (4), 123–30.

Roberts-Holmes, G. and Moss, P. (2021) *Neoliberalism and Early Childhood Education: Markets, Imaginaries and Governance*. New York: Routledge.

Rowe, E., Lubienski, C., Skourdoumbis, A., Gerrard, J. and Hursh, D. (2019) 'Exploring alternatives to the "neoliberalism" critique: New language for contemporary global reform', Discourse, 40 (2), 147–49.

Simpson, D. and Envy, R. (2015) 'Subsidizing early childhood education and care for parents on low income: Moving beyond the individualized economic rationale of neoliberalism', *Contemporary Issues in Early Childhood*, 16 (2), 166–78.

Trnka, S. and Trundle, C. (2014) 'Competing responsibilities: Moving beyond neoliberal responsibilisation', *Anthropological Forum*, 24 (2), 136–53.

Vincent, C., Braun, A. and Ball, S. (2010) 'Local links, local knowledge: Choosing care settings and schools', *British Educational Research Journal*, 36 (2), 279–98.

Whincup, V. A., Allin, L. J. and Greer, J. (2023) 'Challenges and pedagogical conflicts for teacher-Forest School leaders implementing Forest School within the UK primary curriculum', *Education 3–13*, 51 (1), 1–12.

Wood, E. (2019) 'Unbalanced and unbalancing acts in the Early Years Foundation Stage: A critical discourse analysis of policy-led evidence on teaching and play from the office for standards in education in England (Ofsted)', *Education 3–13*, 47 (7), 784–95.

Chapter 3

The Successful Child: Forms of Capital and Childhood

Jeanette Simson

Introduction

As discussed in the previous chapter, the language of neoliberalism (Moss, 2018) has become embedded in our discourse around the successful education and learning of young children, creating an image of the child as yet-to-be-released human capital (Roberts-Holmes and Moss, 2021). In discussions around early childhood education and care (ECEC) today, you may hear the terms assessment, quality, interventions or school-readiness, all of which are passionately discussed by those working in the sector and those studying for early childhood degrees. From an early age, children and their nurseries, preschool settings and schools are assessed and measured, actions which policy-makers deem necessary to ensure that children are receiving a quality early childhood education, one that leads to educational achievement, high employment rates and a stronger economy with fewer social problems (Dahlberg and Moss, 2004). In other words, an education which leads to success.

The attainment bar is raised ever higher and the pressure is building. Children in England were previously reported to be among the most tested in the world (Alexander, 2009). Since then, a progress check at 2-years-old and baseline assessment testing at the start of children's Reception Year have been implemented and recent approaches aimed at children to 'catch up' (DfE, 2021) demonstrate a clear drive towards children meeting measurable standards and targets rather than reflecting a more social and holistic pedagogy. Funded nursery places have been introduced by the government (DfE, 2024a) which less reflect aims to improve children's early experiences and development and more a move to enable parents to work, allowing progression in careers and financial stability.

In this chapter, I aim to challenge dominant conceptions of the successful child, discussing how neoliberal policies exacerbate division within society by framing and measuring the success of children. The concept of *capital* will be introduced and explored, including accepted forms of capital which can promote success for some children and push others to the fringes of our education system and society. The role of policy and media in framing success will be discussed, identifying how dominant narratives cause the marginalisation of communities who do not fit into the preconceived ideas of culture and society. Finally, in the chapter, there will be a call to re-define the successful child, considering whether key solutions for change are hidden in plain sight.

What Is a Successful Child?

As government reports applaud the rising status of England in international rankings for reading for primary age children (IEA, 2021), practitioners complain about the lack of importance given by policy-makers to well-being, creativity, collaboration and critical thinking and a lack of authenticity in acknowledging the unique child. Neoliberalism converts non-economic domains into measurable, competitive and tradable commodities and its reach has extended to encompass early childhood (Roberts-Holmes and Moss, 2021) where there is pressure for children to meet government set age-related standards (DfE, 2024b) set out by a 'one size fits all' approach. This is not easy or even achievable for many children and families who may experience marginalisation due to factors including, but not limited to, class, poverty, ethnicity, gender, age, sexual orientation and immigration status.

Ofsted (2024a, 2024b) sets out the expectation that good leaders in our schools and settings will give children the essential knowledge to prepare them for future success, defining this as *cultural capital*, a term which was first introduced by Bourdieu (1986) but which Ofsted reinterpret through a neoliberal lens. This position suggests that the dominant culture decides what is deemed essential knowledge for future success from an economic, neoliberal standpoint. To examine and debate how this narrative relates to constructions of the successful child, we must aim to understand the term cultural capital from its original meaning (Bourdieu, 1986), to its adoption into early childhood policy.

Capital

Bourdieu (1986) developed the concept of 'capital' to go beyond a meaning solely relating to economics and monetary exchange into a wider sphere, where economic capital could be transformed into immaterial forms of wealth such as cultural and social capital. Bourdieu defined cultural capital as familiarity with the legitimate culture within a society; the knowledge, skills, values and experiences that provide advantage and help one get ahead in life and especially in education. He contested the idea that education raised outcomes for all and tackled disadvantage, calling this *scholastic fallacy* (Bourdieu, 2000) and argued that what formal education considered 'essential knowledge' aligned to the attitudes, dispositions and behaviours of the wealthy classes, enabling them to progress well through education and the workplace. It is problematic to apply such a uniform approach, to define essential knowledge which reportedly leads to success without considering whose essential knowledge this is, where it comes from and the historical, social and cultural perspectives and position it assumes.

Ofsted use the term 'cultural capital' in their documentation, promoting the construction of a '... curriculum that is ambitious and designed to give children, particularly the most disadvantaged, the knowledge and cultural capital they need to succeed in life' (Ofsted, 2024a). This suggests the need for disadvantaged children to 'acquire' accepted forms of capital, reflecting a drive towards one form of culture which certainly would reflect Bourdieu's idea of scholastic fallacy. The inclusion of cultural capital as criteria for judging the quality of provision without a deep consideration of how to use it to sustain children's diverse social and cultural identities is problematic. Bourdieu's ideas acted as a critique of society, rather than a cultural menu outlining skills, attitudes and dispositions deemed appropriate in society by the dominant culture.

In an education system which values 'higher forms' of 'legitimate' cultural capital and where academic results are presented as meritocratic, cultural capital becomes a tool to reproduce inequalities (Torras-Gómez et al., 2021). These inequalities are wide and varied and impact our children at the very beginning of formal education, meaning that some children are more likely than others to achieve the success that our educational policy defines. A discussion of class, poverty and social mobility will explore some of the barriers to success that children meet in their very first years in education.

Class and Poverty

Whilst the UK is deemed one of the richest places in the world, around 4.2 million children (around 3 in every 10) live in poverty (JRF, 2024). This inflicts hardship on children's early years and impacts on their future health, well-being and economic prospects. EYFS profile data recording achievement or 'success' at the end of their Reception Year, show a gap of 18.5% between children in least deprived (76.6%) and most deprived areas (58.1%) attaining a 'good' level of development (DfE, 2023). A good level of development implies that children are 'ready for school', the definition of which is debated amongst policy-makers, educators and those studying Early Childhood. Professionals working in the sector aim to provide children with what they need to thrive in school, supporting children in the development of their curiosity, resilience, empathy, communication and confidence. However, the school readiness agenda links to neoliberal ideas relating to children becoming students who achieve well in the education system and go on to become economically productive adults. Kay (2018: 159) considers that using school readiness as a performance and accountability measure 'further marginalises groups of children who are already marginalised'.

According to Sylva and Eisenstadt (2004: 6), 'the provision of high quality, teacher-led early education, ideally starting from 2 years of age for children from low-income families' is the most important single action for narrowing the gap between lower-income and higher-income families. The recent Conservative government set out plans to enable wider access to nursery places for working families. However, 70% of those eligible for the support for nursery places for 3- and 4-year-olds were from homes in the top half of earners whilst 80% of those eligible for funded places for 1- and 2-year-olds had annual incomes above £45,000 (Sutton Trust, 2024). This seems to perpetuate the advantage of some sectors of society and feeds into a neoliberal agenda to encourage parents back into the workplace, missing the potential of early education to close attainment gaps associated with social deprivation, thereby increasing division.

Class inequality and division has grown since the 1950s with members of the working classes presented as decent, hardworking and successful if they are 'socially mobile' or else failures if not (Reay, 2017). Social mobility refers to a change in a person's socio-economic situation, either in relation to their parents (inter-generational mobility) or throughout their lifetime (intra-generational mobility). The UK has low levels of social mobility, yet there is still a strong discourse around meritocracy, which views social and economic status as determined by individual merit and accomplishment rather than inherited wealth or privilege. However, until recently, many of the highest positions in society were held by those educated in private schools as society's elite which arguably undermines all work to support inclusion and alleviate division and disadvantage and suggests that some children enter school, adulthood and the workplace as already successful. In recent years, many representatives of the working classes have been pushed out of politics to be replaced by middle class politicians, the trade unions have decreasing power and voice, and societal and media discourse has viewed the working classes as 'chavs' (Jones, 2011). There is increasing polarisation in the state sector, where schools and childcare settings in poorer areas are underfunded compared to those in more affluent areas (NAO, 2021), compounding social inequality and children's opportunities for learning and life. When considering historical models of education of the working class, 'the system was designed to provide an inferior education, producing different educational opportunities appropriate to one's station in life' (Reay, 2017: 30) and it could be argued, that this situation continues.

Those who know the rules of the game succeed. Others do not know or are not even aware of the rules of the game, due to cultural contexts, aspirations and dispositions which diverge from the dominant culture and who may hold 'hidden injuries' suffered by families in the past in their treatment by society or the educational establishment (Podesta, 2014). There are many people in society who, based on their identity, culture or needs, experience social exclusion and diverge from the prevalent dominant culture in society – the marginalised.

Marginalised Groups

Children and families may be going through the same education system and be part of the same society, but those who experience marginalisation can experience a lack of recognition and rights, security, an absence of opportunity and exposure to disadvantage and inequality. Many governmental initiatives have been introduced to tackle disadvantage in society, including policies for schools and Early Years settings. These initiatives often take an interventionalist approach, the very term 'intervention' meaning to become intentionally involved in a difficult situation, to improve it or to prevent it from getting worse. This description could be seen to reflect a cultural deficit assumption and an aim to 'fix' children who don't fit into the image of the successful child and who don't hold the required cultural capital. There are many professionals working within educational settings who create powerful, effective relationships with children and families, embracing their identities and cultures and supporting children's holistic development but these connections can be impeded by wider policy and legislation as children proceed through the education system into wider society. More must be done at all levels to look more deeply into the causes and effects of disadvantage, with an authentic curiosity to improve lives, rather than a political narrative to win votes.

In 1990, the UK signed the United Nations Convention on the Rights of the Child (UNCRC), an international agreement setting out the civil, political, economic, social and cultural rights of every child, regardless of their race, religion or abilities (UN, 1989). This convention aims to tackle inequality and provide opportunity for all children to be able to exercise their rights without discrimination of any kind. Many of the articles of the UNCRC are covered by legislation in the UK and this is monitored by the Committee on the Rights of the Child who review progress and publish recommendations for individual countries (see Chapter 4 for further discussion about the UNCRC). In the 2023 review for the UK, the committee raised its deep concern about persistent discrimination against children belonging to minority groups and lesbian, gay, bisexual, transgender and intersex children. In addition, deep concerns were raised for the overrepresentation of children of Asian and African descent and Muslim, Roma, Gypsy and Traveller children in the criminal justice system, with a large proportion of these children living in poverty (United Nations, 2023). These concerns can be linked to Foucault's (Foucault and Gordon, 2001) 'regimes of truth', where certain discourses become dominant over others and the identities and behaviour of those who are not considered 'the norm' is problematised.

Although education has the power to challenge social inequalities and bring about positive change (Freire, 2004), the voices of some members of society, including children, continue to be disempowered and excluded. There is a missed opportunity to recognise forms of capital which may differ from the dominant culture. The 'funds of knowledge' approach (Moll et al., 1992) evolved to challenge the deficit thinking in dominant and accepted forms of capital, highlighting the wealth of skills, knowledge and competencies that children arrive with into schools and settings.

By acknowledging and embracing the rich historical and cultural contexts of all children and their families, the curriculum and society itself is enriched.

The education system and society, including the media, can create tension between communities. It could be suggested that currently the most proactive steps towards inclusion are being taken by people within the sector, striving for an approach which aims to ensure all children are valued and included. Deconstructing stereotypes, working against complex cultural forces and questioning what is deemed 'legitimate' knowledge are important actions to take but this must be supported by policy, legislation and the media.

The Role of Policy and Media in Framing Success

Although currently in a state of crisis and with some changes recently implemented, the mistrust, devaluing and toxic environment that Ofsted has created will leave a long-lasting negative impact across the sector (Perryman et al., 2023). The current spotlight is on the inspection process, but much is to be unpicked, not least the positionality of the government department which drives the neoliberal agenda of meritocracy leading to the success of those in the dominant sector of society. This is not to hope for the demise of anyone but to aim and strive for equity and social justice for all members of our communities.

Ofsted's reinterpretation of Bourdieu's concept of cultural capital to measure and judge the provision and curriculum does not take account of the diversity of children in our schools and settings. If children do not see themselves as someone represented in their wider society, they will feel on the periphery and disempowered. This segregation of society and localities is promoted in the media, where Ofsted reports are shared widely. An unsuccessful Ofsted inspection often equates with an unsuccessful school or setting and an unsuccessful early start in education, often reflecting on staff, families and the local community.

The mass media has a significant role to play in societal attitude formation around conceptions of a successful childhood and the judgement of sectors of society which fall outside constructions of societal norms or accepted forms of capital. Opinion and perspective can be magnified, stories can be altered to fit a narrative and reality can be twisted. Ofcom (2018) reported that a number of minority groups felt unhappy with how they are represented on television, people with disabilities believed there was too much focus on their difficulties, transgender people felt the focus was negative or on medical issues and LGB and Black African and Black African-Caribbean people felt portrayed negatively.

Media representations do not only significantly impact adults in society, but also have a major impact on the thoughts and opinions of children and these opinions can begin to be constructed very early through TV, media platforms and online gaming. Children can inherit social, cultural and political biases which can lead to exclusionary attitudes and behaviours (Nutbrown, 2013). Repeated exposure to stereotyped images can act negatively to construct images of accepted norms or success and work against inclusion of marginalised groups such as people with disabilities, ethnic minorities and LGBTQ+ groups. A report from the Joseph Rowntree Foundation (McKendrick et al., 2008) around media, poverty and public opinion found that the coverage that is most memorable by viewers tends to be the most sensational. This genre has been popular in recent years through programmes which de-humanise sectors of society such as *Benefits Britain: Life on the Dole* (2020), *The Undateables* (2020) and the notorious *My Big Fat Gypsy Wedding* (2015). Those living in mono-cultural communities in a similar socio-economic status may have limited contact with minority groups. As such, there is active engagement between the media and society and this influence is ever growing, gathering momentum through connections with historical perspectives, news reporting, social media and television.

Culture in Focus

Romani (Gypsy), Roma and Irish Traveller communities are often reported as one homogenous group which could be problematic as it could disregard the varied histories, cultural traditions, community identities and social norms for each community. However, by placing these groups in focus, we can aim to highlight the gross inequality, disadvantage and racism directed towards these communities who have rich cultures, experiences and history that may not fit into expected constructions of childhood or adulthood by the dominant sections of society. Showmen and Boaters are also often included in the grouping of these communities.

In the 1960s, the Plowden Report described 'gypsy' children as '... probably the most severely deprived children in the country' (Plowden, 1967: 59). Sir Trevor Phillips, chairman of the Commission for Racial Equality stated in 2004 that: 'The racism suffered by the Gypsy and Traveller community is the last acceptable form of racism, which unlike other forms of racism shows no signs of diminishing' (*BBC News*, 2004) and more recent reports from the Equality and Human Rights Commission, reports that Gypsy, Roma and Traveller children across the UK are more likely to be bullied than other ethnic minority groups (EHRC, 2022). These communities have experienced repeated attack and racism on a scale that would be completely unacceptable against any other ethnic groups. These reports are shocking to most in society but part of the experiences of everyday life for members of these communities.

When referring to EYFS profile data which reports percentages attaining a 'good level of development' by ethnicity, Gypsy Roma (33.6%) and Travellers of Irish Heritage (32.9%) are well below national averages (67.2%) and significantly below that of all other social and ethnic groups. Travellers of Irish Heritage are the only ethnic group which saw a decrease in attainment between 21/22 and 22/23 (DfE, 2023).

The drivers of these poor educational outcomes are complex and interconnected with disadvantages faced by Romani (Gypsy), Roma and Irish Traveller groups in other areas, including in access to healthcare and housing. SEND is also more prevalent in these groups (Equality and Human Rights Commission, 2022) and not only do poverty and ethnicity intersect for some, discrimination from society is fuelled by the media. Over a decade ago, programmes such as *My Big Fat Gypsy Wedding* (2010) and *Gypsies on Benefits and Proud* (2014) ridiculed and ignited tensions directed towards the community. Debates continue with more recent Channel 4 programmes which have received further criticism from the community.

Romani (Gypsy), Roma and Irish Traveller children have reported that the lack of acknowledgement of their ethnicities, cultures and histories within school makes them feel different and excluded, their own valuable and relevant funds of knowledge diverging from those in more dominant sections of society. Although a changing picture, many Traveller children leave school and work in the 'Traveller Economy', traditional Traveller practices distinguished by self-employment and in-family trading (Ryder and Greenfields, 2012). In a recent Traveller Movement annual conference (Traveller Movement, 2023), youth speakers discussed what would help young people access education and then go on to work, highlighting the importance of education being more flexible to accommodate the communities, so that people did not have to choose between their culture and education, and their successes could be valued.

Case Study 3.1

GTRSB Pledge

In 2022, Buckinghamshire University published the GTRSB (Gypsy, Traveller, Roma, Showmen and Boaters) Pledge for schools which was adapted from the Pledge for Higher Education and was developed to support schools to make a firm commitment to support access, retention and outcomes in education for GTRSB pupils (Buckinghamshire University, 2022). An important aspect was to create an open and welcoming environment where members of communities are confident that their culture and learning needs are understood by the school or setting, but this needs to go further, to respect and embrace the funds of knowledge of children and their families (Moll et al., 1992). The Pledge asks schools and settings to commit to ensuring staff development in raising awareness of the barriers pupils face accessing education and more broadly in society, to inclusion and celebration of cultures and communities and data monitoring.

The Pledge is clearly set out, provides support and resourcing for schools and Early Years settings and includes a resource list and a link to a Romani Early Years network. A number of schools and universities have signed up to the Pledge. However, although the Department for Education spoke at the launch of the Pledge and it has been on the agenda for the DfE Gypsy and Traveller Stakeholder meetings, no further action has been taken to promote its implementation through policy or information sharing.

Reflective Questions 3.1

Romani (Gypsy), Roma and Irish Traveller Communities

- What is your understanding of the Romani (Gypsy), Roma and Irish Traveller communities?
- Where did you access information about these communities? Are these accurate sources?
- How do you think the outcomes for these groups can be improved? What action needs to be taken?

Re-Defining the Successful Child: Key Solutions for Change Hidden in Clear View

To re-define the successful child, we must focus on the role of policy, government, the media, the early childhood education sector and most importantly, our constructions of the child. Ofsted's (2023) inspection framework requires schools and settings to *provide* children with accepted forms of cultural capital. This is far from the image of the child as a participatory, empowered child within society. New conceptions of the successful child are needed and for this we must turn to children, recognising the culture, skills, experiences, beliefs and values of all children to feed into policy and education.

Policy

Although achieving true societal equity requires addressing systemic challenges beyond the scope of education alone, central to any move to re-align conceptions of the successful child would be a commitment by all stakeholders to social justice and a central aim to deconstruct disadvantage. Powerful conversations can be uncomfortable and challenging but policy should encourage discussion around providing space and opportunity for developing alternative perspectives, opportunities to embrace the experiences, social practices and histories of all community members.

Past successes which can impact real change at a local level are possible if heeded by policy-makers and politicians. The Labour government's 1999 Sure Start Programme provided holistic support to families with children under the age of 5 in England. It was targeted at the most disadvantaged areas and later became a more universal initiative. Recent research reported by the Institute of Fiscal Studies (Carneiro et al., 2024) reported that access to the earlier Sure Start Local Programmes significantly improved the educational achievement of children, including their GCSE results, with significantly greater impacts for those from the poorest backgrounds and non-white backgrounds. The findings of the report corroborate findings such as those reported by Sylva and Eisenstadt (2024) that the funding and commitment to holistic family support and high-quality early educational provision can effect dramatic changes on the lives of the disadvantaged. To provide this high-quality provision, early childhood education professionals should be more highly valued, and a discussion around status and pay parity with teachers should be considered (Moloney, 2015).

If early intervention is the only approach used, it acts as a cheap fix for social and economic failing (Moss, 2015), aiming for higher exam results, higher university attendance, increased economic gain for the government, entrance into the working economy, etc. However, policy which fully and authentically follows the UNCRC could not only support children's academic learning but embrace and interweave the funds of knowledge held by children and families, and their cultural and social identities, towards the co-construction of societies and communities where success is viewed as holistic and personalised, where childhood is valued in its own right and where new forms and understandings of capital emerge.

Within the Sector

As inclusion and inclusive practice is discussed and referred to in policy and guidance, it is vital that all involved continue to scrutinise practice so that policies, practices, attitudes and values ensure that all children belong, that all needs are addressed and individuality and heritage are understood and respected (Nutbrown, 2023). Anti-discriminatory practices must be integral to this process where discrimination is explored and challenged.

Understanding the idiosyncratic demographic of an educational setting is the framework that gives context to all members of the community. At the heart of this framework is the relationship between the child, parents and carers, educational setting and the community. The relationship should not only seek to benefit children in terms of their development and education but should also aim to develop greater social cohesion and a shared purpose in the school community and beyond, working towards a shared community capital where all members are valued and considered. Policy-makers can learn a great deal from experienced and impassioned professionals within the sector.

The Child

The participatory rights of children is a fundamental consideration in re-defining the successful child. By prioritising a play-based pedagogy, we can enable children to be in control of their own life, to solve problems, develop relationships, be creative and experience true joy (Gray, 2011). There is a pace in the neoliberal education system which aims to accelerate children towards meeting learning objectives, measuring them and ultimately judging them against pre-constructed standards set within a framework for societal economic advancement which is non-inclusive. This considers children as future human-capital. What is needed is to adopt a slow pedagogy (Clark, 2023), to consider the core purpose of early childhood education and to enable a co-construction of accumulating knowledge. An intentional pedagogy considers each child individually and supports a reciprocity of relationship with parents, where there is an integration of services to support children and families (Sylva and Eisenstadt, 2024) and where warm attachments are made.

Conclusion

There is a drive within the sector to promote an image of the successful child as one who is an active participant in their own education, whose cultural capital has worth based on their Funds of Knowledge (Moll et al., 1992) and the co-construction of their accumulating knowledge and skills through a high-quality early education which provides holistic support to families. Experts in the field, students and academics write extensively about the importance of tackling disadvantage, of supporting marginalised groups and of valuing a slow, play-based pedagogy which enables all children to develop curiosity, understanding, relationships and resilience through experiences which promote joy. This would reflect the image of the 'unique' child referred to in the Statutory Framework for the Early Years Foundation Stage (2023) but what is written in policy is not a true reflection of the dominant narrative of policy-makers. The government signed the United Nations Convention for the Rights of the Child (UN, 1989) and has committed to the United Nations Sustainable Development Goals (UN, 2015) but not enough has been done away from the high-profile presence on the global stage.

The values and philosophies embedded in the alternative narratives to the neoliberal agenda are already core beliefs of many working within the sector. A shift in agency is required towards experts in the field, these being practitioners, early childhood students, parents, carers and families and crucially our children to advise policy-makers and politicians. Current constructions of success and ideas of cultural capital drive children towards measurable outcomes and is unfair treatment of our children. It undermines the value of childhood and denies the potential for the co-construction of communities and society, where the successful child is a unique child, whose rights, cultural experiences and social histories are celebrated and integral to the society of which they are part. It is time for politicians and policy-makers to listen.

Further Reading

The Successful Child

The following readings will support you to consider some of the key ideas which have been introduced in this chapter in further detail.

Clark, A. (2023) *Slow Knowledge and the Unhurried Child: Time for Slow Pedagogies in Early Childhood Education*, 1st edn. Oxford: Routledge.

This book encourages deep reflection and promotes vital discussion among practitioners, researchers and policy-makers on the need to slow the pace in ECEC to value childhood in its own right.

Irvine, K. (2022) 'Pierre Bourdieu (1930–2002)', in A. Bradbury and R. Swailes (eds), *Early Childhood Theories Today*. London: Learning Matters, pp. 32–42.

The chapter gives a clear and accessible overview of Bourdieu's main ideas and theory.

Moll, L. C., Amanti, C., Neff, D. and Gonzalez, N. (1992) 'Funds of knowledge for teaching: Using a qualitative approach to connect homes and classrooms', *Theory into Practice*, 31 (2), 132–41. Available at: www.tandfonline.com/doi/abs/10.1080/00405849209543534 (accessed 27 September 2024).

The Funds of Knowledge approach was developed to address deficit thinking in education, where children's poor 'performance' at school is caused by their linguistic, economic and cultural limitations. It calls for the recognition and legitimisation of the lifestyles and cultural practices of all children, particularly those with minority status.

United Nations (1989) *Convention on the Rights of the Child*. Available at: https://downloads.unicef.org.uk/wp-content/uploads/2016/08/unicef-convention-rights-child-uncrc.pdf (accessed 27 July 2024).

This website gives an overview of the UNCRC and contains links to a summary and full report of the UN convention.

References

Alexander, R. (2009) *Children, Their World, Their Education: Final Report and Recommendations of the Cambridge Primary Review*. New York: Routledge.

BBC News (2004) 'CRE examines treatment of gypsies', *BBC News*, 17 October.

Bourdieu, P. (1986) 'The forms of capital', in J. Richardson (ed.), *Handbook of Theory and Research for the Sociology of Education*. Available at: https://doi.org/10.1002/9780470755679.ch15 (accessed 26 February 2025).

Bourdieu, P. (2000) *Pascalian Meditations*. Oxford: Polity.

Buckinghamshire University (2022) *Buckingham University GTRSB Pledge for Schools*. Available at: www.bucks.ac.uk/gtrsb-schools-pledge (accessed 26 February 2025).

Carneiro, P., Cattan, S. and Ridpath, N. (2024) *The Short- and Medium-Term Impacts of Sure Start on Educational Outcomes*. London: Institute of Fiscal Studies.

Clark, A. (2023) *Slow Knowledge and the Unhurried Child: Time for Slow Pedagogies in Early Childhood Education*. Oxford: Routledge.

Dahlberg, G. and Moss, P. (2004) *Ethics and Politics in Early Childhood Education*. London: Routledge Falmer.

Department for Education (DfE) (2021) *Catch-up Premium*. Available at: www.gov.uk/government/publications/catch-up-premium (accessed 24 February 2024).

Department for Education (DfE) (2023) *Early Years Foundation Stage Profile Results: 2022 to 2023*. Available at: www.gov.uk/government/statistics/early-years-foundation-stage-profile-results-2022-to-2023 (accessed 27 March 2024).

Department for Education (DfE) (2024a) *Early Education Entitlements and Funding Update: March 2023*. Available at: www.gov.uk/government/publications/early-education-entitlements-and-funding-update-march-2023 (accessed 25 February 2024).

Department for Education (DfE) (2024b) *Early Years Foundation Stage (EYFS) Statutory Framework*. Available at: www.gov.uk/government/publications/early-years-foundation-stage-eyfs-statutory-framework (accessed 13 June 2024).

Equality and Human Rights Commission (EHRC) (2022) *Educational Challenges Facing Young People from Gypsy, Roma and Traveller Backgrounds*. Available at: www.equalityhumanrights.com/en/our-work/news/response-education-committee-consultation-educational-challenges-facing-children-and-young (accessed 8 March 2024).

Foucault, M. and Gordon, C. (2001) *Power/knowledge: Selected Interviews and Other Writings, 1972–1977*. Harlow: Harvester Wheatsheaf.

Freire, P. (2004) *Pedagogy of the Oppressed*. New York: Continuum.

Gray, P. (2011) 'The decline of play and the rise of psychopathology in children and adolescents', *American Journal of Play*, 3 (4), 443.

IEA (2021) *Progress in International Reading Literacy Study 2021*. Available at: www.iea.nl/studies/iea/pirls/2021 (accessed 24 February 2024).

JRF (2024) *UK Poverty 2024 Joseph Rowntree Foundation*. Available at: www.jrf.org.uk/uk-poverty-2024-the-essential-guide-to-understanding-poverty-in-the-uk (accessed 8 July 2024).

Kay, L. (2018) School Readiness: A Culture of Compliance? EdD thesis, University of Sheffield.

Jones, O. (2011) *Chavs: The Demonization of the Working Class*. London: Verso.

McKendrick, J., Sinclair, S., Irwin, A., O'Donnell, H., Scott, G. and Dobbie, L. (2008) *The Media, Poverty and Public Opinion in the UK*. Joseph Rowntree Foundation. Available at: www.jrf.org.uk/report/media-poverty-and-public-opinion-uk (accessed 21 March 2024).

Moll, L. C., Amanti, C., Neff, D. and Gonzalez, N. (1992) 'Funds of knowledge for teaching: Using a qualitative approach to connect homes and classrooms', *Theory into Practice*, 31 (2), 132–41.

Moloney, M. (2015) Untangling the Knots, (K)not Easy: Professional Identity in the Early Childhood Care and Education Sector. Early Education Alignment: Reflecting on Context, Curriculum and Pedagogy Conference, Trinity College, Dublin, October.

Moss, P. (2015) 'There are alternatives! Contestation and hope in early childhood education', *Global Studies of Childhood*, 5 (3), 226–38.

Moss, P. (2018) *Alternative Narratives in Early Childhood: An Introduction for Students and Practitioners*, 1st edn. London: Routledge.

National Audit Office (NAO) (2021) *School Funding in England*. Available at: www.nao.org.uk/report/school-funding-in-england/ (accessed 6 July 2024).

Nutbrown, C. (2013) *Inclusion in the Early Years*, 2nd edn. Los Angeles: SAGE.

Nutbrown, C. (2023) *Early Childhood Education: Current Realities and Future Priorities*. Los Angeles: SAGE.

Ofcom (2018) *Representation and Portrayal on BBC TV 2018*. Available at: www.ofcom.org.uk/tv-radio-and-on-demand/bbc/representation-portrayal-bbc-tv/ (accessed 21 March 2024).

Ofsted (2023) *Changes Made to School Inspections* (press release). Available at: www.gov.uk/government/news/changes-made-to-school-inspections (accessed 14 June 2024).

Ofsted (2024a) *Early Years Inspection Handbook*. Available at: www.gov.uk/government/publications/early-years-inspection-handbook (accessed 14 June 2024).

Ofsted (2024b) *School Inspection Handbook*. Available at: www.gov.uk/government/publications/school-inspection-handbook (accessed 13 June 2024).

Perryman, J., Bradbury, A., Calvert, G. and Killan, K. (2023) *Beyond Ofsted Inquiry: Final Report*. London: NEU.

Plowden, B. (1967) *Children and their Primary Schools: A Report of the Central Advisory Council for Education (England)*. London: Her Majesty's Stationery Office. Available at: https://education-uk.org/documents/plowden/plowden1967-1.html (accessed 21 March 2024).

Podesta, J. (2014) 'Habitus and the accomplishment of natural growth: Maternal parenting practices and the achievement of "school-readiness"', *Australasian Journal of Early Childhood*, 39 (4), 123–30.

Reay, D. (2017) *Miseducation: Inequality, Education and the Working Classes*. Bristol: Bristol University Press.

Roberts-Holmes, G. and Moss, P. (2021) *Neoliberalism and Early Childhood Education: Markets, Imaginaries and Governance*, 1st edn. London: Routledge.

Ryder, A. and Greenfields, M. (2012) *Roads to Success: Economic and Social Inclusion for Gypsies and Travellers*. London: Irish Traveller Movement in Britain.

Sutton Trust (2024) *General Election Policy Briefing*, Sutton Trust. Available at: www.suttontrust.com/wp-content/uploads/2024/01/Inequality-in-early-years-education.pdf (accessed 14 June 2024).

Sylva, K. and Eisenstadt, N. (2024) *Transforming Early Childhood: Narrowing the Gap Between Children from Lower- and Higher-Income Families*. NESTA. Available at: www.nesta.org.uk/report/transforming-early-childhood/ (accessed 29 February 2024).

Torras-Gómez, E., Ruiz-Eugenio, L., Sordé-Martí, T. and Duque, E. (2021) 'Challenging Bourdieu's theory: Dialogic interaction as a means to provide access to highbrow culture for all', SAGE Open, 11 (2). Available at: https://doi.org/10.1177/21582440211010739 (accessed 26 February 2025).

Traveller Movement (2023) *Annual Conference – Future Voices*. Available at: www.travellermovement.org.uk/november-2023-traveller-movement-conference (accessed 24 July 2024).

United Nations (UN) (1989) *Convention on the Rights of the Child*. Available at: www.unicef.org.uk/what-we-do/un-convention-child-rights/ (accessed 27 September 2024).

United Nations (UN) (2015) *Sustainable Development Goals*. Available at: www.un.org/sustainabledevelopment/sustainable-development-goals/ (accessed 3 September 2024).

United Nations (UN) (2023) *Convention on the Rights of the Child,* 'Concluding observations on the combined sixth and seventh periodic reports of the United Kingdom of Great Britain and Northern Ireland'. Available at: https://documents.un.org/doc/undoc/gen/g23/112/77/pdf/g2311277.pdf

Chapter 4

Children as Rights Holders: Rhetoric or Reality?

Helen Butcher and Jane Andrews

Introduction

In this chapter we explore the ambitions and realities of the United Nations Convention on the Rights of the Child (UNCRC) and its conceptualisation of children as rights bearers in the countries of the United Kingdom (UK) and some associated implications for professional practice with young children. We have chosen this geographical spread for reasons we set out below but we also hope that readers will reflect on other parts of the world that they are already, or want to, become familiar with.

The United Nations adopted the CRC in 1989 and it was ratified by the UK government in 1992 and can be accessed in summary form via the United Nations Children's Fund (UNICEF) website (www.unicef.org.uk/what-we-do/un-convention-child-rights/). At our time of writing, the UNCRC had been ratified by all nations who are members of the United Nations (193 in total), with the exception of the USA, which has signed, but not yet ratified, the Convention. For this chapter we choose to focus our discussion on two specific articles out of the total of 54 and they are:

- Article 19 (protection from violence, cruelty and neglect) and
- Article 30 (children from minority and indigenous groups).

We have chosen these articles because of our own particular interests and because of the challenges they appear to present to all of those working with, living with, developing policies for, and caring for, children in the UK. By this we mean that these articles show how children can encounter varied experiences of growing up due to the locations they are in but also their experiences of the differences between their domestic sphere and that of their early childhood setting or school, as shaped by local or national policy. For Article 19, this can mean being protected from physical abuse or smacking in a setting or school but not in the home, in the case of children growing up in England and Northern Ireland. For Article 30, it can mean using family languages freely in the home setting but being oriented mainly towards English in settings or schools in England.

Although this chapter has a focus on two specific articles, our overriding concern is with the implementation of the Convention as a whole. Article 42 (Knowledge of rights) requires governments to publicise children's rights widely to children and adults. In addition, the convention indicates that children's entitlement is to all of the articles, without exception, and not merely those which governments might find convenient.

In this chapter we explore some challenges which may be perceived by adults as reasons for not implementing the UNCRC holistically and universally for all children. These might relate to ideas such as some children being 'too young' to understand rights or the belief that adults have a better idea of what young children's needs are. To explore these challenges further, we have organised the rest of the chapter in the following way:

- Questions are offered to guide your thinking before reading on.
- Background is provided to the development of the UNCRC on the Rights of the Child.
- Article 19 is unpacked and discussed.
- Article 30 is unpacked and discussed.
- The different approaches taken by the UK's four devolved nations are explored.
- A case study is offered as an opportunity to explore early childhood practice in relation to the UNCRC, specifically Article 42.
- We conclude our chapter with some implications for policy and practice.

Reflective Questions 4.1

Reflecting About Rights

Before we explore the background to the UNCRC here are four questions for reflection:

1. When you were a child did you know you had rights? If you did, how old were you when you knew? Was it a parent, teacher, textbook or other source who informed you?
2. What do you think about the physical punishment of young children by parents or carers? Can you trace where your thinking comes from?
3. What is your daily experience of using, hearing and reading different languages? How is linguistic diversity present in homes or early childhood settings that you are familiar with?
4. How do you feel about children you know or work with having rights? In what ways might living and working with young children be different if they knew they had rights?

Development and Scope of the UNCRC

This section provides a brief summary of arrangements in the UK concerning children's rights and welfare which preceded the UNCRC (UN, 1989). It outlines how implementation of the Convention is monitored and highlights repeated criticism by the review panel regarding aspects of its implementation in the UK.

Children are one of the last social groups to have their civil rights acknowledged and, as explored in Archard and Macleod (2002), it can be said that the concept of children having rights is relatively modern. A key reason for this is that historically children were considered objects, owned by parents or guardians, whose wishes needed to be ignored or subdued (Mayall, 2015). In the UK, campaigning to improve children's lives dates back to the end of the 19th century when 60 years after legislation against cruelty to animals, the Prevention of Cruelty to, and Protection of, Children Act was passed in 1889 to protect children from cruelty and harsh working conditions. Individual campaigners, politicians and charities had vital roles in promoting children's rights and welfare. Benjamin Waugh, the first director of the National Society for the Prevention of Cruelty to Children (NSPCC), drafted The Children and Young Persons Act in 1908 which brought together legislation concerned with children, recognised mental cruelty, and banned denying treatment to sick children. This became known as The Children's Charter.

The charity Save the Children was founded by sisters Eglantyne Jebb and Dorothy Buxton in 1919. Eglantyne's focus expanded from the UK to address children's welfare in Europe in the aftermath of the World War 1, when thousands of children were displaced from their homes and countries. She drafted the first international agreement for children's welfare, adopted by the League of Nations in 1924 – the Declaration of the Rights of the Child – which was the first statement to include the phrase 'the Rights of the Child'. In 1959, the five principles of the Declaration – all children need to be protected, fed, housed and safe from exploitation in the workplace – were increased to ten. The additions included the right to a name and a nationality, free and compulsory elementary education, and the right to play and recreation. These additional principles demonstrate a move away from child as object/possession in need of protection, towards the child as citizen. In 1979, the UN International Year of the Child launched a decade-long drafting of the UNCRC, which was published in 1989. Reflecting on progress towards children as rights-bearing citizens made in the century from 1889–1989, Pascal and Bertram noted: 'A slow but growing acknowledgement of the centrality of the rights of children as citizens is evident in this history' (2002: 252).

What is perhaps concealed in this history is a hierarchy of entitlement in the category of 'children'. Whether it is spoken language behaviour or policy-making, the younger children are, the more they are either overlooked, ignored or otherwise marginalised. As part of monitoring countries' implementation of the CRC, a General Comment (2005) included the observation that in many countries the rights in the Convention's Articles were neither provided nor communicated to children under the age of 8.

> The Committee reaffirms that the Convention on the Rights of the Child is to be applied holistically in early childhood, taking account of the principle of the universality, indivisibility and interdependence of all human rights. (CRC, 2005: 2)

In the next section we explore more of the insights gained from monitoring committee visits carried out to explore how the UNCRC is being implemented in practice.

Monitoring Implementation of the Convention

Countries who sign the UNCRC agree to implement all of its Articles and to self-audit their action. Monitoring visits are conducted every 4 or 5 years in order to ensure the Articles are being implemented and/or that steps towards full implementation are being made. The committee who monitor implementation comprises 18 independent experts on children's rights from different countries who read detailed submissions from each government and charities and public organisations concerned with children's rights. In the UK this includes the Equality and Human Rights Commission (EHRC) and the Children's Rights Alliance in England (CRAE).

Communicating Children's Rights to Adults and Children (Article 42)

Before examining the implementation of two specific Articles (19 and 30) we refer to a third, Article 42 (Knowledge of rights). Self-evidently, unless children, and adults who live and work with children, know of the existence of their rights there is no possibility of them being enjoyed or enacted. We asked Reflection Question 1 above because, in our experience of teaching higher education students over many years, few were aware of the rights they were entitled to and none recalled being aware before they were adolescents. For this reason, we now explore how the UK's four nations have embarked on communicating about the UNCRC and enacting it in practice.

UK Devolution

Following Acts of Parliament in 1998, the four nations of the UK (Northern Ireland, Scotland, Wales and England) each acquired powers to determine a wide range of social and economic policy, including education and children's welfare as well as aspects of equality legislation. This process has resulted in responsibility for determining significant aspects of policy for children and education being interpreted differently in each country. The ways in which the UNCRC has been interpreted differently are outlined in the following section which begins with a deeper discussion of Article 19 (protection from violence, cruelty and neglect).

Unpacking Article 19

Article 19 of the UNCRC requires that:

> Governments must do all they can to ensure that children are protected from all forms of violence, abuse, neglect and bad treatment by their parents or anyone else who looks after them. (UNCRC, 1989)

In the UNCRC, violence is defined as 'any punishment in which physical force is used and intended to cause some degree of pain or discomfort, however light' (Pinheiro, 2006: 2). We think it is important to underline the phrase 'however light' because there has been, in all UK countries, and now only in Northern Ireland and England, a defence of reasonable chastisement for parents and carers accused of child assault. We share an opinion that this defence is unreasonable. Article 19 has been selected for an examination of the UK's commitment to implementing the Convention because, for us, this Article is vital if children's lives and experiences are to be valued equally. Protection from violence is a prerequisite for children's safety and flourishing (Wilson and Conyers, 2013). We argue that enshrining this in law signals full respect for children as rights-bearing human beings.

A number of worldwide campaigns to end violence against children, such as the Global Initiative to End All Corporal Punishment Against Children, established in 2001, were formed. In 2023, the Chief Executive Officer of the NSPCC based in the UK stated: 'It cannot be right that in this country it is illegal to hit an adult, but equal protection is not given to a child' (NSPCC, 2023). Given children's greater vulnerability than adults, both physically and mentally, we assert that the right to bodily integrity needs to be given equal importance to that accorded to adults in the UK.

The first country in the world to ban the physical punishment of children was Sweden, which did so to coincide with the United Nations International Year of the Child, in 1979. This was a decade earlier than the launch of the UNCRC. To date, 63 countries including Scotland (2020) and Wales (2022) and most South American countries have abolished corporal punishment (Aznar, 2022). In Europe, apart from England and Northern Ireland, only Switzerland, Italy and the Czech Republic continue to allow the corporal punishment of children. To answer the question of the extent to which the UK respects children's rights, and is committed to full implementation of all its Articles, it is necessary to look at each of its four countries separately in relation to Article 19. As we shall see, children's experiences of their rights will be different in each of the four countries and this is because of differences in each government's approach towards children's rights.

Scotland

We start by looking at the example of Scotland because it was the first country in the UK to ban physical punishment of children. The Children (Scotland) Act 2020 declared that any of the following actions: hitting, slapping, shaking, throwing, kicking, burning or scalding, drowning, suffocating, biting, fracturing or breaking bones, constitute child assault. Parents and carers charged with assaulting a child, or children, could no longer use a defence of 'reasonable punishment'. Announcing this pioneering legislation, the Scottish government stated:

> We want Scotland to be the best place in the world for children to grow up. Removing the 'reasonable chastisement' defence contributes to that aim. (Scottish Government, 2020a)

Wales

In Wales, the second country in the UK to end the physical punishment of children, ending the defence of reasonable chastisement was included in the title of the legislation. The Children (Abolition of the defence of Reasonable Chastisement) (Wales) Act was passed in 2020. It was implemented in March 2022 when Mark Drakeford, First Minister for Wales at the time, wrote:

> I am delighted the physical punishment of children is now illegal in Wales. This is a historic achievement for children and their rights. The United Nations Convention on the Rights of the Child makes it clear that children have the right to be protected from harm and from being hurt and this includes physical punishment. (Welsh Government, 2022)

Northern Ireland and England

In Northern Ireland and England, the law covering the physical punishment of children is the same. According to Section 58 of the Children Act (2004) it is illegal for a parent or carer to hit a child unless it amounts to 'reasonable punishment'. For us this raises important questions. How is reasonable punishment defined, who defines it, who is advocating for children's perspectives and why are children not protected from assault like adults? As indicated above, charities and pressure groups have played significant roles in progressing children's rights. One pressure group, the Society for Teachers against Physical Punishment (STOPP), was founded in 1968. It lobbied national and local government and supported families taking court action against their children being hit, by adults, in school. The UK government abolished corporal punishment in state schools in 1986 but it was 1999 before it was abolished in independent schools. Rowland et al. (2017) place their arguments for ending the defence of reasonable chastisement firmly in the context of child abuse and safeguarding, and state:

> moves to prevent family violence are progressive but the position of a society where physical punishment of children is permitted yet child abuse is forbidden is not a tenable one. (2017: 166)

In April 2024, as this chapter was being written, the Royal College of Paediatrics and Child Health (RCPCH), published a comprehensive challenge to the existing legislation in England which made the case against maintaining the status quo. The report noted the large evidence base showing that smacking is associated with a range of negative outcomes for children, including physical harm, poorer mental health and increased aggression. Despite the weight of evidence presented in the report the then Conservative government indicated it had no intention to review existing legislation in England. In October 2024, following a fatal case of child abuse, the Children's Commissioner Rachel de Souza, hitherto muted on this issue, called for a ban 'on any type of corporal punishment, including smacking, hitting, slapping, and shaking' (Children's Commissioner, 2024). Media reports suggest that the Labour government may reconsider laws in England on child assault.

Charities working with children and families are united in advocating for children's rights and for continuing to argue for the outlawing of assault against children. Barnardo's and the campaign group Children are Unbeatable are two examples of organisations specifically focusing on protecting children from assault and pushing governments to act. As part of their campaigning work, the National Children's Bureau gathered evidence from children themselves and this quotation comes from a 7-year-old boy:

> Sometimes if you smack, if it was an adult like my daddy, he can smack very hard ... he can smack you like a stone ... and you'll cry. (Willow and Hyder, 1998: 26)

In the section below, we move our consideration to Article 30, regarding children from minority and indigenous families and we focus in particular on linguistic diversity and children's rights to communicate using their family or home language(s) as well as the language of the Early Years setting or school. As with the discussion so far, we consider the contexts of England, Scotland, Wales and the island of Jersey (a British Crown Dependency), as a way of reflecting on, and comparing, how real or rhetorical children's rights are in relation to Article 30.

Unpacking Article 30

'Children have the right to use their own language, culture and religion — even if these are not shared by most people in the country where they live' (UN, 1989). In the children's version of the UNCRC, Article 30, quoted above, asserts a child's right to use their own language, culture and religion. In this part of our chapter we focus the discussion on a child's right to use their own language, although, of course, we recognise how interconnected a child's lived experiences of language, culture and religion are likely to be. For children growing up in the UK, the right to use one's own language is likely to be exercised, or not, in the contexts of the home, within families, and in settings or schools, depending on the age of the child. Families will make their own decisions on how their members interact together in the home environment and academic studies have explored this rich and varied phenomenon under the heading of 'family language policy' (see, e.g., Curdt-Christiansen and Sun, 2022). In determining their individual approaches to linguistic diversity, families will be influenced by their beliefs about language (and culture and religion) and their aspirations for their children in their practices in the home.

Multilingual family interaction, as highlighted in Smidt (2016), can involve translanguaging which refers to speakers moving between several shared languages within a conversation or within a sentence or utterance. Alternatively, adult family members may maintain a consistency of language use, such as always using a chosen home or heritage language, to support children's connection with that language, often referred to by the term 'one parent, one language' or OPOL (see de Houwer, 2009). Aside of which model of multilingual interaction a family engages in, it might be argued that a child's right to use their own languages, as stated in Article 30, can be effectively enabled and supported in the home environment when the family language policy is favourable to multilingual interaction.

When turning to children's experiences of being supported to exercise their right to use their own language in Early Years settings and schools, we may see the emergence of a different picture, if we focus our attention on the policy and practice context of England. In both the Early Years Foundation Stage Statutory Guidance (DfE, 2024) covering practice for children from birth to age 8 and the National Curriculum – Key Stages 1 and 2 (DfE, 2013), covering provision for children from age 5 to 11, it is clear that English is the expected medium of instruction. This is indicated in the following quotation:

> Providers must ensure that children have sufficient opportunities to learn and reach a good standard in English language during the EYFS, ensuring children are ready to benefit from the opportunities available to them when they begin Key Stage 1. (DfE, 2024: 16)

There is recognition of children's linguistic diversity in these documents, as seen in the following two extracts:

> 1.14. For children whose home language is not English, providers must take reasonable steps to provide opportunities for children to develop and use their home language in play and learning, supporting their language development at home. (DfE, 2024: 16)
>
> 4.5. Teachers must also take account of the needs of pupils whose first language is not English. Monitoring of progress should take account of the pupil's age, length of time in this country, previous educational experience and ability in other languages. (DfE, 2013: 8)

Having noted that children's linguistic diversity and their skills in languages other than English are recognised in the extracts above, there is a clear emphasis on the centrality of English within their learning in these early years and school environments. The steer from education policy in England towards prioritising English can be seen to provide a challenge to a child's right to use their own language, as set out in Article 30.

When we look at education policy in Wales and Scotland, we can see that the linguistic landscape differs from England with the presence of additional languages alongside English such as Welsh as the national language in Wales and the use of Gaelic and Scots in different parts of Scotland. In addition, languages used by families and communities who have migrated to Wales and Scotland such as Polish, Urdu, Somali and Arabic, to name but a few, will be commonly used. What does this mean for educational policy and practice in relation to children's home languages? In Wales, the curriculum notes that 'In addition to Welsh and English, all learners should have the opportunity to learn at least one international language at school and to use other home languages and community languages they may speak' (Welsh Government, 2022). This statement suggests that home and community languages may have a place in school and the curriculum guidance then poses a question for teachers asking them to consider how they will build on children's home languages in the classroom. In a similar way, Scotland's Curriculum for Excellence (Scottish Government, 2020b) also prompts teachers to consider how their setting or school will recognise 'that Scotland is a multilingual and diverse society'. In neither Wales nor Scotland are children and families offered an entitlement to use their languages for learning, but it is clear that home languages are considered positively and respectfully.

A final example of a way in which the entitlement to use a language which is different from the mainstream language might be approached is offered in the language policy developed in 2021 by the government of Jersey, an island between the UK and France. This policy provides one document including together a diversity of languages. These are the historic languages used on the island, including English and Jèrriais, modern languages learned in the classroom as part of the curriculum and the languages used by children and families who have arrived in more recent times, such as Portuguese. The inclusiveness of Jersey's approach to linguistic diversity is explained as a holistic approach to multilingualism in schools (Government of Jersey, 2021). Once again, this is not expressed as an entitlement, but it seems to come closer to recognising that linguistic diversity should be respected and encouraged in children's home lives and in their lives in educational settings and school.

We have now reviewed Articles 19 and 30 and the extent to which children can access these rights in contexts in the UK.

What Is the Status of the UNCRC in England?

The Children's Rights Alliance for England (CRAE), established in 1991, has a specific focus on promoting children's rights and monitoring government implementation of the UNCRC. It is an alliance of 97 children's organisations and it submits evidence to the 5-yearly UN Periodic Review of implementation of the UNCRC. In 2022, CRAE wrote in their report:

> … as evidenced in this report, UK government has generally failed to prioritise implementation of the CRC, with regression in many areas. (CRAE, 2022: 13)

This serious criticism of provision for children's rights in England makes an important point regarding the legal status of the Convention. In each of the Periodic Reviews undertaken since the 1991 ratification the Committee have pressed successive governments to sign the Convention into domestic law without success. Doing this would make adherence to all articles a legal requirement and this would greatly strengthen children's rights. In 2010 the UK nearly signed the UNCRC into domestic law, but an unanticipated general election meant that the work done on drafting and reviewing the Bill was 'lost' (Butcher, 2020).

Concerningly, disregarding recommendations made by monitoring committees is not uncommon by the UK government. What does this mean for those of us working with young children? There has been some particularly relevant feedback for practitioners from the Equality and Human Rights Commission (EHRC) report *Children's Rights in Great Britain* (2023) which noted that there was insufficient knowledge about the UNCRC among teachers and that it would be valuable to introduce human rights education as a curriculum area. We see this as a clear-eyed view of the critical role of professional educators in promoting children's rights and improving their, and adults', knowledge of children's rights.

Our critique of policies and practices regarding Articles 19 and 30 should not be taken to suggest that there is a total lack of attention by practitioners to children's rights. In the next section, we offer some case studies of practice which promote children's developing knowledge of their rights.

Rights-Respecting Practice with Children

As indicated above, signatory governments to the Convention are required by Article 42 to include not only reference to the UNCRC, but also, to specific proposals linked to its different Articles. The most recent date in a search for UNCRC of the Department of Education website (March 2024) is 2022. The site offers an infographic entitled, 'How the government is protecting your rights'. While it clearly states children have the right to express themselves and be listened to, the relevant Articles (12 and 13) are not mentioned. Although the title uses the first person 'protecting your rights' the document switches to the third person, e.g., Protecting children from harm. In the section on protection it states:

> The government is creating new laws to help adults and children understand the right way to treat children such as not hurting children or leaving them alone. (DfE, 2022)

In the course of her research into professionals who were knowledgeable and committed to communicating about, and practising within, the UNCRC, Butcher (2020) came across settings which unequivocally expressed their commitment and obligations under the UNCRC. Below she describes an example from a nursery, a school and the work of UNICEF UK as case studies of rights respecting practices.

Case Study 4.1

Rights-Respecting Practice

Nursery

A nursery was located in an inner city with very little outside play space, serving a community experiencing high levels of economic deprivation, most of whom lived in high-rise flats. Parents, carers and children, including some recent arrivals, spoke a wide range of languages. It had over a long period of time enjoyed respect and appreciation from parents, professionals and inspectors. All visitors to the nursery – parents, carers, trainee teachers, social workers, interview candidates, inspectors and advisors – walked through an attractive foyer furnished with bright sofas, fresh flowers and a warm welcome from the reception team. By the welcome desk stood a 6 ft high free-standing scroll entitled, 'Our Children's Rights'. On it were listed some key children's rights: to be listened to, have their opinions respected and to participate in their learning (Articles 12, 13, 28, 29). In addition, there was signposting to clear information on the full UNCRC.

The message was clear for all to see and was communicated daily, in words and actions, directly with young children; this is a setting which respects children's rights, teaches children they have rights and aims to imbue rights respecting values in the children who learned there.

School

Located on the city outskirts, the school served a recently built and expanding housing estate, with an economically diverse population. As the beginning of this new school's first term approached the school hall filled with a range of items, from furniture to toilet rolls, to be distributed to different parts of the school. The Headteacher wondered whether she might receive a proposal to defer introducing the Convention to the children in the second term. She proudly related that even after subtly questioning the whole team about the pressure they were facing they remained resolute in their commitment to children's rights as a non-negotiable aspect of their pedagogical approach.

Rights Respecting Schools Award (RRSA)

An organisation which provided support to both these settings in the form of information, guidance and self-audit materials, is the Rights Respecting Schools Award (RRSA), run by the United Nations Children's Charity, UNICEF UK. Its mission is to put children's rights at the heart of schooling.

Given the woeful record of successive governments in England and Northern Ireland at publicising and promoting children's rights we see these instances of promoting the UNCRC in educational settings as examples of green shoots. These rights-respecting environments help develop children and young people, many of whom will become parents, carers and professionals of the future, to understand human rights.

Conclusion

Having explored and critiqued different ways of implementing, or not, the UNCRC within the four nations of the UK, we strongly believe that it is essential to have, in the words of Lundy (see Kearney, 2020: 4), 'a document like the Convention on the Rights of the Child, which articulates a bespoke set of rights for children.' As Lundy (see Kearney, 2020) goes on to emphasise in the interview, children's right to be heard is at the heart of the UNCRC and that this applies to all children, from babies to young adults.

In answer to the question posed in this chapter's title, regarding whether children's rights in the UK are real or rhetorical, we respond that it depends on which of the four countries children live in. In relation to Article 19, we have discussed how freedom from assault is enshrined in law in Wales and Scotland but not in Northern Ireland or England. Where children living on one side of a street are, for example, in Wales and those on the other in England, they will have different rights to be free from assault. Nor, as we have outlined above, is physical punishment of children the only Article where the UK falls well short of its obligations under the Convention. We suggest this is partly because of a prevailing child-hostile culture noted by the monitoring Committee almost a decade ago (CRC, 2016).

As regards Article 30, the increasingly multilingual communities who make up our society and the children and families who attend early childhood settings and schools will all benefit from the respect and recognition offered by the UNCRC's strong affirmation of the right to interact using their language(s) as well as the majority language(s) of the country they live in.

We end this chapter with a question in the form of a respectful challenge to those of you who either are, or will be, working with young children.

What part will you play in shaping rights respecting practices for children?

Further Reading

Children as Rights Holders

CRAE: https://crae.org.uk/

You may find the website of the Children's Rights Alliance England a useful source of further reading including their proposal of a Children's Rights Charter for the new UK government (July 2024).

Festman, J., Poarch, G. J., Dewaele, J-M. (2017) *Raising Multilingual Children.* Bristol: Multilingual Matters.

This book gives ideas for parents and carers on how to support their children's multilingual skills and identities and suggestions how they can engage with settings and schools to explain their family's approach to linguistic diversity.

References

Archard, D. and Macleod, C. (2002) *The Moral and Political Status of Children*. Oxford: Oxford University Press.

Aznar, A. (2022) 'Smacking children: What the research says', *The Conversation*, 18 May. Available at: https://theconversation.com/smacking-children-what-the-research-says-182733 (accessed 16 October 2024).

Butcher, H. E. (2020) Realising Young Children's Rights: Researching Conversations with Rights Respecting Early Childhood Leaders. Doctoral dissertation, University of the West of England. Available at: https://uwe-repository.worktribe.com/output/1491158 (accessed 27 February 2025).

Equality and Human Rights Commission (2023) *Children's Rights in Great Britain*. London: EHRC.

Children's Commissioner (2024) *Statement from the Children's Commissioner on Removing Reasonable Physical Punishment of Children*. Available at: www.childrenscommissioner.gov.uk/statement/statement-from-the-childrens-commissioner-on-removing-reasonable-physical-punishment-of-children/ (accessed 25 October 2024).

Committee on the Rights of the Child (CRC) (2005) *General comment No. 7 (2005): Implementing Child Rights in Early Childhood*. Available at: www.refworld.org/legal/general/crc/2006/en/40994 (accessed 25 October 2024).

Committee on the Rights of the Child (CRC) (2016) *Concluding Observations on the 5th Periodic Report of the United Kingdom of Great Britain and Northern Ireland: Committee on the Rights of the Child*. Available at: https://digitallibrary.un.org/record/835015?ln=en&v=pdf (accessed 25 October 2024).

CRAE (2022) *UK Implementation of the UN Convention on the Rights of the Child - Civil Society Alternative Report 2022 to the UN Committee – England*. London: CRAE.

Curdt-Christiansen, X. L. and Sun, B. (2022) 'Establishing and maintaining a multilingual family language policy', in A. Stavans and U. Jessner (eds), *The Cambridge Handbook of Childhood Multilingualism*. Cambridge: Cambridge University Press, pp. 257–77.

De Houwer, A. (2009) *An Introduction to Bilingual Development*. Bristol: Multilingual Matters.

Department for Education (DfE) (2013) *National Curriculum in England: Key Stages 1 and 2 Framework Document*. Available at: www.gov.uk/government/publications/national-curriculum-in-england-primary-curriculum (accessed 16 October 2024).

Department for Education (DfE) (2022) *How the Government is Protecting Your Rights*. Available at: www.gov.uk/government/publications/infographic-on-the-united-nations-convention-on-the-rights-of-the-child (accessed 16 October 2024).

Department for Education (DfE) (2024) *Early Years Foundation Stage Statutory Framework*. London: Department for Education.

Government of Jersey Communications Team (2021) *Our Children, Our Languages – Language Diversity in Jersey Schools*. Jersey: Government of Jersey. Available at: www.gov.je/Education/Schools/ChildLearning/pages/languagepolicyjerseyeducation.aspx (accessed 16 October 2024).

Kearney A. (2020) 'An interview with Professor Laura Lundy', *Kairaranga*, 21(1), 3–6. doi:10.54322/kairaranga.v21i1.320.

Mayall, B. (2015) 'The sociology of childhood and children's rights', in W. Vandenhole, E. Desmet, D. Reynaert and S. Lembrechts (eds), *Routledge International Handbook of Children's Rights Studies*. Abingdon: Routledge.

NSPCC (2023) *Majority of Public Want Children in England to Have Same Protection From Assault As Adults*. Available at: www.nspcc.org.uk/about-us/news-opinion/2023/majority-of-public-want-children-in-england-to-have-same-protection-from-assault-as-adults/ (accessed 25 October 2024).

Pascal, C. and Bertram, T. (2002) *Early Years Education: An International Perspective*. London: Qualifications and Curriculum Authority.

Pinheiro, P. S. (2006) *World Report on Violence Against Children*. Geneva: UN Publications.

RCPCH (2024) *Equal Protection from Assault in England and Northern Ireland: Prohibiting the Physical Punishment of all Children*. Available at: www.rcpch.ac.uk/resources/equal-protection-from-assault-england-and-northern-ireland (accessed 10 October 2024).

Rowland, A., Gerry, F. and Stanton, M. (2017) 'Physical punishment of children: Time to end the defence of reasonable chastisement in the UK, USA and Australia', *The International Journal of Children's Rights*, 25, 165–95. doi:10.1163/15718182-02501007

Scottish Government (2020a) *Physical punishment and discipline of children: how the law is changing – Factsheet*. Available at: www.gov.scot/publications/physical-punishment-and-discipline-of-children-how-the-law-is-changing/ (accessed 16 October 2024).

Scottish Government (2020b) *Curriculum for Excellence Learning Through 2 (+1) Languages*. Available at: https://education.gov.scot/resources/a-1plus2-approach-to-modern-languages/ (accessed 9 October 2024).

Smidt, S. (2016) *Multilingualism in the Early Years – Extending the Limits of our World*. London: Routledge.

United Nations (UN) (1989) *Convention on the Rights of the Child*. Available at: www.unicef.org.uk/what-we-do/un-convention-child-rights

Welsh Government (2022) *Physically Punishing Children Becomes Illegal in Wales* (press release). Available at: www.gov.wales/physically-punishing-children-becomes-illegal-wales (accessed 16 October 2024).

Welsh Government (2022) *Curriculum for Wales*. Available at: https://hwb.gov.wales/curriculum-for-wales/ (accessed 9 October 2024).

Willow, C. and Hyder, T. (1998) *It Hurts You Inside – Children Talking About Smacking*. London: National Children's Bureau.

Wilson, D. and Conyers, M. (2013) *Five Big Ideas for Effective Teaching: Connecting Mind, Brain, and Education Research to Classroom Practice*. New York.: Teachers College Press.

Chapter 5

Policy: For Children or About Children?

Eleri John and Joanne Munyard

Introduction

Early childhood professionals and settings play a crucial role in influencing who a particular policy is for and what the policy is about. This chapter will show that policy formation, which happens at the outset of the policy-making process, connects to a more path-dependent approach underpinned by neoliberal and performative ideas. Policy enactment, on the other hand, takes place towards the end of the process, and produces a more contestable, ambiguous and context dependent pathway as the policy hits the real world. It is then that the act of trying to match ends and means becomes problematic, as the policy is 'made sense of, mediated, struggled over (and sometimes ignored) or in other words enacted' (Ball et al., 2012: 4). By opening up the policy to new voices – the practitioner's view, for instance – enactment takes on a more 'for' the child focus whilst the policy-forming 'about' the child decreases.

At the heart of this chapter is a case study which highlights how constructions of childhood in policy-making have been framed by neoliberal and performative considerations ultimately leading to children being viewed as 'becomings' rather than 'beings'. The chapter will go on to demonstrate that policy formation and policy enactment 'about' and 'for' children become disconnected as *in situ* enactment takes over. The chapter, however, begins with a brief discussion of the conceptual ensemble that wraps around policy-making before moving to explore the historical and political context within which policy-making has been set. The chapter ends with some implications for both policy and practice.

Definitions and the Policy Ensemble

The term policy is often used in various contexts without clear definition. We frequently use the term in our everyday language and interpret it within the literature we read based on a set of assumptions and ideologies (Ball, 1993; Forrester and Garrat, 2016). We may think of policy as a physical document, a text on a website or a government speech, for instance. Sometimes, we might think of policy as being written by the managers of our settings; a set of guidance and procedures that we must follow in our practice. When writing academically about policy, it is therefore important to be able to define what we mean by the word and how authors have influenced our understanding of this. To begin, we will introduce a limited range of influential writers and researchers within the field of educational policy.

We will set the ball rolling with one of the most influential – Stephen Ball, who has written extensively about educational policy, and provides many definitions and theoretical frameworks by which we can start to explore its multiple meanings. Ball (1994: 10) asserts that policy is 'text and action, words and deeds, it is what is enacted as well as what is intended'. In this sense, Ball describes policy as either 'text' or 'discourse'

(Ball, 1993: 44), suggesting that policies may take the form of written documents or 'texts' or they may focus more specifically on the language used, and the ways in which that influences the way we behave, think and communicate. Likewise, Trowler (2003: 95) defines policy as a 'specification of principles and actions' which set out to guide us, provide rules and to enable specific functions and goals to be achieved. This frames policy as a concept which continually evolves and changes due to the complexity of society and education; policy is never truly complete or achieved. As a result, we often refer to the 'policy cycle' which recognises the ever-changing nature of policy in response to the subjective nature of changing contexts.

Moreover, Levin (1997) suggests that policy can be used to state government intentions, actions, practices or status. When considering policy as an intention we may think of policy documents such as political manifestos, White Papers, or a speech from a Member of Parliament. Policy may be used to set out a course of action regarding a specific issue or need such as a response to the Covid Pandemic or the allocation of funding to support parents back into work (e.g., the Thirty Hours Funded Childcare scheme legislated by the 2015 Childcare Bill (DfE, 2015)). We are also familiar with policies within organisations – locations where we might be employed or educated even. These are usually used to set out the practices to be actioned within a particular setting, for example, a safeguarding policy. In this sense, policy is intended to set out the values, aims and processes within an organisation in order to shape practice. Finally, Levin (1997) suggests that policy is sometimes intended to acknowledge and set out the status of a particular action or practice; the very phrase 'government policy' indicates that a particular position has been adopted and is intended to be enacted by those stakeholders concerned (e.g., Early Years qualifications requirements (DfE, 2024)). Levin's framework acknowledges that policy can be a formal document or the spoken word which aligns to Ball's (2005) definition of policy, and an evolving phenomenon as suggested by Trowler (2003). Some useful definitions therefore are:

- *Policy:* A statement of actions and intentions to follow. A set of guidelines intended to produce a specific outcome.
- *Social policy:* Policies intended to address social needs (e.g., education, housing, justice, etc.).
- *Policy as discourse:* The language that we use to discuss policy and the influence this has on our everyday practice.
- *Policy as action:* Policy reflected in our actions (e.g., practice) and in response to specific issues.
- *Policy as text:* A policy document which is read and intended to meet a specific need or outcome.

When exploring the phenomenon of policy, we should also recognise that Early Childhood Education and Care (ECEC) policy is a major form of public policy. This perspective relates to the extent to which education policy contributes to the welfare of children and families and the whole of society. Levin (1997) further suggests that social policy is a form of 'intent' and 'action' serving a range of needs linked to issues such as employment, the economy, health and social mobility. Recent policies related to funded hours for children whose parents are in employment, serve to address a range of issues linked to the economy, employment, gender pay gaps, health and well-being, equality of access and social mobility. Implementation of these policies impacts on social issues such as the recruitment and retention of practitioners as well as the qualifications of staff, their well-being and the ratios of practitioners to children. This example highlights the complexity of early ECEC policy and the relationship that it has to wider social policy as well as the potential that effective ECEC policy has in addressing social issues (Di Stasio and Solga, 2017).

The Historical and Political Context

Early childhood education and care has traditionally been characterised as a mix of three strands of provision which form part of the policy context from which it is developed. These three strands have underpinned the policy approaches over recent decades and include: social welfare services for poor children; universal Early Years education; and childcare for children with employed parents. These elements demonstrate the multi-disciplinary nature of ECEC, which has historically been reflected in the diversity and complexity of early childhood policy. The variety of government departments in debating and drawing up early childhood policy includes, but is not limited to, the Department for Work and Pensions, Department for Education and HMRC. In addition, this is further complicated by the devolutionary powers that exist in the UK for Wales, Scotland and Northern Ireland which result in differences of policy across curricula, funding streams and rules surrounding qualifications of the Early Years workforce. For instance, instead of promoting change, ECEC policy formation may institutionalise split administrative systems, where government responsibility remains allocated partly to education, but shared with other departments often along age-related boundaries (Kaga et al., 2010).

The decades of the Blair–Brown administrations, for instance, saw considerable transformations in early childhood, including significant reductions in child poverty, increased access to free childcare and a real terms increase in child benefit of over 70%. The Blair administration (1997–2007) therefore marked a significant turning point in UK early childhood policy, characterised by substantial investment and a holistic approach to child well-being, with a clear focus on delivery. Blair's government also introduced forward-looking comprehensive initiatives such as *Sure Start* centres, the National Childcare Strategy and the *Every Child Matters* framework, with a focus on community and responsibility (Ball, 2021). These policies reflected a view of children as valuable members of society in their own right deserving of support and investment. The focus on reducing child poverty, expanding early education and providing integrated services demonstrated a commitment to improving children's immediate lives and long-term prospects. This approach aligned with a societal view of children as 'beings' – individuals with present needs and rights – rather than merely as future economic contributors.

Following the Labour administration between 1997 and 2010, the coalition government's early childhood policy agenda was slow to emerge and was largely absent in both Conservative and Liberal Democrat manifestos. Set against a backdrop of austerity measures and tax benefit reforms, families with children under five took a significant hit along with considerable cuts to spending on early childhood education and care, and *Sure Start* (Stewart and Obolenskaya, 2015).

The years of the coalition government (2010–2016) were followed by Theresa May's administration (2016–2019) with an initial 'commitment' to social mobility as highlighted in her speech outside Downing Street about the 'burning injustice' of social inequality (May, 2016). Set against a backdrop of abolishing the child poverty unit and poverty income targets, May was encouraged to expand the childcare component of universal credit and in April 2017 introduced tax-free childcare. This policy allowed working parents to apply for two new government childcare schemes – tax-free childcare and 30 free hours in the September of that year. Following May's tenure in government, the focus on early childhood policies went into retreat.

Boris Johnson's reign in Downing Street (2019–2022) was dominated by Brexit and the Covid pandemic. During his turbulent term in office, there was a slight increase in funding for the Early Years; however, such an increase failed to match years of underfunding during the period of austerity (Education Committee, 2023). His tenure was characterised by a shift to more localised politics in which local authorities were expected to take on more ownership of Early Years provision, despite decreasing funding levels in real terms (Eyles, 2022). There were also significant policy changes relating to the EYFS. Johnson's government updated the *Development Matters* Framework in 2021 as part of their broader education reforms. These included reducing paperwork and the administrative burden on Early Years practitioners whilst simplifying guidance to make it more accessible. There was also a focus more explicitly on language development and an alignment between Early Years and later key stages of education.

However, the Early Years sector's response to these changes was notably critical, leading to the creation of *Birth to 5 Matters* (Early Years Coalition, 2021). This alternative framework represented a significant vote of no confidence in the government's approach to Early Years policy. The sector expressed serious concerns about multiple aspects of *Development Matters* (DfE, 2021), particularly noting that it was developed with limited consultation with Early Years experts. Practitioners argued that the simplified approach fundamentally undermined the complexity of child development and worried about the reduced emphasis on play-based learning, which they viewed as essential to Early Years pedagogy. There was widespread criticism that the framework was too closely aligned with later key stages rather than being distinctly Early Years focused, suggesting a misunderstanding of the unique nature of early childhood development (Gibbon, 2020). *Birth to 5 Matters* was therefore created as a sector-led alternative, developed by the Early Years Coalition. This represented an unprecedented move of collective action by the sector to create its own guidance, effectively challenging the government's vision for Early Years education (Archer, 2024). The existence of two competing frameworks highlighted the significant tension between government policy and professional expertise in the Early Years sector. The fact that many settings chose to use *Birth to 5 Matters* either instead of, or alongside *Development Matters* demonstrated the lack of confidence many practitioners had in the government's understanding of Early Years education and child development. This situation reflected a broader pattern of concern about the government's approach to Early Years policy under Johnson's leadership, where decisions were often seen as being made without sufficient consultation with or understanding of the sector itself.

The years following the pandemic saw considerable economic uncertainty followed by successive failures in government marked by high inflation rates, considerable increases in the price of consumer goods as well as grossly inflated gas and electric prices. However, in 2023, amid the backdrop of economic uncertainty, a cost of living crisis and the country on the verge of recession, Rishi Sunak's government published their plans to invest £8bn every year which represented the single biggest investment in childcare in England. This was set against a backdrop of increasing practitioner–child ratios for 2-year-olds, going from 1:4 to 1:5, meaning fewer staff were needed in settings, as well as a change in the required qualifications for Level 3 practitioners no longer needing Level 2 (GCSE equivalent) in maths, leaving such requirements for managers only. Despite it being presented as a significant investment in the Early Years, such proposals continue to worsen the recruitment and retention crisis in the Early Years sector (Nutbrown, 2021).

Path-Dependent Policy Formation

Having outlined a brief recent history of early childhood policy changes, we now move to consider the impact of these policy developments in order to understand whether early childhood policy has been created 'for' children or 'about' children. The evolution in policy approaches outlined above can be understood through the concept of path dependence. Path dependence, first coined by Pierson (2004), is a concept that explains how the set of decisions one faces for any given circumstance is limited by the decisions one has made in the past, even though past circumstances may no longer be relevant. In the context of UK early childhood policy, path dependence has played a significant role in shaping approaches that often prioritise economic considerations over children's immediate well-being and rights (Rigby et al., 2007; Lloyd, 2015).

The UK's historical approach to early childhood, which has long been dominated by neoliberal ideology and viewed as a means to enable parental employment alongside economic and financial productivity, rather than as a critical developmental service for children, has created a policy path that is difficult to deviate from (Brewer et al., 2014; Moss, 2014; Lloyd, 2015; Archer, 2020, 2022, 2024). This path began with the post-war emphasis on women entering the workforce, leading to policies focused on providing care to free up parents for work. Over time, this initial trajectory has been reinforced by subsequent policies, creating a self-perpetuating cycle where new initiatives tend to build upon and extend this work-centric approach. The initial steps taken during the Blair years (1997–2007) to link childcare with economic policy established an infrastructure, funding mechanisms, and policy frameworks that made it more straightforward for later administrations to build upon the economic aspects of early childhood policy while gradually side-lining the more holistic, child-centred elements. This historical inertia makes it ever more challenging to implement radical shifts in policy even when new research or societal changes suggest the need for a different approach. This has also been further impacted by the complex system of institutions, regulations and funding mechanisms around ECEC here in the UK. These established structures create vested interests and operational norms that resist significant changes. For example, the mixed economy of childcare provision (including private, public and voluntary sectors) that has evolved over decades makes it difficult to implement universal, state-funded models seen in some other European countries, Finland being a classic example.

It could therefore be argued that the theory of path dependence significantly impacts early childhood policy formation in the UK (Lloyd, 2015). This is also reinforced through policy feedback loops, for instance, policies that prioritise workforce participation and economic considerations tend to produce outcomes that further justify and entrench this approach. Policies that expand childcare availability, for example, may lead to increased maternal employment, which in turn creates more demand for childcare services and strengthens the economic argument for such policies. These self-reinforcing cycles make it difficult to shift focus towards alternative priorities, such as child-centred developmental approaches or the intrinsic value of early childhood experiences. This therefore creates a cognitive and cultural 'lock-in' from governments and policy-makers; a trap that continues that long-standing focus on childcare as an economic rather than an educational enabler. This cognitive lock-in also makes it difficult to conceive of and gain support for radically different approaches such as extended parental leave or reduced formal childcare for very young children.

Lloyd (2015) argues that this path dependence therefore makes radical reform to Early Years provision difficult, as new initiatives and policies tend to build on existing frameworks and modify policies rather than fundamentally reimagining them. This theory of path dependence in early childhood policies therefore suggests that instead of providing early childhood policy the opportunity to promote change, too often it exemplifies the divided systems of government in which early childhood policy is set (Kaga et al., 2010; Lloyd, 2015). As a result, policy formation institutionalises 'ethical and value-laden positions and dominant paradigms ... which influence subsequent social and policy debates' (Lloyd, 2015: 147).

Understanding path dependence in UK early childhood policy settings therefore helps explain why certain approaches persist and why achieving significant policy shifts can be challenging. It highlights the need for policy-makers and advocates to not only propose new ideas but also to actively work on dismantling the historical, institutional and cultural barriers that maintain the current policy trajectory. Recognising these path-dependent elements is crucial for anyone seeking to understand, influence or reform early childhood policy in the UK. It also underscores the importance of addressing systemic issues and long-standing assumptions during the process of policy formation.

Performativity and Ideological Orthodoxy

To recap, this path-dependent approach arguably reflects and reinforces society's view of children as 'becomings' – future adults who can be moulded to meet society's needs rather than 'beings' in their own right. By consistently framing early childhood policies in these terms – such as school readiness, workforce preparation and long-term economic benefits – policy-makers implicitly construct childhood as a preparatory phase rather than a period of life with intrinsic value. The difficulty in breaking from this path is evident in the resistance to alternative approaches that prioritise children's current experiences, rights and well-being. Calls for more play-based learning, lower staff-to-child ratios, or longer parental leave often struggle to gain traction against the entrenched narrative of childcare as an economic enabler. This path dependence not only shapes policy decisions but also influences societal attitudes, creating a self-reinforcing cycle.

While children gained unprecedented recognition as rights-bearing individuals with their own agency at the turn of the 21st century, they simultaneously faced intensifying institutional oversight and regulation. This paradox manifested through expanding policy frameworks and professional practices that sought to monitor, shape and control children's experiences (Proud, 2000). Such institutional control is made possible as societies typically have a collective vision of desired outcomes for their children and what they consider suitable for them. This vision is shaped by two main factors: the societal aspirations for children's future roles and the current understanding of child development. This perspective implies that children are malleable and that childhood can and should be structured in specific ways to achieve desired outcomes and financial productivity (Archer, 2022). In essence, societies tend to design childhood experiences and developmental support with particular outcomes in mind reflecting their values, expectations and beliefs about children's nature and potential. The political climate therefore significantly influences its childhood policies. In the UK, the performative and neoliberal ideology has been a dominant force during and since the Thatcher government which promoted an individualistic world view. This perspective has shaped how children are perceived – as autonomous individuals rather than products of their social environment.

Performativity is defined as a mode of regulation that employs judgements and displays as a means of control based on particular rewards and sanctions (Gray and Seiki, 2020). Performativity also reduces social processes into numerical categories that can measured by the mechanics of monitoring. Put simply by meeting the demands of external policy regulators. As discussed in Chapter 2, neoliberalism, the prevailing political paradigm in the UK, emphasises individualism and rejects societal explanations for personal circumstances. It dismisses the impact of social factors like class, gender or ethnicity on individual outcomes. Instead, it promotes the belief that anyone can succeed through personal effort and maximising their potential and failure is likewise the fault of individual flaws. This ideology has profound implications for how childhood is conceptualised and is limited and instrumental (Roberts-Holmes and Moss, 2022). Within the neoliberal framework, parents are expected to provide optimal opportunities for their children. Simultaneously, children are also, in part, given responsibility for making wise life choices based on the opportunities presented to them – despite being too young and unformed to make such decisions. Crucially, these neoliberal ideas about childhood and individual responsibility have become deeply ingrained in society. They are often accepted as self-evident truths, making it difficult to consider alternative perspectives on childhood and social development.

Context-Dependent Policy Enactment

Despite the prevailing ideological orthodoxy, policy adoption is still a contested domain. Policies do not tell you what to do directly because putting policy into practice is a more sophisticated, creative and often more disruptive than policy-makers realise (Ball, 1994). Usually set in coded texts embedded in various documents they become problematic when they are put into action. In the early childhood world, educators become the key actors as they endeavour to enact the various policy pronouncements. It is here that context plays a crucial role; where the micro-elements of a classroom or a play setting force the policies to be interpreted, re-thought, translated, deleted or simply rejected. Of crucial importance is what 'texts and voices are included in the policy documents, and which are excluded, and what is the significance of absences?' (Fairclough, 2003: 47).

It is here that the linear 'road map' metaphor of policy formation and adoption becomes challenged. The environment for enactment becomes fraught with uncertainty, ambiguity and contingency when the adult, carer or practitioner engages with young children. Policy enactment therefore becomes skewed towards the 'for' children as outlined in the title of this chapter while the linear rational choice approach of policy formation with its optimal based solutions approach tends towards the 'about' children highlighted in the title. The latter is influenced by broader social factors, where individual children are often subject to policy decisions that may not always prioritise their best interests. The perspective of children as 'beings' emphasises their inherent value and potential for agency recognising them as individuals in their own right. This viewpoint aligns with the United Nations Convention on the Rights of the Child (UNCRC), acknowledging children's rights and their capacity to contribute meaningfully to society. However, the mere existence of these rights does not guarantee their automatic implementation or benefit to children. In the UK, societal attitudes towards children and childhood have led to a reluctance in granting children opportunities to participate in policy-making processes. This hesitancy arguably stems from a persistent view of children as incapable of making rational decisions.

The concept of children as 'becomings' – focusing on their future potential rather than their present capabilities – remains deeply ingrained in UK society. This perspective often overshadows the recognition of children's current abilities and rights, impacting how they are involved in decisions that affect their lives. These societal changes have paradoxically created conditions that lead to increased regulation of children's lives. This phenomenon aligns with Foucault's observations about the state's growing interest in population management and bio-politics (Wells, 2011). It also facilitates what Smith (2014) describes as the 'government of childhood' – a concept where the state takes an active role in shaping children's experiences and development. This increased involvement partly stems from viewing children primarily as 'becomings' rather than 'beings' and education policy becoming standardised (Ball, 2021). In this perspective, children are seen more as future workers, citizens, taxpayers, or potentially, problems to be managed. Consequently, it can be argued that the state perceives childhood as a process to be guided and controlled to produce certain accepted outcomes.

Case Study 5.1

Changes to Staff-to-Child Ratios

In 2023, the UK government announced changes to staff-to-child ratios in early childhood settings, allowing providers in England to increase the number of 2-year-olds one staff member can care for from four to five. This policy change, implemented in January 2024, provides a clear illustration of how economic considerations have come to dominate early childhood policy in the UK, often at the expense of child-centric approaches.

- Before the changes the ratios in England were:
  - 1:3 for children under 2 years old
  - 1:4 for 2-year-olds
  - 1:8 for 3–4-year-olds.
- Proposed changes: In 2023 the UK government proposed changing the ratios for 2-year-olds from 1:4 to 1:5 in England.
- Implementation: These changes were officially implemented in January 2024 but are optional. Providers can choose whether to adopt the new ratios or maintain the previous ones.
- Rationale outline by government:
  - Increase availability
  - Reduce costs for parents
  - Address staffing shortages in the sector

The primary motivation behind this policy shift was to address the economic challenges facing the early childhood sector. Chronic underfunding has led to significant recruitment and retention difficulties, with providers struggling to attract and retain qualified staff due to low pay and challenging working conditions. By allowing providers to care for more children with fewer staff, the government aimed to alleviate some of the financial pressures on settings, potentially enabling them to offer more competitive wages or reduce costs for parents.

However, it can be argued that this policy change reflects a prioritisation of economic factors over considerations of child well-being and developmental needs, making this policy more *about* children rather than *for* children. Early Years experts and professionals have voiced concerns that increased ratios could compromise the quality of care, reduce individualised approaches in ECEC, and potentially impact child safety. With fewer staff members responsible for more children, there are worries that individual attention and responsive and active learning opportunities may be compromised. As outlined in the *Birth to 5 Matters* document, practitioners should be supporting the *unique* child whilst developing *positive relationships* and *enabling environments* (Early Years Coalition, 2021). This reduction in staffing levels will reduce the personalised approach of practitioners and could potentially hinder children's social–emotional development, language acquisition and overall well-being. It might also limit opportunities for rich, meaningful interactions between practitioners and children, which are crucial for cognitive development and secure attachment formation. This policy change therefore arguably negates the principles of the EYFS, reducing opportunities for supporting the unique child and decreases opportunities for the development of positive relationships.

The changes also raise serious concerns about increased stress for staff. Early childhood educators already face significant challenges in managing groups of young children, and the increased ratios may exacerbate this stress. Overworked and overwhelmed staff are more likely to experience burnout, potentially leading to higher turnover rates in an already strained sector. Additionally, safety concerns arise from the reduced ability of staff to adequately supervise and respond to the needs of more children simultaneously. Moreover, the willingness to potentially compromise on care quality and individualised attention reflects a view of young children as malleable and resilient, capable of adapting to less-than-ideal circumstances without significant long-term effects which is often not the case.

This perspective undervalues the critical importance of early experiences in shaping children's development, attachment and well-being. It prioritises future outcomes – such as school readiness and eventual workforce participation – over children's current emotional needs, opportunities for play, and rights to high-quality care. These concerns highlight the tension between economic pragmatism and child-centred policy-making as well as the complex interplay between government decisions, provider practices and societal views on childcare and learning. In essence, this policy shift demonstrates a societal willingness to treat early childhood as a phase to be optimised for future benefit, rather than a period of life to be respected and nurtured, thus reinforcing the argument that policy-making in the UK is designed to be *about* rather than *for* children.

Implications and Conclusions

To return to the question posed in the title of the chapter, it has become clear in the preceding analysis that policy formation is driven by particular ideological intent: neoliberalism and performativity. As has been shown, looking at policy through the other end of the lens, enactment becomes crucial and context is central. The former opens up difference by bringing other voices into the enactment process – the practitioner's, for instance (Ball et al., 2012: 4), thus resulting in the policy being re-framed 'for' children as it becomes owned by the practitioner or carer.

Having the two interlocking processes for policy development – formation and enactment – operating at different points in the policy cycle, makes the whole process more akin to a series of overlapping rings rather than a linear process. For example, the formation process instanced in the case of early childhood policy, is underpinned by competing paradigms that reflect the political and economic demands of the day. Spillane (2004) in a large-scale study supports this view and shows that in conventional accounts too often there is a tendency to highlight the role of the policy agents and their explicit or implicit use of rational choice theories – all aimed at 'utility maximisation' (2004: 8).

Of crucial importance, however, is the way these goals and demands are re-moulded when they enter the orbit of the practitioner. In his research, Spillane (2004) demonstrates that policies are implemented, changed, adapted, interpreted, understood or discounted even according to the 'sense making' of individual actors in various contexts. This approach challenges the many 'taken for granted assumptions' on the part of the policy-makers (Maguire et al., 2011: 494) and makes policy enactment more 'for' children than the utilitarian 'about' children which is often the preserve of the state-driven policy formation phase.

Reflective Questions 5.1

Early Childhood Policy

- How well does current government policy align with the values of the Early Childhood Education and Care sector? What challenges and tensions arise during this process?

- Who ultimately holds decision-making power in early childhood policy? How might this affect outcomes? And how do economic and political interests influence whether policies truly centre children's needs and perspectives?
- How often are children's voices and lived experiences incorporated into the policy development process? And to what extent are policies being created based on adult assumptions about children's needs?
- Reflect on the policies you have used within your own practice. Can you apply Ball and Levin's theories about the purpose and enactment of policy? And are there limitations to these perspectives?

Further Reading

Policy: For Children and About Children

Ball, S. (2021) *The Education Reform*. Bristol: Bristol University Press.

This book explores the complexity of social policies and the ways in which they have developed in recent decades.

Garrat, D. and Forrester, G. (2016) *Education Policy Unravelled*, 2nd edn. London: Bloomsbury Academic.

This book of policy development throughout education has a specific chapter dedicated to Early Childhood Education and Care policy.

References

Archer, N. (2020) Borderland Narratives: Agency and Activism of Early Childhood Educators. Doctoral dissertation, University of Sheffield.

Archer, N. (2022) 'Uncovering the discursive "borders" of professional identities in English early childhood workforce reform policy', *Policy Futures in Education*, 22 (2), 187–206.

Archer, N. (2024) 'The development of Birth to Five Matters guidance: Reflections on the critical agency and collective advocacy of an English early childhood coalition', *Early Years*, 44 (5), 999–1013.

Ball, S. (1993) 'What is policy? Texts, trajectories and toolboxes', in S. J. Ball, *Education Policy and Social Class: The Selected Works of Stephen J. Ball*. London: McGraw-Hill Education

Ball, S. (1994) *Education Reform: A Critical and Post-Structural Approach*. Buckingham and Philadelphia: Open University Press.

Ball, S. (2005) *Education Policy and Social Class: The Selected Works of Stephen J. Ball*. London: Routledge.

Ball, S. (2021) *The Education Reform*. Bristol: Bristol University Press.

Ball, S., Maguire, M., Braun, A., Hoskins, K. and Perryman, J. (2012) *How Schools Do Policy: Policy Enactment in the Secondary School*. London: Routledge.

Brewer, M., Cattan, S. and Crawford, C. (2014) 'State support for early childhood education and care in England', in C. Emmerson, P. Johnson and H. Miller (eds), *IFS Green Budget 2014*. London: Institute for Fiscal Studies. Available at: www.ifs.org.uk/budgets/gb2014/gb2014_ch8.pdf (accessed June 2014).

Department for Education (DfE) (2015) *Childcare Bill: Policy Statement*. Available at: https://www.gov.uk/government/publications/childcare-bill-policy-statement (accessed 27 February 2025).

Department for Education (DfE) (2021) *Development Matters*. Available at: www.gov.uk/government/publications/development-matters--2 (accessed July 2024).

Department for Education (DfE) (2024) *Early Years Qualification Requirements and Standards*. Available at: www.gov.uk/government/publications/early-years-qualification-requirements-and-standards (accessed July 2024).

Di Stasio, V. and Solga, H. (2017) 'Education as social policy: An introduction', *Journal of European Social Policy*, 27 (4), 313–19.

Early Years Coalition (2021) *Birth to 5 Matters*. Available at: https://birthto5matters.org.uk/ (accessed July 2024).

Education Committee (2023) *House of Commons Education Committee Support for Childcare and the Early Years: Fifth Report of Session 2022–23*. London: Stationery Office.

Eyles, A. (2022) *The Johnson Legacy: Education – UK in a Changing Europe*. Available at: https://ukandeu.ac.uk/the-johnson-legacy-education/ (accessed May 2024).

Fairclough, N. (2003) *Analysing Discourse Textual Analysis for Social Research*. London: Routledge.

Forrester, G. and Garrat, D. (2016) *Education Policy Unravelled*, 2nd edn. London: Bloomsbury Academic.

Gibbon, A. (2020) 'New early years guidance has serious flaws', *TES*, 3 September. Available at: www.tes.com/magazine/archive/new-early-years-guidance-has-serious-flaws (accessed September 2024).

Gray, P. and Seiki, S. (2020) 'Institutional performativity pressure and first-year teachers', *Frontiers in Education*, 5 (71), 1-10.

Kaga, J., Bennett, J. and Moss, P. (2010) *Caring and Learning Together – A Cross-National Study on the Integration of Early Childhood Care and Education Within Education*. Available at: www.researchgate.net/publication/44841473_Caring_and_learning_together_A_cross-national_study_on_the_integration_of_early_childhood_care_and_education_within_education (accessed June 2024).

Levin, P. (1997) *Making Social Policy: The Mechanisms of Government and Politics, and How to Investigate Them*. Maidenhead: Open University Press.

Lloyd, E. (2015) 'Early childhood education and care policy in England under the Coalition Government', *London Review of Education*, 13 (2), 144–56.

Maguire, M., Perryman, J., Ball, S. and Braun, A. (2011) 'The ordinary school – What is it?', *British Journal of Sociology of Education*, 32 (1), 1–16.

May, T. (2016) *Statement from the new Prime Minister Theresa May*. Available at: www.gov.uk/government/speeches/statement-from-the-new-prime-minister-theresa-may (accessed May 2024).

Moss, P. (2014) 'Early childhood policy in England 1997–2013: Anatomy of a missed opportunity', *International Journal of Early Childhood Education*, 22 (4), 346–58.

Nutbrown, C. (2021) 'Early childhood educators' qualifications: A framework for change', *International Journal of Early Years Education*, 29 (3), 236–49.

Pierson, P. (2004) *Politics in Time: History, Institutions. and Social Analysis*. Princeton and Oxford: Princeton University Press.

Proud, A. (2000) 'Children's participation: Control and self-realisation in British late modernity', *Children & Society*, 14 (4), 229–325.

Rigby, E., Tarrant, K. and Neuman, M. (2007) 'Alternative policy designs and the socio-political construction of childcare', *Contemporary Issues in Early Childhood*, 8 (2), 98–108.

Roberts-Holmes, G. and Moss, P. (2021) *Neoliberalism and Early Childhood Education: Markets, Imaginaries and Governance*. Abingdon: Routledge.

Smith, K. (2014) *The Government of Childhood: Discourse, Power and Subjectivity*. Basingstoke: Palgrave.

Spillane, J. (2004) *Standards Deviation: How Schools Misunderstand Education Policy.* Cambridge, MA: Harvard University Press,

Stewart, K. and Obolenskaya, P. (2015) *The Coalition's Record on the Under Fives: Policy. Spending and Outcomes 2010-2015.* London School of Economics. Available at: https://sticerd.lse.ac.uk/dps/case/spcc/wp12.pdf (accessed August 2024).

Trowler, P. (2003) *Education Policy.* London: Routledge.

Wells, K. (2011) 'Politics of life: Governing childhood', *Global Studies of Childhood*, 1(1), 1–25.

Chapter 6

The Commercialisation of Childhood

Katrina Diamond and Melissa Arrowsmith

Introduction

This chapter seeks to explore the implications of a neoliberal, capitalist ideology on children and childhood, in particular, consumer culture and levels of materialist behaviour in modern day society (for a full discussion on neoliberalism and childhood see Chapter 2). Consumerism is defined as 'the prolonged, habitual buying pattern of individuals, slowly grasping society in epidemic proportions irrespective of class boundaries' (Ghosh and Gaur, 2020: 1). Increasingly, materialism is bound up in ideas of identity formation and self-image, and the attribution of ideas of success and self-worth, to extrinsic possessions and external motivators (Allsop et al., 2020). Children display a consummate level of involvement in materialistic behaviour which arguably leads to a construct of the child as a fully fledged and agentic consumer (Ghosh and Gaur, 2020). This is achieved via a process of 'mediatisation' by corporate interests whose primary purpose is the framing of human activities in such a way as to obtain the maximum amount of data about their customers, with children as no exception (Krotz, 2018). Thus, debates around the commercialisation of children are concerned with ideas of agency and empowerment which, whilst perhaps aligning with concepts of children's rights around provision and participation, may conflict with the concept of protection, specifically with regards to parental rights, and potentially increases opportunities for exploitation and adversarial relationships for and between both parties (UN,1989; Sanders, 2020; van der Hof et al., 2020). The chapter will explore these issues with regards to issues of parental versus children's rights and the parent–child relationship, with a focus on the tensions between protection and enablement. This includes discussion of the increasing commodification and sexualisation of children, and the commercialism of play, with a view to a potential erosion of the Global North's social construction of childhood. It will explore the continuing growth of capitalism and the omnipresence of technology and media in children's lives and question whether children are indeed agentic, powerful consumers and online entrepreneurs as a result, or more vulnerable and exposed to even greater exploitation.

Children as Consumers

Children are regularly and actively involved in purchasing-driven strategies, now not only in traditional retail, but also across a range of platforms and channels, including television, social media and online advertising (Ghosh and Gaur, 2020). Increasingly, multinational organisations use peer-to-peer marketing and sponsorship campaigns often led by influential figures – known as 'influencers' – for example, the famous child vlogger Ryan of Ryan's World, who at age 7, had more than 19 million viewers

(De Veirman et al., 2019). These organisations realise the impact of these influencers on their peers, evoking a keen awareness of children, of themselves as consumers, and the significance and importance of money. The opportunity for children to earn their own money is important to them, as is evident from the *Good Childhood Report* (The Children's Society, 2023) which states that from a list of seven potential future issues, children and young people rate money as their top worry, with 61% of the children in the study claiming that having enough money was a 'very important' factor in their future. With the explosion of interactive consumer technologies, children's abilities to interact with, and access, these media, the opportunity and appetite for materialism and consumerism has increased exponentially (Backholer et al., 2020; Ghosh and Kaur, 2020; Watkins et al., 2022). The ability for children to earn income from interacting with online content, may position them as passive victims (Dastbaz et al., 2018) of developing technologies. Conversely, others (Whitaker, 2019) argue that children (albeit always vulnerable to exploitation in some respect) can also act as agentic and empowered agents in their interactions with consumerism and the evolving digital play landscape. Children are exercising agency to take control of their own futures, through a recognition of the potential to earn money for themselves and their families, and the opportunity to achieve an unprecedented, earlier financial independence. However, the extent to which children are aware of the language of persuasion and possess an adequate level of advertising literacy, particularly in children under 12, is questionable, as is the degree to which safety and rights are protected and upheld in the online, consumer world (De Jans et al., 2017). The tensions between the boundaries of a child's right to access and participation as a consumer, versus problems of excess and protection, are key to discussions of agency and exploitation (De Veirman et al., 2019; van der Hof et al., 2020).

Although 15 years old, The Buckingham Report (DCSF, 2009) is still a seminal piece of evidence in the analysis of the impact of the commercial world on the well-being of children. The report explores how the commercial world positions children as subjects of complex marketing campaigns in contemporary society, that far exceed traditional media advertising that children would have been more familiar with in the past. In terms of the potential for exploitation, arguably young children lack the ability to recognise persuasive intent, leaving them vulnerable to influence, surreptitious data collection and the creation and sharing of a profile to corporations whose singular objective is profit (Radesky et al., 2020). The report outlines both the risks posed by the commercial world as well as the potential benefits, concluding that the evidence for either perspective is rarely definitive or refutable due to the ever-changing constructions of childhood within society and the digital age. Children are neither vulnerable and helpless in their consumer role, nor are they the autonomous and empowered entrepreneurs that economists and big corporations might like to portray them as (De Veirman et al., 2019). In engaging in this discussion of contemporary childhoods and their capability as consumers, it is important not only to acknowledge the focus on a Global North perspective, but also to recognise that advancements in online technologies and increased commercialisation, may further accentuate inequality and inequity around access, creating a wider gap of disadvantage and limiting life opportunities further for many children (Nawaila et al., 2018; Backholer et al., 2020). The continuing advancement of the digital age alongside an expanding and increasingly competitive economic market ensures that commercialism will continue to be a key consideration in contemporary childhood discourse. A focus on additional resourcing that promotes digital and media literacy and equity, needs to ensure that parents, children, educators and other professionals are better informed with a view to the adequate safeguarding of children and their rights – online and off (Livingstone and Third, 2017; van der Hof et al., 2020).

When Does Commercialisation Start?

Arguably the child's introduction into consumer cultures begins with the commodification of motherhood. Patterns of consumption are heavily influenced by celebrity mothers and social media influencers (Krzyżanowska, 2020). This materialism around pregnancy and birth is promoted further via pamper parties, gender reveal parties and baby showers, with pictures and videos of babies uploaded to social media via new age 'sharenting' practices (Steinberg, 2017), along with a plethora of accompanying consumer goods, all signified as vital to the successful development and assimilation of the child into society. This serves to emphasise a dominant economic model of motherhood and arguably a relinquishing of what it means to be a good mother to a market positioning itself as the authority responsible for ensuring this (Krzyżanowska, 2020). This neoliberal idea of motherhood as the property of the market, contrasts with the individual and personal experience and subsequent interactions historically associated with the idea of motherhood and arguably embeds the mindset of consumerism at the forefront of daily mothering decisions and actions (Krzyżanowska, 2020). This drives patterns of consumption and arguably encourages the same materialism of children.

Neoliberalism, Consumerism and the Parent–Child Relationship

The term 'sharenting' is a term that has emerged in the past decade due to the increasingly invasive nature of social media on the parent–child relationship (Steinberg, 2017; Sanders, 2020). Arguably, it is the role of the parent in the first instance to protect the child from the vulnerability afforded by advertising and the media. However, it is often the parent, and overwhelmingly, the mother, that is exposing their child to these risks of exploitation, which combined with technology, results in 'sharenting' and sends a message to the child that social media is part and parcel of their daily lives (Krzyżanowska, 2020; Sanders, 2020). The relationship between the parent and the child is instrumental to the child's development and outcomes, and the degree of parental consumerism and materialism impacts on that complex relationship (Sanders, 2020). This 'sharenting' can present as an adversarial parent–child relationship, where conflict can potentially arise between the right of the child to participate in social media and consumerism, and the role of the adult in protecting the child's privacy, identity and well-being from online influences (Van der Hof et al., 2020; Pacht-Friedman, 2022). Moreover, a neoliberal model of motherhood implies that ideas of satisfaction and happiness of and within the relationship, is externally motivated by third parties. This is concerning when research shows that when people identify with satisfaction and contentment as externally motivated, via consumerism for example, they are less likely to connect with others in a close, authentic and interpersonally trusting way (Kasser and Ryan, 2001; Allsop et al., 2021). Almada and Panozo suggest that parents are to blame with regards to the over commercialisation of their children, through a lack of responsibility and ownership of the 'marketer's exploitation of their children's vulnerabilities' (2023: 3). However, it is important to consider whether the parents are aware of any exploitation and whether they themselves may be subject to the same. Similarly, we must consider that children now have different choices with regards to how and for what purpose they use technology, and that restrictions on children's technological access and participation either from parents, teachers or policy-makers must balance the risk whilst acknowledging children's perspectives and rights (Nawaila et al., 2018). Furthermore, Keddie (2016) reinforces the ideas of exploitation via a neoliberal agenda that seeks to position children as agentic consumers in the guise of empowerment, taking 'pester power' to a new level (Lawlor and Prothero, 2011). This increased agency and independence creates an antagonistic parent–child relationship where children perceive adults as getting in the way of what they want. From a rights perspective therefore, tensions result around Article 5 of the UNCRC around respecting the evolving capacities of the child and their increasing ability to make decisions about those matters that concern them, along with Article 12 stating that 'Every child has the right to express their views, feelings and wishes in all matters affecting them, and to have their views considered and taken seriously' (UNCRC, 1989). Ideas of participation and its interpretation are contentious therefore, balancing the parental role as protector and the child as a right bearing consumer, with purchasing awareness, power and consumption (Clark and Ziegler, 2014; Krzyżanowska, 2020). Significantly, the impact of any subsequent 'anti-adult' strategies and antagonistic parent–child relationships, resulting from conflicting ideals around participation and agency, is damaging, potentially manifesting in attachment disorder, anxiety and depression (Allsop et al., 2021. There is a delicate balance between access rights and protection from corporate *and* parental financial interests, particularly with younger children. This involves the successful navigation of parents or carers when moving from gatekeeper to scaffolder in ensuring alignment with the child's 'evolving capacity' (UNCRC, 1989), to ensure harmony with the relationship and avoid any potential estrangement from the parents (Allsop et al., 2021).

The Acceleration of Consumerism and Sexualisation via Evolving Digital Technologies and Media – Complex Ideologies and Consumer Identity

In modern day consumer culture and rampant capitalism, innocence is often the target of exploitation, meaning that Rousseau's construction of the child as innocent can be problematic. By constructing the child as innocent, we are positioning them as vulnerable and potentially attractive to corporate exploitation (Egan and Hawkes, 2009) via vehicles such as 'pester power' and the effects of parental comparison. However, consumerism also seeks to destroy the separate innocent identity of the child and reassume the adult identity, particularly around sexuality for financial gain (Taylor, 2010). Positioning the child as an adult consumer with the accompanying agency and purchasing power, exposes them to, and perhaps permits, increased exploitation through an early sexualisation, particularly of girls, and supports a growing 'corporate paedophilia' movement (Rush and La Nauze, 2006; Egan and Hawkes, 2008). Sexually exploitative advertising towards young children has taken place for decades. As early as 1975, the 'Love Cosmetic' advertisements for children's bath gels shows girls in mature make-up with the tagline 'Innocence is sexier than you think'. The sexualisation of the child takes place through the provision of a multitude of products and merchandise, and their continual exposure to them through increased media advertising. Vänskä,(2020) suggests that clothing is a key product when it comes to sexualising children. Outfits alluding to increased sexual attraction and other adult themes around sex and nudity are instrumental in shaping and constructing perceptions and understandings of childhood as sexualised. In early 2024, clothes retailer H & M were accused of sexualising young children through their school uniform campaign featuring two primary aged schoolgirls and the slogan 'Make those heads turn in H & M's Back to School Fashion' (BBC, 2024). Similarly, the Balenciaga Gift Collection holiday campaign in 2022 featured two separate campaigns with different images. The first showed children holding teddy bears in leather bondage gear, and the second 'office' themed advertisement included papers relating to a Supreme Court case on child porn and highlighted pornography usage in an advertising context (Jin, 2023). Chinese clothes manufacturer Just Naturally Be Yourself (JNBY) were accused of irresponsible messaging to children with phrases such as 'let me touch you' and 'Welcome to Hell' on one of their T-Shirts created for children. The increase in using children for marketing purposes will be subject to the ongoing debate regarding the related ethical implications. Arguably, this ongoing sexualisation of children results in an expansion of paedophile culture, leaving children vulnerable and at increased risk, and impacts on the notion of childhood itself, leaving it extremely fragile (Jin, 2023).

In the context of this fragility and increased opportunity for exploitation, an argument for early sexuality education and the possession by young children of a 'self-chosen and explored sexuality' may afford some protection (Brennan and Epp, 2014: 2). A small study by Stein et al. (2018) suggests that parents argue for sexuality education as a proactive strategy for both typically and non-typically developing children in fostering awareness, independence and the prevention of victimisation, with 89.5% of parents of children in the study believing that their children would benefit from sexuality education. This once again identifies the fine line between a child's agency and rights in their present state as sexually developing 'beings', and an increased awareness of those threats and dangers that may arise with this image. The role of the parent in protecting their child from sexual exploitation by corporations and/or individuals (often with online access to the child) requires further challenge as this aspect of child empowerment evolves (Brennan and Epp, 2014). Any attempt of the child to present themselves as older, 'more grown-up' or aspiring to be more like teenagers, perhaps unwittingly leads to adult perceptions of them as sexual, whilst they, arguably, are simply seeking to be seen as being 'more cool'. These ideas can be linked to the evolution of and exposure to new types of toys, media sharing and advertising of collectables such as the Bratz dolls brand, that represent tweens appearance, with 'provocatively stylish – some even say "street-walker" clothes' (Macpherson, 2005: 1), and where children aspiring to be 'hot' (Taylor, 2010) are perhaps confusing it with 'cool', but which 'reflect and amplify the association of young girls' self-identity with commodities', and the pleasure that children feel from the consumer experience (McCallister, 2007: 1). Increased use of technology and exposure to advertising (in conjunction with their emerging identities), mean children can make purchasing and relational decisions for themselves. This is an ongoing and complex process that involves communication, respect for children's agency and a continued discussion around ethics and the protection rights of parents to keep children safe from harm – both physically and psychologically (Egan and Hawkes, 2009).

The Commercialisation of Play

Historically and by way of remedy to this neoliberal and adult oriented environment, play has always been instrumental in supporting the healthy development of children, and a function that we naturally associate with childhood (Doek, 2021; Kourti et al., 2021). From a rights perspective, Article 31 of the UNCRC (1989) and General Comment 17 states the rights of the child to rest and leisure, to engage in play and recreational activities appropriate to the age of the child, and to fully develop his/her personality, talents, and mental and physical abilities to their full potential (Doek, 2021; Brooker and Woodhead, 2013). However, when discussing the commercialisation of children, it is important to consider the changing landscape of play and the inescapable reach of the market (Mesce et al., 2022). Recent unprecedented events such as the pandemic and increases in digital technology have resulted in increased multi-media use by children (Cowan et al., 2021; Egan and Beatty, 2021). Kourti et al. (2021)

chart a review of literature to suggest that during the Covid-19 pandemic, children's play opportunities were mostly indoors, with increases in screen time, and preferences for video games over board games and reading, where 'restrictions on normal life have left a space which [children] are filling with social media, gaming and watching content' (Ofcom, 2020: 4). It was reported that children continued to immerse themselves in imaginative play both on and offline and play emerged as a common coping strategy in times of stress and anxiety for young people (Mesce et al., 2022). However, these online play spaces also provided a market opportunity and social context that often bore a financial element or invitation to buy and spend, further commercialising children during a time when alternative play choices and locations were restricted (Casey and McKendrick, 2022). That is not to say that the digital environment for play does not afford positive impacts for children. Cowan et al. (2021) discuss the multimodality of play and cite the '100 languages of the child' as highlighted by the Reggio Emilia approach and suggesting that digital play is one more means of children's expression and meaning making. However, not all children experienced the shift to the online environment in the same way. According to Ofcom (2021), digital exclusion is affecting children in the UK, with evidence that 6% of households do not have access to the internet. Research including that of Holmes et al. (2022) suggest that children who are excluded from access to the internet and media are experiencing disadvantage and disconnection from play and learning opportunities, with their participation rights compromised, indicating that we tread carefully and do not adopt a deficit model of digital engagement.

Indoor Versus Outdoor Play

In addition to impacting on children as play 'consumers', increasingly neoliberal policies also impact on places and spaces for play. While post-pandemic influences may dictate that more play is taking place indoors now, additional factors relating to play and leisure funding may also be a contributing factor to a decrease in outdoor play in the UK. Outdoor play is instrumental to children's health and well-being, with research demonstrating a range of benefits, from self-esteem and confidence to stress reduction and resilience (McCormick, 2017; Roberts et al., 2020). In 2011, Play England, who had been acting as the government's national 'play strategy delivery partner', had their funding cut and contract terminated after 3 of their 5 years of the contract by the UK government. The partnership was initially introduced to align with the government's 'Big Society' with the intention that the play organisation would work with local communities to help to design and provide children and families with play facilities and spaces. Opposition to this move at the time highlighted concerns over the decision believing it created social dysfunction rather than addressing it and calls for prioritising children's health and well-being through these play opportunities were largely ignored, contravening Article 31 of the UNCRC and children's right to play. NHS data (Newlove-Delgado et al., 2022) reports that 18% of children aged 7–16 years old had a probable mental health disorder, showing an increase over time and suggesting that more play opportunities and facilities would help in supporting children through more challenging experiences and addressing poor mental health in children and young people. Despite research evidencing the importance and benefits of free and accessible play and movement opportunities for all (Haga, 2021), we are still seeing funding cuts in this area, with green spaces deprioritised to social infrastructure and economic growth, leading to the monetisation of these important spaces for children's play (Mell, 2018). Smith (2018) reports that there is an increasing political pressure to use parks and open spaces as event venues which is therefore challenging the way these spaces are governed and managed. He points to the processes of neoliberalism as the culprit, although this summation may 'oversimplify the nuances of park commercialisation' (2018: 533). Moreover, in recent years, in the UK we have seen an inflation of new business offering play opportunities to children (or more accurately, to parents). These may include indoor play spaces, stay and play activities or sessions such as forest school, and arts and crafts. These play-focused businesses offer paid experiences to enhance childhood opportunities for learning, development and entertainment, from infancy. These businesses aimed at the childhood market may include activities such as baby sensory classes, art sessions and physical movement groups, but it can also be argued that this level of commercialisation starts pre-birth in such sessions as ante-natal yoga (see previous section on the commodification of motherhood). This argument supported by Nairn (2008) begins to question whether what we are seeing is the commercialisation of parenthood which in turn leads to a consumerism focused on childhood or, indeed whether the line between childhood and adulthood is blurring, intentionally due to consumerist drivers and priorities.

Case Study 6.1

Jade's Story

Children's engagement with digital technology is particularly pertinent in considering the extent to which childhood is monetised. It can be argued that childhood now exists as an explicit economic market with children as the main unit of currency. From conception to birth, and beyond, childhood has become an increasingly economically focused space. This may start in the form of gender reveal paraphernalia and nursery designs and baby shower gifts but the main vehicle for showcasing these is via social media. Children are now being invited to take on roles in the digital world that they would perhaps not be afforded in the 'real' or offline world. Connecting with strangers online, being paid for content and being influenced into purchases are some examples of the many ways that children's online roles are evolving. Modes of employment in online and paid work has become a form of acceptable child labour – children are encouraged to take up space in the world of online consumerism, voyeurism, gaming and incessant consumption.

Jade, at 7 years old in central London, has been introduced to the world of social media, influencing and making money through online content, from a young age. She lives in an area with high levels of anti-social behaviour, poor local play and leisure facilities and high volumes of traffic. She is often encouraged to stay indoors in her free time to keep her safe; plentiful posts on local social media pages suggest that the risk of harm from predatory adults is high in her neighbourhood. Her mum has a lifestyle page on a popular platform and an account on a short form video hosting service, on which Jade has made appearances since she was born, often involved in advertising posts for children's toys and clothes. At the age of 5, Jade was set up with a profile on a video sharing platform by her family and she began to post videos of herself unboxing the latest toys, games and collectables. This venture has meant that Jade has been able to amass a considerable amount of paid work, including lucrative deals from big companies. This has increased in the last year in line with her increased number of followers. With in excess of 50,000 followers on many platforms, Jade is focused on increasing followers to ensure that she is paid more for her content. As Ofcom (2023) reports, compared to previous years (before 2023), children are now using a range of strategies to get more attention online. They do this by engaging with popular trends, using hashtags or tagging other users in their posts to ensure that more people were viewing their posts, more people were hearing what they had to say, and talking about them as a result. The report also found that girls were more likely than boys to post videos on video sharing platforms. This may suggest a link to the increased risk of sexualisation or harm from others. It also leads into a wider debate around body image and emotional well-being.

In sharing an increased number of posts, Jade has been able to generate regular income, which her mother has used to start a savings account for her. Jade's interactions with digital technology amount to more than 4 hours a day and her average spend on the online games she plays exceeds £30. This is in line with the most recent Ofcom data suggesting that children are spending an average of £38 a month on video games (Ofcom, 2023).

This case study highlights the debate between children constructed as exploited consumers vs. being viewed as empowered and agentic consumers. These further fuels the conflicting narrative around participation and protection rights for children, relating to their life choices and opportunities as outlined in the introduction to this chapter.

Reflective Questions 6.1

Children and Commercialisation

1. How can we protect children against the negative influences of advertising and consumerism, whilst protecting and respecting their rights as agentic consumers?
2. How are children's rights and safeguarding considered and enabled in a virtual world and how does this compare to the ways we protect children and their rights in the real world?
3. How is children's consent considered when involved in marketing, influencing and paid advertising if they are too young to make their own choices? Should the child's 'future self' be considered in making the decisions in the best interests of the child?
4. Is there a perceived gender difference when we consider the impact of children in an online workplace? Would this case study prompt different answers to the questions above, if Jade was a boy? What legislation might exist in the offline world to protect children's rights relating to labour and work and is there anything that protects the type of paid work outlined in the case study above?

Summary

Commercialisation is increasingly enhanced by developing digital technologies.

Digital technology appears to be serving as the perfect vehicle for capitalism and therefore consumerism. The ease with which children can access a digital world and the lack of safeguarding or up to date legislation to consider these relatively new interactions, means that children are yet to be sufficiently protected from harm whilst also being enabled to participate.

Parental cycle of perpetuating consumerism.

In reflecting on this area of contemporary Western society, it is imperative to consider the impact or parenting norms and the interactions of trusted adults with digital technologies and consumerism. With so much of the global population addicted to consumption, it is important to challenge the perceived impact on children and consider ways to better support the understanding of these elements.

Rise of anti-adultism and anti-parentism – Are we seeing the erosion of childhood?

In a world where children and young people can connect, realise their rights and claim increasing levels of independence, the societal construction of childhood and an identity of childhood as separate to adulthood, is shifting.

Prioritising children's rights to consider what these mean in a digital age.

Does the rights agenda suggest that children should be empowered to be involved and lead the commercialisation of childhood by identifying their own opportunities and making choices that influence how companies provide products for children? A future challenge is to consider children's participation and provision relating to commercialisation and how we ensure that the protection of children is upheld but not used to challenge their autonomy.

Conclusion

Whilst the chapter sets out the difficulties that children and parents face in a world of capitalism, digitalisation and consumerism, it is important that we recognise the positives that these elements can bring to the lives of children For example, research states that during the pandemic children were able to feel connected via the use of social media and the ability to study and reach out to their friends and family through technology, with positive impacts on their well-being (Goldschmidt, 2020). Whilst we acknowledge the increase of screen time, we must consider that this was for educational as well as leisure purposes and provided many children worldwide with the opportunity to continue to learn and play, albeit it in a different space. Similarly, if the advent of technology and peer influencers can show children a positive way to be confident and independent and provide a platform for some children to have a voice (Article 12, UNCRC 1989), this must be viewed as beneficial (de Vierman et al., 2019). As the use of technology grows and the focus on material growth continues, we must consider the difficult role of the parents and the challenges that they face in raising their children and, from a rights perspective, respecting the rights of their children around voice, freedom of expression and participation. This ongoing conflict is echoed by the Sonia Livingstone and the 5 rights foundation (5Rights, n.d.) whose work suggests that the original UNCRC and existing rights and safety measures for children are not fit for purpose in an ever-developing digital world. Livingstone (see 5Rights, n.d.) advises that digital rights must now be considered in order that children are both protected and empowered in the play spaces in which they are now interacting.

Due to the exponential increase of the internet and online media, parents themselves have had to accommodate these changes into their parenting, in what are previously unchartered waters (Benedetto and Ingrassia, 2021). We must be clear about our priorities for our children, namely their health and well-being, and support them in navigating the neoliberal, material world with caution. We must ensure that our children are confident and comfortable in their identity, with sufficient advertising literacy to recognise those online elements that are beneficial for them and those that disserve them, whilst acknowledging the instrumental role of parents, caregivers and society in the realisation of this.

Further Reading

The Commericalisation of Childhood

Almada, S. J. and Panozzo, G. (2023) 'Is marketing an adverse childhood experience? Practical Implications and suggestions for community psychologists', *Global Journal of Community Psychology Practice*, 14 (3).

Here, the authors position marketing to children as an adverse childhood experience, due to the adverse impacts on children's health and psychological well-being through the unregulated neoliberal economic power and government inaction. The article argues the need for protection for children from this damaging, invasive influence – one which convinces them that their identity is inextricably linked to their purchasing power and interaction with media.

Balaban, D. C., Mucundorfeanu, M. and Mureşan, L. I. (2022) 'Adolescents' understanding of the model of sponsored content of social media influencer Instagram stories', *Media and Communication*, 10 (1S2), 305–16.

The authors consider the concept of 'advertising literacy' to assess children and young people's understanding of the economic model behind social media influencing. The article considers the impact of understanding this model in relation to willingness to support a brand.

Bussy-Socrate, H. and Sokolova, K. (2024) 'Sociomaterial influence on social media: Exploring sexualised practices of influencers on Instagram', *Information Technology & People*, 37 (1), 308–27.

This article begins to explore the drivers of social influences, suggesting that these are not always controlled by explicit human actions but instead suggests that it is more likely that technology-driven algorithms are leading the contemporary understanding of social norms. The article includes analysis of the impact on influencer culture on our modern era with a particular focus on the sexualisation of females.

Whitaker, L. (2019) 'Vulnerable AND agentic? The failure of binary constructions of childhood in online games regulation', *Media Education Research Journal*, 8(2), 54–73.

This article aims to question the positioning of the child as vulnerable within an economy of gaming. The authors suggest that the existing protectionist perspective is not fit for purpose in the changing times of evolving technologies and commercialisation. The paper also argues that alternative perspectives presenting children as agentic are equally problematic as they avoid ethical issues around fair monetisation and working practices.

References

5Rights (n.d.) *Building the Digital World that Young People Deserve*. Available at: https://5rightsfoundation.com/ (accessed August 2024).

Almada, S. J., and Panozzo, G. (2023) 'Is Marketing an Adverse Childhood Experience? Practical Implications and Suggestions for Community Psychologists', *Global Journal of Community Psychology Practice*, *14*(3).

Allsop, D. B., Wang, C. Y., Dew, J. P., Holmes, E. K., Hill, E. J. and Leavitt, C. E. (2021) 'Daddy, mommy, and money: The association between parental materialism on parent–child relationship quality', *Journal of Family and Economic Issues*, 42, 325–34.

Backholer, K., Gupta, A., Zorbas, C., Bennett, R., Huse, O., Chung, A., ... and Peeters, A. (2020) 'Differential exposure to, and potential impact of, unhealthy advertising to children by socio-economic and ethnic groups: A systematic review of the evidence', *Obesity Reviews*, 22(3), e13144.

BBC News (2024) *H&M pulls school uniform advert after being accused of sexualising children*. Available from; https://www.bbc.co.uk/news/business-68054060 (accessed 20 March 2024).

Benedetto, L. and Ingrassia, M. (2021) 'Digital parenting: Raising and protecting children in media world', in L. Benedetto and M. Ingrassia, *Parenting: Studies by an Ecocultural and Transactional Perspective*. London: InTech Open, pp. 127–48.

Brennan, S. and Epp, J. (2014) 'Children's rights, well-being, and sexual agency' in A. Bagattini and C. Macleod (eds), *The Nature of Children's Well-Being: Theory and Practice*. Dordrecht: Springer Netherlands, pp. 227–46.

Brooker, L. and Woodhead, M. (2013) *The Right to Play*, Vol. 9. Maidenhead: The Open University with the support of Bernard van Leer Foundation.

Casey, T. and McKendrick, J. H. (2022) 'Playing through crisis: Lessons from COVID-19 on play as a fundamental right of the child', *The International Journal of Human Rights*, 27 (9–10), 1369–88. doi: 10.1080/13642987.2022.2057962

Clark, Z. and Ziegler, H. (2014) 'The UN Children's Rights Convention and the capabilities approach – family duties and children's rights in tension', in D. Stoecklin and J. M. Bonvin (eds), *Children's Rights and the Capability Approach. Children's Well-Being: Indicators and Research*, Vol. 8. Dordrecht: Springer.

Cowan, K., Potter, J., Olusoga, Y., Bannister, C., Bishop, J. C., Cannon, M. and Signorelli, V. (2021) 'Children's digital play during the COVID-19 pandemic: Insights from the Play Observatory', *Journal of e-Learning and Knowledge Society*, 17 (3), 8–17.

Dastbaz, M., Arabnia, H. and Akhagar, B. (2018) *Technology for Smart Futures*. Cham: Springer International Publishing.

DCSF (2009) *The Impact of the Commercial World on Children's Wellbeing*. London: DCSF.

De Jans, S., Hudders, L. and Cauberghe, V. (2017) 'Advertising literacy training: The immediate versus delayed effects on children's responses to product placement', *European Journal of Marketing*, 51 (11/12), 2156–74.

De Veirman, M., Hudders, L. and Nelson, M. R. (2019) 'What is influencer marketing and how does it target children? A review and direction for future research', *Frontiers in Psychology*, 10, 498106.

Doek, J. (2021) 'The right of the child to play with special attention to COVID-19 and the digital world', *International Journal of Play*, 10 (4), 344–54.

Egan, R. D. and Hawkes, G. (2008) 'Girls, sexuality and the strange carnalities of advertisements', *Australian Feminist Studies*, 23 (57), 307–22.

Egan, R. D. and Hawkes, G. (2009) 'The problem with protection: Or, why we need to move towards recognition and the sexual agency of children', *Continuum*, 23 (3), 389–400.

Egan, S. M. and Beatty, C. (2021) 'To school through the screens: The use of screen devices to support young children's education and learning during the COVID-19 pandemic', *Irish Educational Studies*, 40 (2), 275–83.

Ghosh, S., & Gaur, M. J. (2020). 'Consumerism engulfing childhood and youth', in *Indian Institute of Management Kozhikode 04th International Conference on Marketing, Technology & Society 2020*. Available at: https://forms.iimk.ac.in/research/markconf20/Proceedings/114.pdf

Goldschmidt, K. (2020) 'The COVID-19 pandemic: Technology use to support the wellbeing of children', *Journal of Pediatric Nursing*, 53, 88–90.

Haga, M. (2021) 'Body and movement in early childhood: Spaces for movement-based play', *Journal of Physical Education and Sport*, 21, 526–29.

Holmes, H., Karampour, K. and Burgess, G. (2022) *Digital Poverty in the UK: A Review of Literature*. Cambridge: Cambridge Centre for Housing and Planning Research. Available at: www.landecon.cam.ac.uk/sites/default/files/2024-02/digital_poverty_in_the_uk.pdf (accessed 20 February 2024).

Jin, Z. (2023) The Potential Crisis and Response Behind the Sexualisation of the Girl in the Advertising of the 2023 Balenciaga Spring/Summer Collection. 2nd International Conference on Public Culture and Social Services. Amsterdam: Atlantis Press, pp. 19–27.

Kasser, T., and Ryan, R. M. (2001) 'Be careful what you wish for: Optimal functioning and the relative attainment of intrinsic and extrinsic goals',. in P. Schmuck and K. M. Sheldon (eds.), *Life goals and well-being: Towards a positive psychology of human striving. Oxford*: Hogrefe & Huber Publishers, pp. 116–131.

Keddie, A. (2016). 'Children of the market: Performativity, neoliberal responsibilisation and the construction of student identities', *Oxford Review of Education*, 42(1), 108–122.

Kourti, A., Stavridou, A., Panagouli, E., Psaltopoulou, T., Tsolia, M., Sergentanis, T.N. and Tsitsika, A. (2021) 'Play behaviors in children during the COVID-19 pandemic: A review of the literature', *Children*, 8 (8), 706.

Krotz, F. (2018). 'Explaining the mediatisation approach', in I. Tomanić Trivundža, H. Nieminen, N. Carpentier, and J. Trappel (eds), *Critical Perspectives on Media, Power and Change*. Abingdon: Routledge, pp. 86–101.

Krzyżanowska, N. (2020) 'The commodification of motherhood: Normalisation of consumerism in mediated discourse on mothering', *Social Semiotics*, 30 (4), 563–90.

Lawlor, M. A. and Prothero, A. (2011) 'Pester power: A battle of wills between children and their parents', *Journal of Marketing Management*, 27 (5–6), 561–81.

Livingstone, S. and Third, A. (2017) 'Children and young people's rights in the digital age: An emerging agenda', *New Media & Society*, 19 (5), 657–70.

Macpherson, K. (2005) 'Barbie vs. Bratz: Who's no. 1?', *Knight Ridder Tribune Business News*, 27 November, 1.

McAllister, M. P. (2007) '"Girls with a passion for fashion": The Bratz Brand as integrated spectacular consumption', *Journal of Children and Media*, 1 (3), 244–58.

McCormick, R. (2017) 'Does access to green space impact the mental well-being of children: A systematic review', *Journal of Pediatric Nursing*, 37, 3–7.

Mell, I. (2018) 'Establishing the costs of poor green space management: Mistrust, financing and future development options in the UK', *People, Place and Policy*, 12 (2), 137–57.

Mesce, M., Ragona, A., Cimino, S. and Cerniglia, L. (2022) 'The impact of media on children during the COVID-19 pandemic: A narrative review', *Heliyon*, 8 (12), e12489.

Nairn, A. (2008) '"It does my head in ... buy it, buy it, buy it!": The commercialisation of UK children's web sites', *Young Consumers*, 9 (4), 239–53.

Nawaila, M. B., Kanbul, S., and Ozdamli, F. (2018) 'A review on the rights of children in the digital age', *Children and Youth Services Review*, 94, 390–409.

Newlove-Delgado, T., Marcheselli, F., Williams, T., Mandalia, D., Davis, J., McManus, S., Savic, M., Treloar, W. and Ford, T. (2022) *Mental Health of Children and Young People in England, 2022*. Leeds: NHS Digital.

Ofcom (2020) *Children's Media Lives: Life in Lockdown*. Available at: www.ofcom.org.uk/__data/assets/pdf_file/0024/200976/cml-life-in-lockdown-report.pdf

Ofcom. (2021) *Children and parents: media use and attitudes report*. Available at: www.ofcom.org.uk/siteassets/resources/documents/research-and-data/media-literacy-research/children/childrens-media-literacy-2021/children-and-parents-media-use-and-attitudes-report-2020-21.pdf?v=326330 (accessed 20 March 2024).

Ofcom (2023) *Children's Media Lives*. London: Ofcom. Available at: www.ofcom.org.uk/__data/assets/pdf_file/0025/255850/childrens-media-lives-2023-summary-report.pdf (accessed 28 February 2025).

Pacht-Friedman, J. (2022) 'The monetization of childhood: How child social media stars are unprotected from exploitation in the United States', *Cardozo Journal of Equal Rights and Social Justice*, 28 (2), 361–88. Available at: https://heinonline.org/HOL/Page?handle=hein.journals/cardw28&collection=journals&id=379&startid=&endid=406

Play England (n.d.) *Play England: Freedom to Play*. Available at: www.playengland.org.uk/ (accessed 28 February 2025).

Radesky, J., Chassiakos, Y. L. R., Ameenuddin, N. and Navsaria, D. (2020) 'Digital advertising to children', *Pediatrics*, 146 (1).

Roberts, A., Hinds, J. and Camic, P. M. (2020) 'Nature activities and wellbeing in children and young people: A systematic literature review', *Journal of Adventure Education and Outdoor Learning*, 20b(4), 298–318.

Rush, E. and La Nauze, A. (2006) *Corporate Paedophilia: Sexualisation of Children in Australia*, Discussion paper no. 90, The Australia Institute. Available at: www.tai.org.au/?q=node/8&offset=2 (accessed 30 September 2008).

Sanders, R. (2020) 'The impact of capitalist-led neoliberal agenda's on parents and their children', *Children Australia*, 45 (2), 101–8.

Smith, A. (2018) 'Paying for parks: Ticketed events and the commercialisation of public space', *Leisure Studies*, 37 (5), 533–46.

Stein, S., Kohut, T. and Dillenburger, K. (2018) 'The importance of sexuality education for children with and without intellectual disabilities: What parents think', *Sexuality and Disability*, 36, 141–48.

Steinberg, S. B. (2017) 'Sharenting: Children's privacy in the age of social media', *Emory LJ*, 66, 839.

Taylor, A. (2010) 'Troubling childhood innocence: Reframing the debate over the media sexualisation of children', *Australasian Journal of Early Childhood*, 35 (1), 48–57.

The Children's Society (2023) *The Good Childhood Report 2023*. London: The Children's Society. Available at: www.childrenssociety.org.uk/information/professionals/resources/good-childhood-report-2023 (accessed 28 February 2025).

United Nations (UN) (1989) *Convention on the Rights of the Child*. Available at: www.unicef.org.uk/what-we-do/un-convention-child-rights.

Van Der Hof, S., Lievens, E., Milkaite, I., Verdoodt, V., Hannema, T. and Liefaard, T. (2020) 'The child's right to protection against economic exploitation in the digital world', *The International Journal of Children's Rights*, 28 (4), 833–59.

Vänskä, A. (2020) 'Sexualising fashion? An introduction to the special theme issue', *Sexualities*, 23 (5–6), 692–701.

Watkins, L., Gage, R., Smith, M., McKerchar, C., Aitken, R. and Signal, L. (2022) 'An objective assessment of children's exposure to brand marketing in New Zealand (Kids' Cam): A cross-sectional study', *The Lancet Planetary Health*, 6 (2), e132–8.

Whitaker, L. (2019) 'Vulnerable AND agentic? The failure of binary constructions of childhood in online games regulation', *Media Education Research Journal*, 8 (2), 54–73.

Chapter 7

Children's Health and Well-being

Jackie Musgrave

Introduction

If babies and children aren't given the opportunity to develop good physical and mental health habits in early childhood, they have an increased risk of poor health outcomes across the lifespan. And if children don't feel fit and healthy, they are less likely to be able to learn and are less likely to have good well-being. However, health and well-being are complex issues, which are sometimes oversimplified – this chapter 'unpacks' some of the issues.

This chapter will give an overview of contemporary issues relating to the health and well-being of babies and young children both within the UK and globally. Such conditions include communicable health conditions, for example, infectious diseases, and non-communicable health conditions which include mental health difficulties, obesity, increasing levels of dental decay and chronic health conditions.

Bronfenbrenner's (1979) ecological systems will be adopted to frame some of the factors within children, the family, the community and society that can and do influence health. Factors will address the diversity of children and families and will highlight social, cultural, economic and religious influences on health.

The content places the child and their health needs at the centre of the chapter and will illustrate the valuable contribution that *all* adults including professionals and students, as well as carers and parents can make to improving children's health. A key message will be that working with parents in sensitive and supportive ways are critical to addressing health-related issues.

The influences that can impact on children's health are examined in detail, and the complexities of how the influences inter-relate and overlap are illustrated in three case studies that highlight the economic, cultural and social influences on diverse families. Detailed information about specific health conditions is not explored, but there are resources relating to common contemporary conditions in the 'Further Reading' section.

The chapter is designed to provoke thinking and ignite a desire to develop knowledge about children's health. The reflective questions and further reading are designed to develop knowledge and understanding of the role we all have in promoting the health of babies and children.

What Is 'Health'?

We often do not consider what is meant by health until we are unwell and feeling unhealthy. The World Health Organisation's definition of health that states 'health is a state of complete physical, mental, and social well-being and not merely the absence of infirmity' (World Health Organisation, 1948) is still relevant today. The definition points out that our health is influenced by many factors; it suggests that physical and mental health are affected by society and people within our communities.

There are numerous definitions of what mental health means and a selection are included here:

> Mental health can be defined as a state of well-being in which every individual realises his or her own potential, can cope with the normal stresses of life, can work productively and fruitfully, and is able to make a contribution to her or his community. (WHO, 2022)
>
> Child mental health, the complete well-being and optimal development of a child in the emotional, behavioural, social and cognitive domains. (NHS England, 2024)
>
> A problem experienced by a person which affects their emotions, thoughts or behaviour, which is out of keeping with their cultural beliefs and personality and is producing a negative effect on their lives or the lives of their family. (Patel and Hanlon, 2017)
>
> An interpretation of illness and the medicalisation of behaviours considered to be beyond the norm. (Burton et al., 2014: 4)

When thinking about these definitions in relation to children's mental and physical health, it is important to consider that children may have minimal influence on controlling the factors that affect their health, and limited agency in the factors within their communities. Consequently, it is critical that the adults who care and educate children, both professionally and personally, are aware of their responsibilities in relation to creating environments for children that help them to experience the best health they possibly can. To be able to understand the complexities of children's health and to be able to debate the contemporary issues affecting children's health, let's look at the historical context of children's health.

Looking at Children's Health in the Past

Up until the first half of the last century it was still a common occurrence for children to die in infancy and early childhood, that is between birth and age 5. This remains the case in many parts of the world, but in high income countries child mortality has reduced significantly. The reason for the improvements in child survival rates are attributable to many reasons.

Reflective Questions 7.1

Children's Health

1. Why do you think that children's mortality has decreased in high income countries? Write a list. To help you do this, you may want to have a conversation with someone who is over the age of 80 and ask their thoughts.

The next section outlines some of the reasons you may have included:

> *Improved infrastructure*, such as sanitation, sewerage systems and the provision of safe water supplies and safer roads. Living conditions have improved for many people, and most homes have running water, toilets and heating.

Legislation to improve the air quality and reduce pollution caused by heavy industry. Legislation to limit how children are used as labour in industries such as coal mining and factories. Greater awareness of how to protect children from harm.

Health and social care services being made freely available in many high income countries for children.

Medical advances such as improved ante-natal care, safer births, surgical and medical procedures, the development of life-saving medication such as antibiotics. The development of paediatrics as a medical speciality.

Health promotion The development of knowledge about how to prevent some health conditions, through immunisations and understanding about the importance of good handwashing.

You may have come up with other reasons why children are less likely to die in the 21st century than was the case in recent history. If you were able to have a conversation with a person aged over 80, they may have mentioned how the introduction of the United Kingdom's National Health Service (NHS) in 1948 was a turning point in improving health for everybody. Before the NHS, medical treatment had to be paid for, and this meant that many poor families were unable to afford medical fees, and consequently, children either died or suffered from conditions that negatively affected their health.

Undoubtedly, all the reasons listed above have reduced child mortality; however, this doesn't mean that children are enjoying good health. There are many factors that are contributing to reduced levels of health for young children and these are examined in the following section.

Factors That Influence Babies and Children's Health

There are many factors that can influence children's health, either in a positive or negative way. Some of the factors are within the child, others are factors within the family, wider community, society and globally. The following activity is designed to help you think about some of the factors.

Reflective Questions 7.2

Ecological Systems Theory

Using a similar approach to Bronfenbrenner's (1979) ecological system (see Chapter 1), write down some of the factors in each of the 'layers' listed in Figure 7.1 that you think can of.

You have probably come up with several factors within each of the layers that have a significant impact on children's health. Table 7.1 summarises some of the factors that you may have included in your list. The first column looks at the focus of each of the layers. The middle column includes some examples of the potential factors or causes, the third column gives a brief description of some of the possible implications of the factor or cause. As you read the content, think in depth about how potential implications can influence children's health.

Figure 7.1 ▪ Using Bronfenbrenner's (1979) Ecological System to Identify Factors That Can Impact on Children's Health

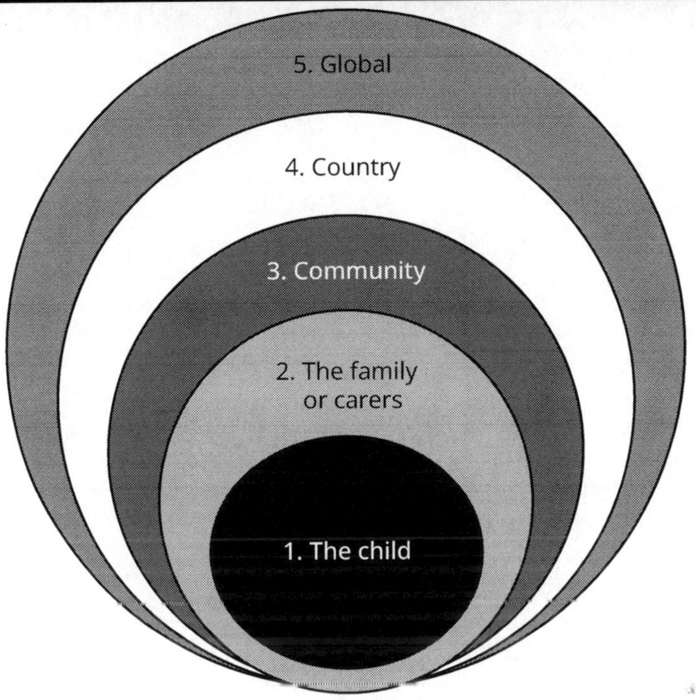

Key:

- Microsystem – within the child
- Mesosystem – within the family
- Exosystem – within the community
- Macrosystem – within the country a child lives in, or globally

Table 7.1 ▪ Factors influencing children's health

Layer	Potential factors	Potential implication
Child	Pre-conception, pregnancy and childbirth	Inadequate maternal nutrition can impact on infant weight and health. Trauma in pregnancy or during childbirth can lead to disability.
	Genetics	Some inherited conditions can cause disability and/or complex medical needs.
	Age and understanding	A child's age and level of development can affect their understanding and influence their health.

(*Continued*)

Table 7.1 Factors influencing children's health (*Continued*)

Layer	Potential factors	Potential implication
Family and carers	Social, economic, religious and cultural influences	Families may have health beliefs that are influenced by culture and/or religion. Living in poverty adversely affects children's health.
	Family structure	Single parent families *may* find managing children's health more of a challenge.
	Looked-after children	Children in the care of the state are likely to have less favourable health (DfE, 2015). Half of looked-after children have a diagnosable mental health condition, partly because of previous experiences attributable to abuse and neglect.
Community	Geographical location	Inner city and remote rural areas can have positive or negative influences on children's health.
	Provision of play areas	Well-equipped and well-maintained play areas have a positive impact on children's health and well-being.
	Children's services	Reduced funding has led to cuts in services.
	Voluntary services	Can provide advice and guidance for families.
	Shopping facilities	Access to shops that provide healthy and affordable food.
Country	Economic status of the country	High income countries have lower levels of child mortality. Low and some mid income countries tend to have no or few child health services.
	Civil status of the country	Conflict and war all impact negatively on children's health.
	Child-centred policies	Education and health policies for children can improve health, for example, in England, the Early Years Foundation Stage (DfE, 2024) includes aims and principles that are health related.
Global	Children's status as citizens	The way a country regards children is an influence on their health. The United Nations Convention on the Rights of the Child (1989) includes the child's right to health.

Poverty and Child Health

Whilst all of the factors outlined in Table 7.1 can influence children's health, the single most negative influence on children's health is poverty. Poverty affects children across the world, and in many high income countries, such as the United Kingdom, levels of poverty are increasing. 'The poor health associated with child poverty limits children's potential and development, leading to poor health and life chances in adulthood' (Wickham et al., 2016: 1).

Poverty in mid and low income countries can be magnified by climate, for example, droughts in countries where many families rely on home-grown crops can cause famine, and consequently, poor nutrition and starvation in children.

The effects of the lockdown to curtail the spread of the Covid-19 pandemic meant that many families who were poor before the pandemic became poorer and increased levels of poverty is having a disproportionate impact on children's health and well-being.

Health and Social Consequences of Child Poverty

Children living in poverty in the UK are more likely to:

- die in the first year of life
- be born small
- be bottle fed
- breathe second-hand smoke
- become overweight
- suffer from asthma
- have tooth decay
- perform poorly at school
- die in an accident. (Wickham et al., 2016)

The content of this chapter so far has given a brief overview of the factors that have improved children's health particularly those that have occurred over the last century. Better infrastructure, legislation, medical advances and the provision of health services have all made significant contributions to improving children's health. However, there are significant challenges to the health of children, and this is the case in low, medium or high income countries across the world. These are explored in the following section.

Contemporary Health Issues

People who were alive at the time of the creation of the National Health Service in the UK may be surprised to hear reports about poor levels of children's health, both physically and mentally. A report by The Academy of Medical Sciences in February 2024 (AMS, 2024) highlighted wide-ranging evidence of declining health among children under five in the UK, and calls on policy-makers to take urgent action to address the situation. The following sections summarise some of the contemporary conditions, both non-communicable and communicable, affecting children's health.

Non-Communicable Health Conditions

Many physical causes of poor health in children can be described as non-communicable, meaning they are not passed on by organisms such as bacteria, viruses and fungi. Many health conditions are avoidable.

One example of a physical health condition that is mostly avoidable is *tooth decay* which affects a quarter of all children in the UK. Oral health is frequently under-regarded in young children; this may be because children's first teeth fall out and are replaced, and consequently adults are not aware of the importance of good diet and oral hygiene starting during the first year of life when the first tooth appears. The extraction of decayed teeth in young children is the most common reason that they are admitted to hospital. However, for some children, oral hygiene is more challenging, for instance some medication used to control epilepsy can cause gum problems that make maintaining oral health very difficult.

Childhood obesity is a global issue, and it is potentially seen as being a preventable health condition. The prevalence of obesity in children aged 4–5 in the UK is reported as being 9.2%, and for children aged 10–11, as many as 22.7% are classed as obese. Levels of childhood obesity are increasing amongst young children living in poverty. The reasons why this is so are difficult to unpick, but this is attributable to food insecurity in low income homes. Many children live in obesogenic environments, meaning there is more access to poor quality, filling, relatively inexpensive and quickly available foods. Advertising of such foods is a feature of an obesogenic environment, and again, areas of deprivation are more likely to be obesogenic.

Chronic health conditions can be described as lasting for more than three months, and the effects of such conditions can negatively impact on children's well-being. The most common childhood chronic health conditions include asthma, diabetes, eczema and sickle cell disease (please see Further Reading for more information about these conditions). As many as 20% of children have an ongoing health condition. Each of these conditions have a set of signs and symptoms that help diagnosis, and in turn help to identify ways to manage the condition so that the effects on the child are minimised. This can present some challenges, for example, a child who has asthma, may 'trigger' the symptoms of asthma, namely cough, wheezing and shortness of breath by encountering substances such as animal fur, or physical activity. A natural response to prevent triggering asthma symptoms may be to limit activities that trigger a reaction; however, this may mean that a child with asthma is excluded from enjoyable learning experiences such as stroking animals on a farm trip with nursery. This is likely to mean that the child feels excluded, and this can impact negatively on their sense of inclusion and well-being. Limiting a child's physical activity may mean that they spend their time outdoors sitting with the adults and not running around and playing with their friends. As well as the possible emotional effect on them, reduced physical activity can lead to lower levels of physical development and increased risk of the child becoming overweight.

Understanding the way that a chronic health condition affects a child is critically important. Working with parents and carers to understand what triggers the signs and symptoms of a child's condition, will mean that adaptations can be made to maximise their inclusion in activities (Musgrave and Levy, 2019). It is also important to bear in mind that that many children have more than one chronic condition.

Mental health difficulties in young children are increasingly being identified and diagnosed. As many as 'one in five children and young people in England aged eight to 25 had a probable mental disorder in 2023' (NHS, 2023). It is estimated that 10% of children aged 5–16 have a clinical diagnosable mental health problem (Mental Health Foundation, 2023). The incidence of mental health conditions in younger children is also increasing.

The range of conditions and reasons that can cause mental health difficulties in babies and young children is very broad. Unlike some physical health conditions, the signs and symptoms are not always easily attributable to a mental health condition. For example, an infectious disease, such as the aforementioned measles has very clear signs, including a distinctive rash, which makes it relatively straightforward to diagnose. Babies and children with an infectious illness will show signs such as a high temperature, they can be tired and sleepy, and off their food. The presence of pain is likely to make them grumpy and affect their behaviour. Mental health difficulties in young children rely on less obvious physical signs such as a temperature and so on. Babies and young children are less likely to be able to articulate how they feel, and of course, they may not be aware that their feelings and behaviour are outside the 'norm' – although this is a word that should be used with caution.

Some of the mental health difficulties that are being experienced by babies and young children are potentially preventable. Children respond to well organised and predictable routines that meet their physical and emotional needs, such as sleep, food, drink, safety and positive relationships with reliable adults. Adults providing opportunities for children to play, be physically active, with access to safe outdoor spaces, being listened to and generally giving them the time they need to be independent and take things at their pace are all factors that contribute to a sense of good well-being. In turn, good well-being can contribute to good mental health. However, the reality is that many children's lives are not conducive to good well-being.

It is important to bear in mind that there are mental health difficulties which if diagnosed can be controlled with interventions such as medications, thus reducing the impact of the condition on the child and potentially preventing the escalation of the condition.

Communicable Diseases

Communicable diseases such as mumps, rubella, measles, diphtheria and polio, are passed on by bacteria, viruses and fungi. They are largely preventable. However, many of the diseases that are caused by infections are on the rise in the UK. In January 2024, an outbreak of measles cases in the West Midlands, in England, was causing concern (UK Health Security Agency, 2024), especially as England has had measles-free status.

Measles is very unpleasant and can leave a legacy of disability and is a cause of death. Measles had been largely eradicated in the UK; however, outbreaks of measles have started to emerge. Measles, like many other previously common childhood infections, are mostly preventable through immunisation. Like many high income countries, the UK has a national immunisation programme that is provided free of charge. Despite the schedule of immunisations that is available through the National Health Service, the uptake of immunisations by parents is declining.

There are many reasons for this decline and can be briefly summarised by what the World Health Organisation (2014) describes as the '3Cs' (complacency, convenience and confidence). Complacency is caused by a lack of knowledge about the impact of childhood infectious diseases. Accessing the free immunisation programmes is not always convenient for parents, and many parents have concerns about the safety of immunisations.

This section has looked at some of the specific contemporary health conditions that are affecting children in the UK and globally. It is important to note that although there is a distinction between physical and mental health conditions, it is not always easy to separate them out. For instance, for a child who has a physical condition, such as very troublesome eczema, the symptoms may be triggered by everyday substances like sand, water, soap and chemicals in many products. Eczema can cause intense itching that is temporarily relieved by scratching. The itching can impact on sleep, resulting in sleep deprivation, which can lead to lack of concentration and what could be seen as unacceptable behaviour, all of which can reduce the child's well-being and predispose to poor mental health.

When the Factors That Influence Children's Health Come Together

The points in Table 7.1 are an attempt at unpicking the complex features that impact on children's health. However, you may have had some difficulty in locating a factor, or influence, into neat layers. This is because many of the factors overlap each other and are inter-related. The following case studies aim to illustrate the way that the various factors come together, and how they can influence children's health. As you read the case studies, please link back to Figure 7.1, where Bronfenbrenner's ecological system has been adapted to identify factors that can impact on children's health, and consider where you would locate the factors.

Case Study 7.1

Family Living in an Affluent Area in a High Income Country

Please read each of the following case studies. Please note that there is no element of judgement or stereotyping in the content of the case studies; they are meant to illustrate the factors that can influence children's physical and mental health.

Jim and Paramjit and their twins, Nisha and Arun who are 9 months old, live in an affluent urban area. Both parents work full time in professional jobs in the nearby financial area of the big city where they live. Paramjit became unexpectedly pregnant and then she had a difficult pregnancy and birth – the twins were born 8 weeks early and she hadn't started maternity leave when she went into labour. Paramjit had to return to full time work when the twins were 4 months old because she is the main earner and Jim is working hard to start his own business, and his income isn't steady and reliable.

The twins attend a private nursery where Anya is their key person. Anya is concerned because Paramjit is often rushed when dropping the twins off, and she appears flustered and exhausted. The twins are handed over in their car seats and are often in their sleepwear when they arrive. Paramjit has mentioned that she has started to introduce solid foods to the twins but is finding it time consuming and messy. She has also mentioned that she is having difficulty getting an appointment to get the immunisations for the twins.

1. Consider the factors that may influence the twins' health; start with Paramjit's pre pregnancy time (pre-conception). Can you link them back to the factors described in Figure 7.1 and Table 7.1?
2. What are the routines and context of the family that may influence the twins' health?
3. If you were Anya, how do you think you could support the family to address some of the factors that could have an immediate and longer-term impact on the twins' health?

Comment

Going right back to the pre-conception period, as Paramjit became pregnant unexpectedly, it may be the case that she hadn't prepared for the possibility of becoming pregnant. Pre- conception – the period before conception – has been receiving more attention in recent years. Previously the importance of the health and habits of would-be parents was under regarded. It is now acknowledged that there are many factors that can influence the pregnancy and the health of the child. Such factors can link back to Bronfenbrenner and the microsystem (see Figure 7.1) and include lifestyle habits and choices including smoking, alcohol intake, quality of diet and whether illegal drugs are taken prior to becoming parents.

Pregnancy can be an opportunity to concentrate on maternal health, ensuring that as much is done to prevent complications that could affect the health of the mother and baby. Antenatal health care, an example of a service which may be provided by a country, can help to identify risk factors, such as high blood pressure. It sounds as if Paramjit didn't have much time to prepare for the arrival of her babies. And as the pregnancy was unplanned, the news that she was expecting not just one, but two babies must have been a huge shock. The early arrival of the babies will have meant that they will have been physically separated from their parents while they received additional support in hospital having been born at 32, instead of the usual 40 weeks of gestation.

Paramjit may have found it difficult to adjust to becoming a mother, and she may even have experienced a degree of resentment towards her babies. In turn, this can impact on how she bonded and formed an attachment with Nisha and Arun. And Jim as the father may have had similar responses.

Paramjit and Jim's financial situation has meant that she needed to return to work early, and as the babies were only 4 months old, it is unlikely that they were settled into a routine where they sleep well, and of course if babies don't sleep neither do the parents. Not surprisingly it sounds as if Paramjit is exhausted and is feeling the effects of being short of time.

Regarding the babies and introducing solids, Anya may consider working with Paramjit to start the weaning process so that the twins have a safe and unhurried introduction to solid foods. Anya could point Paramjit to guidance such as the National Health Service online resources 'Better Health, Start for Life', another example of guidance available within the macrosystem. Anya could also explain how she would ensure that mealtimes at nursery could be adapted for the babies, and gently suggest how the parents could follow a similar routine at home.

Many babies spend long periods of time in 'containers' such as car seats, and it sounds as if this is the case for Arun and Nisha as they are transported from home to nursery. Being contained in car seats, buggies, highchairs and so on can have a negative impact on the level of physical activity that babies have. In turn, this can impact on the level of physical development, especially in the case of babies who are born early. The World Health Organisation's (2020) guidelines on physical activity stress the importance of providing opportunities to stretch and wriggle, and also to have up to 30 minutes 'tummy time' each day.

And finally, Paramjit has mentioned that she's having difficulty accessing an appointment to get the babies immunised against some of the infectious diseases that can cause children to be very unwell, leave a legacy of disability, or even be a cause of death. The difficulty may be that as the parents are both working full time, the appointments that are being offered may clash with their working schedules. This is an example of where services may be 'hard to reach' for some families. As it is so important that babies are immunised, Anya may take the opportunity of exploring with Paramjit and Jim to find out if there are reasons other than the practical one of not being able to get a convenient appointment.

The parents may be concerned that the babies' early birth and may see this as a reason for not immunising them. As vaccine hesitancy is a common concern, Anya could send a communication that includes up to date government guidance about immunisations to all parents. Health Visitors are very well placed to support parents and advise about immunisations.

Case Study 7.2

Family in a Rural Area in the UK

Dan and Lucy are farm tenants and live in a remote rural area. The farm is not profitable, and Dan and Lucy need to diversify to find ways to earn enough money for the family to live on. Council cuts have resulted in the local bus service ending. Lucy has a part time job at a bakery which is 10 miles away in a small town and Lucy drives to work each day. Lucy can buy unsold produce at discounted prices, and this is a major benefit of the job because it reduces their food bill.

Ben is six and has special needs; he is also highly anxious and is finding school life a struggle. He attends the local primary school, but the school is finding it a challenge to meet Ben's needs. Moving Ben to a special school may be the best thing for him, but in the short term, not a good suggestion for the family, because the school is 20 miles in the opposite direction to Lucy's work. The only place that Ben feels relaxed and happy is when he works with Dan on the farm.

Nelly is four and she has recently been diagnosed with asthma which is mostly well controlled as long as she is given her preventer inhaler twice a day. Getting the repeat prescription for the inhalers can be difficult because the pharmacy in the village has closed, and the family now have to go to the town to pick up the prescription. The farmhouse is old and dusty, and there is mould in Nelly's bedroom; the house needs renovation, but there isn't the money or time available to do so. The family's cash reserve has been dwindling, and things have become worse because the car, which is old and unreliable at the best of times, has been badly damaged because of being driven into a pothole and is now off the road.

1. How do you think the family's situation could impact on Ben's health and well-being?
2. How do you think the family's situation could impact on Nelly's health?
3. Can you link them back to the factors described in Figure 7.1 and Table 7.1?

Comment

This case study highlights the impact of several factors on children's health. The geographical isolation of where the family lives is having an impact on their access to employment opportunities and in turn, their finances and economic situation; these examples could be located in the mesosystem. The uncertainty of their future is probably a source of great concern and additional stress for Dan and Lucy.

The local community can't provide suitable education for Ben. And the lack of local and reliable transport means that they rely on their car which is hard to maintain because of its age, and the cost of fuel is a big expense. The lack of shops to meet the needs of the community mean that affordable and healthy food are less easy to access. The closure of the pharmacy means that Lucy must plan carefully how to get a supply of Nelly's inhalers; without them, she runs the risk of having an asthma attack.

The case study also illustrates the uniqueness of children. The farm is Ben's happy place, he feels relaxed when working with his dad, he loves being outside and working with the animals. When at school, he feels anxious and unhappy. In contrast, Nelly's health is probably being negatively affected by living on the farm. The dust and mould in the house are possible triggers of her asthma symptoms, as is contact with the animals. The family know that the current state of affairs is unsustainable, but the parents are acutely aware that whatever they decide about their future will impact negatively on one of their children's health.

Case Study 7.3

Refugee Family

Mahamat and Mariam have come to the UK as refugees from Chad, one of the poorest African countries. Chad has been affected by war and famine for many years which has meant many families have had to flee their homes. Mahamat and Mariam have three children and Mariam is pregnant. The family are to join relatives who have lived in England for a few years in an inner-city area which has several services aimed at supporting refugee families. There is a stay-and-play group for the youngest child, and the others are settling well into nursery and school.

1. What are the potential risks to the children's health as a consequence of the family and the context of their lives?
2. What factors are likely to make a positive contribution to the health of the children?
3. Can you link them back to the factors described in Figure 7.1 and Table 7.1?

Comment

The family have had to leave their home and country and move to a country which has many different social and cultural practices; this factor can be located in the Macrosystem. The high income status of the UK contrasts sharply with that of Chad which is a low income country.

Chad has experienced conflict, and the family may have experienced traumatic events prior to their departure. The journey to the UK is likely to have been arduous and the family are likely to have been scared about their safety and concerned about the future. All these factors can take an emotional toll which can impact on well-being and mental health. However, the family is joining a community where there are well thought out services that are aimed at helping refugee families to settle into their new life. The support of their relatives and the community will give them a social network and will help them as they become familiar with new ways, and as they start to learn English.

As the family won't have been used to accessing health services that routinely provide antenatal care and immunisations for children, this is likely to require careful explanation to the family to encourage them to attend. As previously mentioned, giving immunisations to babies is something that can be difficult to comprehend if you are from a different culture. Why would you take a very healthy baby to have an injection, which is likely to make him cry, and possibly make him grumpy and give him a fever?

Many religions have objections to immunisations, for example, a public health emergency was declared in an Orthodox Jewish neighbourhood in Brooklyn, in the United States of America in 2019. This was attributed to a small but vocal group of 'anti-vaxxers' who were opposed to immunisations (Kendall-Raynor, 2019).

Conclusion

The content of this chapter has given a broad overview of the complexities surrounding children's health and the factors that can influence children's health. The case studies and the questions raised are provocations to enable you to think about the role that we all have to support and promote the health of our youngest citizens. Professionals working in services relating to children's health, education and care are well placed to work with parents and carers to achieve better health for our children, they deserve no less.

Further Reading

Children's Health

If you would like to read more about the topics discussed in this chapter, consider the following resources and readings:

Musgrave, J. and Payler, J. (2023) *Early Childhood Health Promotion: A Toolkit for Early Childhood Education and Care Practitioners*. Maidenhead: The Open University. Available at: https://oro.open.ac.uk/95887/ (accessed 28 February 2025).

A resource to support your practice in improving the health of children in preschool settings.

Open Learn Create (2024) *Antenatal Care*. Available at: www.open.edu/openlearncreate/course/view.php?id=10 (accessed 28 February 2025).

Open Learn Create (2024) *Health Education and Training*. Available at: www.open.edu/openlearncreate/course/index.php?categoryid=23 (accessed 28 February 2025).

Open Learn (2020) *Supporting Children's Mental Health and Wellbeing*. Available at: www.open.edu/openlearn/education-development/supporting-childrens-mental-health-and-wellbeing/content-section-overview (accessed 28 February 2025),

Open Learn (2023) *Supporting Physical Development in Early Childhood*. Available at: www.open.edu/openlearn/health-sports-psychology/supporting-physical-development-early-childhood/content-section-overview (accessed 28 February 2025).

Free courses available as part of a collection of 17 courses.

References

Academy of Medical Sciences (2024) *Prioritising Early Childhood to Promote the Nation's Health, Wellbeing and Prosperity*. Available at: https://aimh.uk/wp-content/uploads/2024/02/The-Academy-of-Medical-Sciences-Prioritising-early-childhood-to-promote-the-nations-health-wellbeing-and-prosperity-Feb-24.pdf (accessed 5 April 2024).

Bronfenbrenner, U. (1979) *The Ecology of Human Development: Experiments by Nature and Design*. Cambridge, MA: Harvard University Press.

Burton, M., Pavord, E. and Williams, B. (2014) *An Introduction to Child and Adolescent Mental Health*. London: Sage.

Department for Education (DfE) (2015) *Promoting the Health and Well-being of Looked-after Children*. London: DfE.

Department for Education (DfE) (2024) *Early Years Foundation Stage (EYFS) Statutory Framework*. Available at: www.gov.uk/government/publications/early-years-foundation-stage-framework--2 (accessed 19 April 2024).

Kendall-Raynor, P. (2019) 'Measles outbreak: Misinformation and poverty fuelling quadrupling of worldwide cases', *Nursing Children and Young People*, 31 (3).

Musgrave, J. and Levy, R. (2019) 'Including children with chronic health conditions in early childhood education and care settings', *The Journal of Early Childhood Research*, 18 (2), 159–73.

Mental Health Foundation (2023) *1 in 10 children have no one to talk to in school when they are worried or sad*. Available at: www.mentalhealth.org.uk/about-us/news/1-10-children-have-no-one-talk-school-when-they-are-worried-or-sad

NHS England (2023) *One in Five Children had a Probable Mental Disorder in 2023*. Available at: www.england.nhs.uk/2023/11/one-in-five-children-and-young-people-had-a-probable-mental-disorder-in-2023/ (accessed 28 February 2025).

NHS England (2024) *Infant and Early Years Practitioner (IEYP) training: for the early years' workforce and the broader children and young people's mental health community*. Available at: https://view.officeapps.live.com/op/view.aspx?src=https%3A%2F%2Fwww.hee.nhs.uk%2Fsites%2Fdefault%2Ffiles%2Fdocuments%2FCYP%2520PT%2520-%2520Infant%2520and%2520Early%2520Years%2520Practitioner%2520%2528IEYP%2529%2520Training%2520Curriculum.docx&wdOrigin=BROWSELINK

Patel, V., & Hanlon, C. (2017) *Where there is No Psychiatrist: A Mental Health Care Manual* (2nd ed.). Cambridge: Cambridge University Press.

UK Health Security Agency (2024) Confirmed cases of measles in England by month, age, region and upper-tier local authority: 2024. Available at www.gov.uk/government/publications/measles-epidemiology-2023/confirmed-cases-of-measles-in-england-by-month-age-region-and-upper-tier-local-authority-2024

United Nations (1989) *Convention on the Rights of the Child*. Available at: www.unicef.org.uk/what-we-do/un-convention-child-rights/

Wickham, S., Anwar, E., Barr, B., Law, C. and Taylor-Robinson, D. (2016) 'Poverty and child health in the UK: Using evidence for action', *Archives of Disease in Childhood*, 101, 759–66.

World Health Organization (WHO). (1948). *Constitution of the World Health Organization*. New York: World Health Organization.

World Health Organization (2014) *Report of the SAGE Working Group on Vaccine Hesitancy*. Available at: www.asset-scienceinsociety.eu/sites/default/files/sage_working_group_revised_report_vaccine_hesitancy.pdf (accessed 28 February 2025).

World Health Organization. (2022) *Mental Health*. Available at: www.who.int/news-room/fact-sheets/detail/mental-health-strengthening-our-response

World Health Organisation (2020) *Guidelines on Physical Activity and Sedentary Behaviour*. Available at: www.who.int/publications/i/item/9789240015128 (accessed 8 April 2024).

Chapter 8

Play: Investment or Pleasure?

Zoe Lewis and Vina Patel

This chapter takes a historical view of children's play from the relative freedom of early 20th century city streets, through the development of kindergartens, nurseries and infant schools. It explores the question of whether play might be considered as an investment for society or as a pleasurable activity for children themselves. The work of Foucault is used to consider the power relations that challenge children's right to play when it becomes a pedagogical approach and how that produces children as passive recipients of education and an investment in the future workforce.

A place-based approach is taken to trouble the binaries of nature/culture, work/play, adult-led/child-initiated play and ultimately investment/pleasure. The chapter concludes with a case study demonstrating the intergenerational potential of a forest school space where power is distributed and the boundaries between investment and pleasure are blurred.

What Is Play?

Play is widely associated with early childhood, but its complexity, unpredictability and fleeting nature make it almost impossible to arrive at a singular or precise definition. Therefore, it is perhaps more helpful to explore play through several different lenses and perspectives. The first, and perhaps most common of these lenses, is play as understood through its key characteristics.

Play is usually considered to be a spontaneous process, active, imaginative, social, but also aimless and the opposite of work (Moyles, 2015). In their play, children produce their own narratives, set their own boundaries for the action, and determine their own rules (Wood, 2013). When play takes place outdoors, children identify their own challenges and learn to balance them with a level of risk that they can manage for themselves (Solly, 2014). Play is often described as being child initiated, child led or self-directed. Free from any rules and controlled by the players. It is not possible to force anyone to play because play is an intrinsically motivated, spontaneous and freely chosen activity, valued for its own sake, serving its own ends and purposes. There are often high levels of concentration and engagement because children find their play pleasurable and meaningful, but there is also uncertainty in the absence of any contextual or social factors that might constrain the play. Play is a way of knowing and being.

Romantic interpretations of play are connected to a view of childhood as being innocent and play being a natural process. From this perspective, play is always positive, frequently taking place in open green spaces with natural materials such as trees, stones, mud and water being the main resources. It might be argued that this is a nostalgic view, overlooking the possibility that play can also be 'coercive, cruel and dangerous' (Burman, 1994: 166), disturbing for adults to watch, and more likely to be based on idyllic adult memories of childhood rather than the realities of children's experiences today (Taylor, 2013).

Outdoor spaces may have the potential to offer more freedom to play and less pressure than indoor learning environments where adults hold more power and control. Therefore, children frequently seek out these spaces to play away from the adult gaze and in ways that they find personally meaningful. Adults may also see outdoor play as a positive experience, supporting children's health and physical development and a potentially more suitable activity than sedentary indoor play with computer games and the internet. Or perhaps children have become disconnected from nature, are suffering from 'nature deficit disorder' (Louv, 2005) and need more play opportunities which adults are expected to provide. These romantic, largely Western, discourses of play suggest natural, active, joyful activities that are pleasurable for children to engage in.

Reflective Questions 8.1

Experiences of Play

- What are your memories of play in childhood?
- What does play mean to you now?

Play and Learning

A contrasting understanding of play is derived from psychological theories of children's development. Piaget's theories (1951) dominate Western thinking about child development whereby children's learning is understood to pass through predetermined stages towards agreed, normative outcomes (Burman, 1994). In this context, play is reduced to an instrumental process in which young children explore and assimilate new knowledge and skills to make sense of the world. Similarly, Vygotsky's theory (1978) suggests a pedagogical approach where adults or peers have a mediating role in guiding children's learning through play. Vygotsky (1978: 102) argues that play provides the context for learning, in which the child acts 'as though he were a head taller than himself'. Together, these developmental and pedagogical perspectives combine to produce a dominant discourse of play being harnessed in early childhood education as an investment in children's learning on what might be described as a linear, individualised journey towards adulthood.

Play Cultures

More recent perspectives recognise the social and material relations that shape children's play. It is through their playful interactions that children create their own cultures and practices. However, limitations can occur through adult unconscious bias, leading to decision-making being based on the dominant culture and not the children themselves. Adults must reflect carefully to ensure that each child can see themselves in play opportunities that represent their own religion, race and culture (Louis and Betteridge, 2024).

Furthermore, children are always entangled with and attuned to the spaces in which they play, adapting them for their own purposes and at the same time developing their own identities from within them. In a relational context, play becomes a means of challenging the power dynamics, rules and norms of the adult world, creating disorder and taking a degree of control. There is also an emotional and sensory dimension to these connections between children, spaces and places through the embodied ways in which play is entangled with the material world (Rautio and Winston, 2015). Children derive their own hidden and secret knowledges (Norman, 2017) from their play in the more neglected and often overlooked spaces and materials of the urban environment, but the meanings they derive from these spaces may no longer be accessible to adults.

Historical Discourses of Play

Historical perspectives from the pioneers of play in early childhood education chart the development of several potentially competing discourses originating in the Global North. As the unstructured play of working-class children moved from the streets and gutters of the city to the newly formed spaces of the free kindergartens and then to nursery schools, children's opportunities for intrinsically motivated and pleasurable free play were transformed into play as a way of learning (Read, 2010).

Romantic ideals of the innocent child playing, growing and developing in nature were encapsulated in the concept of the 'kindergarten' which was celebrated as a safe, protected garden space in which children could play and learn (Duhn, 2012). A founding pioneer of the kindergarten approach was Friedrich Froebel (1782–1852), who saw play and nature as being central to childhood, development and learning. His kindergarten activities included the study of nature so that children would understand the fundamental interconnection between all living things. Froebel particularly valued outdoor play because it gave children the autonomy to express themselves freely and contributed to their emotional well-being as well as their learning (Wall and Owen, 2021). Therefore, Froebel's (1897) pedagogy of the kindergarten produced outdoor spaces as sites for play-based learning and play became valued as children's 'work'.

Following Froebel's ideas, from 1900 new 'free' kindergartens began to open for working-class children. However, their aims were broader than the earlier fee-paying kindergartens of the middle classes, and perhaps guided by different political motives (Read, 2010). Their founders sought to improve the lives of poor children in urban areas by addressing their health and welfare needs through outdoor experiences. Despite their good intentions, these developments led to new tensions and discontinuities in the discourses of play in relation to early education.

Social Discourses of Play

Margaret McMillan (1901: 79) drew upon Froebel's romantic model of the garden as the natural learning environment for young children when claiming that '... fields, the woods and meadows, and the brook-sides are the best school rooms'. Together with her sister Rachel, she founded the Open-Air Nursery School in Deptford, again emphasising the importance of fresh air, exercise and healthy living. Like Froebel, she encouraged children to care for nature as that would also encourage them to care for themselves and others (McMillan, 1904). Although McMillan clearly wanted to improve working-class childhoods, Steedman (1990) questions the lack of agency afforded to poor children who had previously been able to play in the relative freedom of the city of streets. Images of them playing in dirty, foul-smelling and potentially immoral conditions contrasted sharply with romantic conceptions of the child playing happily in nature (Read, 2010). There may also have been social reasons to move children's play from the streets to the kindergarten within these aims of 'child-saving'. Read (2010) argues that there was a hidden political desire to control children through their play and to socialise them into middle-class values of cleanliness and order whilst training them to become useful members of an increasingly industrialised workforce. The change of terminology from the '*kindergarten*' to the open-air '*nursery school*' indicates an important shift in the discourse of play which could be interpreted as an investment in the economic future of the country and its ability to compete in the 20th century (Read, 2010). At the same time, the concept of the nursery school also began to redefine what was socially acceptable as 'good and appropriate play', while other working-class, street-based forms of play became morally and physically undesirable (Read, 2015: 135).

In 1905, a Board of Education investigation (cited in Read, 2015: 142) reported that conditions in public elementary schools were 'totally unsuitable for young children, including rigid adherence to timetables, formal teaching styles, lack of physical activity, limited changes in environment, and disciplinary regimes requiring children to sit still with folded arms'. There was a need to expand free nursery school provision, although this was largely limited to the children of poor families. Children's play spaces in the streets and gutters of the city, where they had once been an annoyance to adults and often referred to as guttersnipes or street urchins, were moved into more suitable, safer, cleaner and healthier settings. The mud, dust and debris of the streets were replaced with dedicated gardens, educational objects to explore, drawing exercises and writing slates. However, many of the original romantic ideals of the kindergarten were lost as play acquired an educational purpose.

Similar patterns continued through the early 20th century where acceptable modes of play and play spaces were increasingly linked to educational outcomes while unregulated public spaces began to be seen as being dangerous to children. By 1914, Hendrick (1997: 36) suggests that 'a recognisably "modern" notion was in place: childhood was legally, socially, medically, psychologically, educationally and politically institutionalized'. There was now a socially agreed definition of where and how children should play.

Welfare reformers continued to argue for the provision of appropriate play spaces that would remove children from the dangers of adult society and where they would not interfere with adult activities. Writing in 1930, Susan Isaacs argued again for the importance of play in education, re-claiming it as a 'child's work', and suggesting that play was 'nature's means of education' (1930: 9). However, it is important to note that Isaacs (1930: 81) did not have any planned outcomes for the youngest children's play. Instead, she was guided by their questions and interests, which were then followed 'for their own sake'.

Outdoor Play, Safety and Sustainability

The 1930s also saw the development of dedicated play areas with swings, slides, sand and perhaps a paddling pool, while more naturalistic spaces with trees, hedges, birds and wildlife were often set aside to make space for these new playgrounds. Soon afterwards, safety concerns led to metal playground equipment being replaced by coloured plastic, and asphalt bases replaced by rubber matting. However, an adult overemphasis on safety and control took much of the challenge out of play and many children returned to the adventure and excitement of the bombed city streets around the war period.

The 1967 Plowden Report recognised the value of play as the most appropriate way for young children to learn, arguing in favour of the child-centred approach that had been established by nursery schools (McDowell Clark, 2016), while away from education, the play of 1970s childhoods remained a fairly 'free range' outdoor experience. New adventure playgrounds briefly challenged the sanitised play spaces of the past but were then closed during the risk averse period of the 1980s and 1990s. These ongoing safety concerns were reflected in investment to provide 'more safe places to play' through the policies of the 2000s (DCSF, 2007: 31). However, by the start of the 21st century, children's access to outdoor play was still limited. Arguments that they are becoming disconnected from nature (Louv, 2005) and losing their natural love of it have led to a new role for outdoor play in supporting ecological sustainability. Whilst current campaigns (for example Children & Nature Network, 2024) for children's right to regular access to play in natural spaces are focused on the future, they could also be interpreted as a return to romantic notions of the kindergarten as an investment in the health and well-being of both children and the planet.

Power Relations in Play

The philosopher Michel Foucault (1977) offers a helpful framework to analyse some of the inherent assumptions in the varied discourses of play considered so far. Foucault was a poststructuralist thinker, which means he was interested in applying critical perspectives to explaining the inter-relations between power, discipline and knowledge. He argues that knowledge, people and society are never neutral. They are always shaped through politics and language. For example, the ways in which their play is thought about and discussed as being 'natural', 'educational', 'developmental' or 'risky' shapes the ways in which young children are understood, how they behave, how they understand themselves and what becomes possible, acceptable or unthinkable in their play. Foucault's ideas about 'governmentality' (2000) and 'disciplinary power' (1977), help to understand how rather than there being generalised 'truths', understandings of play have all emerged from within particular social contexts and become normalised so that they are seen as 'common sense' and therefore they are taken for granted. The social and historical analysis above raises several questions:

- What kinds of spaces and places are suitable for young children's play?
- What is too risky or dangerous for play?
- Which play materials and resources are appropriate for young children, and which are not?
- What is acceptable as educational play in Early Years settings, and which kinds of play are discouraged?

Using Foucault's ideas as a theoretical framework, these questions guide the remaining analysis of play in this chapter. It aims to trouble the binary of play as investment or pleasure and to explore how children themselves are governed and their subjectivities are produced through complex and often competing discourses of play.

How and where children can play reflects cultural values. Assumptions are made about how to play properly. Language and discourses of educational play favour particular groups in society, while the play of others is deemed unsuitable or unacceptable. Play has become increasingly entangled with learning agendas and political drives for measurable outcomes in return for financial investment. The pleasurable, intrinsic, but unpredictable and uncontrollable nature of play makes these outcomes impossible to guarantee. As a result, the role of play within education is marginalised in favour of more adult-led, formal instruction that is more easily linked to learning intentions and normative developmental expectations. The power of adults to control children's choices, use of time and access to play materials and spaces within educational policy and accountability regimes produces play as an investment in human capital, and children's futures as a return on that investment (Moss and Petrie, 2002).

Although it was not their original intention, Froebel and Isaacs have contributed to another dichotomy between work and play that serves to separate children from the adult world. Play is trivialised when understood as 'child's play' and the dichotomy becomes a powerful 'regime of truth' (Foucault, 1977) in early childhood education where work and play are normalised as being opposing activities. Arguments that early childhood educators 'just play' add to this trivialisation and contribute to a deficit view of young children as incomplete – adults in the making.

Furthermore, adult agendas focus on adult fears, including stranger danger, increased traffic, normative interpretations of what is 'good parenting' and worries about children's development, health and physical fitness. Adult interpretations of socially acceptable and 'normal' play experiences regulate children's bodies, again separating them from adult society for their own protection. They keep children's play out of the way of adults and shape their behaviour towards more sedentary, disciplined ways of being. This produces a regime of truth where socially constructed, adult discourses of play as an investment in society become the obvious, unquestioned and common-sense way in which it 'should' be understood.

Regulating Educational Play

In the highly regulated space of the classroom, discourses of play shift to institutionalised and individualised aims of school readiness. Early childhood education is governed by predetermined and normative outcomes that are defined and legitimated by policy. The expectations of school, where children must learn how to follow routines, to sit still, raise their hand before speaking and only use 'inside voices', regulate play within the wider school culture of performativity (Roberts-Holmes, 2015). Consequently, for much of the day children must resist the temptation to engage in their own play (Hattingh, 2024), or at least avoid getting caught doing so. Recent Covid lockdowns have created additional concern for children's 'delayed' development, leading to political calls for more structured learning environments and even fewer opportunities for free play. The result is a 'schoolification' (Moss, 2012) of children and an institutionalisation of their play which constructs them as passive, under-developed, future members of the workforce.

Paradoxically, play is also understood as a developmentally appropriate way for children to learn. Playful and play-based pedagogical approaches seek to harness the engagement and focus that are afforded by play to motivate children to learn in the classroom. Policy discourses and classroom practices combine to produce an illusion of classroom-based play as being a controllable, ordered and coherent process in which adults direct the play according to the knowledge they wish to impart. Children's right to engage in what matters to them is simultaneously marginalised and governed by a hurried curriculum and tight timetables. Free play time is only permitted after learning outcomes have been met and the work is done. Consequently, an unhelpful work/play binary is produced in education, where investment in play is only worthwhile if its outcomes lead to increased levels of cognitive development or to aspects of life that are socially valued in the adult world (Norman, 2017).

Reflective Questions 8.2

Play and the School Readiness Discourse

- In what ways does the school readiness discourse impact on play?
- How might practitioners resist this discourse and support children's right to meaningful, self-directed play?

Children's Right to Play

Throughout historical discourses, play can be seen as being potentially challenging to an adult society which seeks ownership and control. Furthermore, children's play is not always understood or valued by policy-makers and other adults (Moss and Petrie, 2002). There has been little consensus on how to value and promote children's right to play for their own pleasure. Under Article 31 of the United Nations Convention on the Rights of the Child (1989), children have a right to relax, play and take part in cultural, artistic and recreational activities. Similarly, for children, their play affords opportunities to make their own choices and to slow down from busy lives where their leisure time is often dominated by hurried journeys between organised out-of-school group lessons and activities.

In 2013, the United Nations expressed concern that there was insufficient recognition given to children's rights under Article 31 and that '… poor recognition of their significance in the lives of children results in a lack of investment in appropriate provision …' (UN, 2013: 3). This lack of investment in both time and financial resources, for outdoor play in particular, is likely to be due to a number of issues. Children spend increasing amounts of their time in education and care settings, and parents have less time to take their children to parks and public play spaces due to working long hours and/or long distances away from home. Safety concerns around road traffic accidents, crime and pollution have increased due to population growth and a move to more urban ways of living. Children's pleasure in play thrives on challenge, risk and adventure but these adult fears have led to a reluctance to allow them free access to outdoor play. Normalised views of parenting where children should be supervised at all times have resulted in overprotection and conceptions of 'cotton wool children' (Nikiforidou, 2017) who lack the confidence to judge the safety of play situations for themselves. All these barriers to children's access to outdoor play challenge the romantic notion of 'natural' childhoods of the past and there remains an ongoing need for investment in more safe but challenging play spaces.

Play Spaces and Places

When considering the development of new play spaces, children are not always included in local planning processes, and where they do participate, it is often only at a superficial level (McDowell-Clark, 2016). Most public spaces reflect adult values and intended purposes, and even when they are intended for children's play, they are determined by the dominant culture, placing them clearly within adult control (Taylor 2013). Alternatively, when children seek out their own play spaces, they identify very different features as being interesting or meaningful (McDowell Clark, 2016), often choosing messy or neglected spaces, alleyways and hidden places away from the adult gaze. Their connection with these spaces is founded on the enjoyment and pleasure they derive from their play. They explore power dynamics, imbue status on people and objects, and stake claims on particular places and materials as a means of taking control of their play. Regular opportunities to play in these spaces of their own choosing can develop children's cultures and sense of belonging, connection, neighbourhood and well-being.

However, children's play spaces remain under threat. In his argument for children's right to free play in nature, Louv (2005: 27) cites the example of 'no ball games' signs as evidence of this adult control of children and their play, going on to suggest that 'natural play' is being 'criminalised' through such adult restrictions. There is potential for intergenerational conflict over play due to adult concerns about noise and disturbance, while children's access to outdoor play is also influenced by their own age, gender, socio-economic status and location, and it is particularly limited for babies and children with disabilities.

Lack of play space is an increasing issue for campaign groups such as Play England (2023) who found that regular opportunities for children to play out in their streets have been in dramatic decline in a society. Children want to play outdoors but their play is not always welcome. In 2002 the Welsh government began to address children's rights by investing in the first specific national policy for children's play. Play Wales (2024) now states, 'We envision a future where play is valued in Wales for being crucial to a healthy and happy childhood. A country where children can freely explore, discover, develop and grow through play'. Similarly, Play Scotland (2024) has a national strategy aimed at 'realising the right to play' and articulating a core belief that 'play is fundamental to a healthy and happy childhood'. These policies reflect a renewed commitment to play as a source of children's welfare and well-being and therefore, an investment in both individuals and wider society.

Jobb (2019) combines Foucault's ideas about power relations with a focus on space and place that is offered by geographical research and place-based pedagogies (Duhn, 2012). Jobb (2019) explains that space can be understood as the physical environment, which is fixed and bounded. Place, on the other hand, is a more fluid, relational assemblage of the social and the material context. A place is constructed as meaningful and valued through the activities and interactions, such as play, that occur within it. When children shape spaces through their play, they are creating a 'place' that they value through the embodied connections and attachments they form during that play and the feelings, sensations and memories they make in the process. Therefore, when play is interpreted as a place-based activity, rather than being imposed by adults on children, power becomes something that is constructed and shaped through the relations and interactions between children, adults and the physical environment. This shifts the perspective of adults holding all the power over children's play to recognise that young children are acutely attuned to their play spaces and shape them in their own ways.

From a relational, place-attuned perspective, children's right to play can only be realised within a supportive political, financial and environmental policy framework (UN, 2013). This requires an 'optimum environment' in which children are afforded time and space to play in spaces that are free from the hazards of traffic and pollution (UN, 2013: 10) and in which they can create a 'culture of childhood' through their own 'languages, games, secret worlds, fantasies and other cultural activities' (UN, 2013: 5). If children's rights are to be respected, adults must invest and engage on a more equal, intergenerational level, working with children as genuine partners in planning for and supporting play. In this way, play has the potential to produce children as being powerful, strong and capable through their interactions with adults who respect them as children with their own cultures and interests.

Reflective Questions 8.3

Play and Choice

- Why should children have choice over their play spaces and places?
- In what ways can young children be powerful in play?

Case Study 8.1

From Kindergarten to the Forest School

In this forest school space, in the Midlands region of England, the boundaries between education and play as work are blurred with those of a leisure time afforded by an outing to a public visitor attraction. The space is described as a forest school, but this is an informal educational setting and its informality brings a freedom from work and the performative systems of schooling for both children and adults. This is a space designed for children but also for people of all ages to socialise, create and connect within the parkland landscape.

I feel my spirits lifting as I take a deep breath of the cool fresh air on my walk along the imposing avenue of mature giant redwood trees between the car park and the forest school entrance. I feel a sense of relief, having left my usual indoor workplace to research and play in the freedom of the outdoors.

The space is arranged as a circle of tents and play areas where children can choose to engage with a range of natural materials provided by the practitioners or to source their own. Beyond the tents lies a blue tape marking the boundary of the play space. Nobody mentions or crosses it. A few parents and carers choose to accompany the children as they play in the mud kitchen, paint with natural materials, or dig for 'dinosaur' bones. They share memories of family activities and past experiences that come to mind in this space. An old rowing boat prompts stories of adventure, while a central circle of logs invites children to jump around carefully without falling into the 'crocodile infested' waters below. The circular space within the logs provides a regular meeting space where parents, grandparents, carers and practitioners frequently stop to socialise. They gather and chat easily, leaving the children to move freely in and out of the various tents and activities. They are supervised, but not always visible to the adults.

There is great concentration as very young children struggle to transport pots full of water across the uneven terrain without spilling it. Mud cakes are baked and served to passers-by. The sound of drumming emerges from metal pots and pans in the music area. It reverberates across the whole site. A calm, purposeful atmosphere pervades the setting as children and adults play and socialise together, enjoying the pleasure of having the space, time and materials to think, explore and create in the many possibilities afforded by this forest school space.

In the case study above, play serves its own purpose and is an end in itself. In the complex interaction between adults, children and the material space, there are no predetermined, individualistic developmental goals or concerns about future school readiness. Instead, there is a trust in children to determine their own needs in the present moment. They are learning and developing by playing alongside adults who foster their creativity and afford them the autonomy to follow their own interests and make their own choices. The right of very young children and babies to create their own play spaces and direct their own play is valued and respected. There is no separation between work and play, nature or culture or what is deemed adult or child led play in this space. Investment and pleasure are brought together in the production of a place that is meaningful across the generations.

Investment or Pleasure?

This chapter has explored social, historical and place-based conceptualisation of play to consider whether it is an investment in society's future or for children's pleasure. Thinking with Foucault's ideas about power and normative discourses has revealed a series of socially constructed and potentially unhelpful binaries including work/play, nature/culture and adult/child. Power relations between children and adults have challenged children's right to play at home, in their communities and in education. These binaries and power relations produce children as passive in social processes that limit their potential to being an investment in the future workforce. However, by exposing and reconsidering these power relations the chapter has shown that children's rights and their contribution to society are only genuinely valued when their independent, free play is taken seriously.

Reflective Questions 8.4

Reflecting on Play

- What assumptions are made about children's play in educational settings?
- How would you justify increased investment in children's play and play spaces in your local area?
- How do play experiences impact on the ways in which children understand themselves?

Further Reading

Play

If you would like to read more about the topics considered in this chapter, we recommend the following:

Owen, K. (2021) *Play in the Early Years*. London: Sage.

This book provides a comprehensive introduction to key debates in the field of play. Separate chapters provide a focus on historical perspectives, outdoor play and children's right to play.

Louv, R. (2005) *Last Child in the Woods: Saving our Children from Nature-Deficit Disorder*. New York: Chapel Hill.

This key text draws upon romantic discourses of play to argue that children are suffering from nature-deficit disorder. Louv is also the co-founder of the Children & Nature Network.

Play Scotland's website provides a range of resources for practitioners, families and communities, all aimed at fostering children's right to play: www.playscotland.org.

References

Burman, E. (1994) *Deconstructing Developmental Psychology*. New York: Routledge.

Children & Nature Network (2024) *Our Work*. Available at: www.childrenandnature.org/about/ (accessed 13 March 2024).

DCSF (2007) *The Children's Plan: Building Brighter Futures*. London: DCSF.

Duhn, I. (2012) 'Making "place" for ecological sustainability in early childhood education', *Environmental Education Research*, 18 (1), 19–29.

Foucault, M. (1977) *Discipline and Punish: The Birth of the Prison* (A. Sheridan, Trans.). Harmondsworth: Penguin.

Foucault, M. (2000) 'Governmentality', in J. D. Faubion (ed.), *Power: The Essential Works of Foucault 1954-1984*, vol. 3. London: Penguin, pp. 201–22. [Original work published 1978.]

Froebel, F. (1897) *Pedagogics of the Kindergarten* (J. Jarvis, Trans.). London: Appleton Press.

Hattingh, L. (2024) 'Time to play, time to think: Meaningful moments in the forest', *European Early Childhood Education Research Journal*, 32 (1), 22–3.

Hendrick, H. (1997) *Children, Childhood and English society 1880–1990*. Cambridge: Cambridge University Press.

Isaacs, S. (1930) *Intellectual Growth in Young Children: With an Appendix on Children's Why Questions by Nathan Isaacs*. London: Routledge.

Jobb, C. (2019) 'Power, space, and place in early childhood', *Canadian Journal of Sociology*, 44 (3), 211–32.

Louis, S. and Betteridge, H. (2024) *Let's Talk About Race in the Early Years*. Abingdon: Routledge.

Louv, R. (2005) *Last Child in the Woods: Saving our Children from Nature-Deficit Disorder*. New York: Chapel Hill.

McDowell Clark, R. (2016) *Childhood in Society for the Early Years*, 3rd edn. London: Sage.

McMillan, M. (1901) *Early Childhood*. London: Swan Sonnenschein & Co.

McMillan, M. (1904) *Education Through the Imagination*. London: Swan Sonnenschein & Co.

Moss, P. (2012) *Early Childhood and Compulsory Education: Reconceptualising the Relationship*. London: Routledge.

Moss, P. and Petrie, P. (2002) *From Children's Services to Children's Spaces*. London: RoutledgeFalmer.

Moyles, J. (2015) 'Starting with play: Taking play seriously', in J. Moyles (ed,), *The Excellence of Play*, 4th edn. Maidenhead: Open University Press, pp. 14-24.

Nikiforidou, Z. (2017) 'The cotton wool child', in A. Owen (ed.), *Childhood Today*. London: Sage, pp. 11–22.

Norman, G. (2017) *The Sociology of Early Childhood: Critical Perspectives*. SAGE: ProQuest Ebook Central. Available at: http://ebookcentral.proquest.com/lib/bcu/detail.action?docID=4810400.

Piaget, J. (1951) *Play, Dreams and Imitation in Childhood*. London: Heinemann.

Play England (2023) *Play England 2023 Playday Report, Findings from the 2022 Survey*. Available at: www.playengland.org.uk (accessed 14 March 2024).

Play Scotland (2024) *Realising the Right to play*. Available at: www.playscotland.org/about/ (accessed 18 February 2024).

Play Wales (2024) *About Us*. Available at: https://play.wales (accessed 18 February 2024).

Rautio, P. and Winston, J. (2015) 'Things and children in play: Improvisation with language and matter', *Discourse: Studies in the Cultural Politics of Education*, 36 (1), 15–26.

Read, J. (2010) 'Gutter to garden: Historical discourses of risk in interventions in working class children's street play', *Children & Society*, 25, 421–34.

Read, J. (2015) 'Working with children: An integrated approach', in M. J. Kehily (ed.), *An Introduction to Childhood Studies*, 3rd edn. Maidenhead: Open University Press, pp. 135–53.

Roberts-Holmes, G. (2015) 'The "datafication" of early years pedagogy: "If the teaching is good, the data should be good and if there's bad teaching, there's bad data"', *Journal of Education Policy*, 30 (3), 302–15.

Solly, K. (2014) *Risk, Challenge and Adventure in the Early Years: A Practical Guide to Exploring and Extending Learning Outdoors*. London: Routledge.

Steedman, C. (1990) *Childhood, Culture and Class in Britain, Margaret McMillan 1860–1931*. London: Virago.

Taylor, A. (2013) *Reconfiguring the Natures of Childhood*. London: Routledge.

United Nations (1989) *Convention on the Rights of the Child*. Available at: www.unicef.org.uk/what-we-do/un-convention-child-rights/?sisearchengine=284&siproduct=Campaign_G_02_Our_Work&gad_source=1&gclid=EAIaIQobChMIyOmfl-uehAMV5qloCR3CXQLaEAAYASAAEgLXOPD_BwE (accessed 13 March 2024).

United Nations (2013) *General Comment No. 17*. Available at: www.playboard.org/wp-content/uploads/2023/02/UNCRC-General-Comment-17.pdf (accessed 4 March 2024).

Vygotsky, L.S. (1978) *Mind in Society: The Development of Higher Psychological Processes*. Cambridge, MA: Harvard University Press.

Wall, S. and Owen, K. (2021) 'Play in the great outdoors', in K. Owen (ed.), *Play in the Early Years*. London: Sage, pp. 75–94.

Wood, E. (2013) *Play, Learning and the Early Childhood Curriculum*, 3rd edn. London: Sage.

Chapter 9

Measuring Childhood: The Good, the Bad and the Ugly

Kate Irvine

Introduction

Over the last two decades, the language of 'standards', 'frameworks', 'targets', 'benchmarks' and 'baselines' has become a prominent and accepted way of talking about, viewing and understanding early childhood. The rise of these narratives to describe the quality of experiences of children in early education reflects how a measurement culture focused on numbers has come to dominate not only the lives of young children but also the practitioners who work with them. This chapter critically examines key features of this measurement culture and considers the tensions this creates between educators' responsibility to support the children they work with and the demands of accountability systems for data and results. It considers the implications this has for young children's educational experiences and the agency of Early Years educators to enact the practices that support all children to thrive in our settings.

The issues raised by the concepts, practice and implications of measurement are explored through three themes – The Good, the Bad and the Ugly – to help unpick the positive aspects of measurement and assessment that are intrinsic to the teaching and care of young children from the misinformation and unintended consequences which can distort early education and care. In response to the challenges raised, this chapter will also introduce evidence for alternative perspectives that will support practitioners to reflect on the diversity and complexity of children's learning and development, and to navigate a balanced and purposeful way forward in a quickly changing and expanding early educational landscape where regular and critical reflection is important.

Throughout the 20th and 21st centuries governments have increasingly taken a stronger interest in, and control of, education, including in Early Years with the introduction of standardised curriculum guidance and operational frameworks. The first standardised framework in England appeared in the 1990s following increasing pressure from three main cultural and political angles:

- Education of the masses should be undertaken for the benefit of the economy.
- Child-centred education is unpopular with those in privileged positions.
- Early educational settings should provide care and nurture in addition to that provided by the family. (Male and Palaioglogou, 2016)

The lens of social history helps educators to better understand the current policies and systems of early childhood and the challenges faced in navigating the best practices for children (Nutbrown and Clough, 2014). Unlike much of Europe where 4- and 5-year olds are firmly embedded in a child-centred and play-based early education system until they are 6 or 7, in England these Reception-aged children are usually in state-controlled primary schools, following state-prescribed reading programmes and measured against 17 government-mandated early learning goals. How did this fundamental rift in the concept of childhood happen? According to Aynsley-Green (2019), a cultural divide emerged between England and Europe in the 18th century, in which England rejected the theories of Rousseau and Froebel that view children as capable learners and value play, and embraced John Locke's 'tabula rasa', 'blank slate' perspective of the helpless child in need of instruction. The tension between these two fundamentally opposite paradigms of children and childhood is evident in England's current socio-cultural and political pressures on early childhood and the experiences of young children in Early Childhood Care and Education (ECEC) settings.

The dominance of this deficit view of the child in English ECEC policy together with five decades of neoliberal-driven early education policy (Moss and Cameron, 2020), has resulted in an Early Years system that is more concerned with controlling what children learn and the way this is delivered than the well-being of young children and families. Such concerns are not new. In the opening chapter of *Assessment in Early Childhood Settings* (2001), Margaret Carr identifies several assumptions about assessing young children's learning and development that operate to serve the system, not the child or the educator's professional practice. Carr references a model of 'convergent assessment' (Torrence and Pryor, 1998) that excludes the holistic and interdependent aspects of child development, reducing learning to a linear path of predetermined goals. In contrast Carr (2001) advocates a 'divergent view' where progress is identified in supporting the increasing complexities of the child's participation in the world. The continuing friction between these opposing models of the measurement of early childhood fuels renewed interest in the discourses on early childhood, as well as societal and political demands to review the status of early childhood and family life (Early Education and Childcare Coalition, 2024).

The importance of high-quality early education as being essential to reducing the impacts of social deprivation and financial poverty is increasingly coming to the attention of policy-makers. Longitudinal evidence from SureStart policy of the Labour Government 1997 to 2009 shows not only a positive impact on GSCE outcomes of children who attended these centres as under-fives, but also an economic saving on overall education spending (Carneiro et al., 2024). The social and political narratives of early childhood are now framed through a lens of an economic need for childcare and early learning with a growing acceptance across political divides of the value of high-quality provision. There is less consensus however about what this might look like and how to measure it.

The Good: Getting Measurement Right

Assessing children's development and learning is a necessary part of responsive high quality early education and care and as educators we are accountable to the children, families and societies we serve. Effective early childhood systems celebrate the child and family, their interests and development pathways within a multi-dimensional understanding of childhood and learning which enables educators to understand how best to support their progress.

> Assessment is all about reflecting on observations and other knowledge of the child to decide what it means in terms of the child's interests, current focus of learning ways of thinking, emotional response, and level of development. Quite simply assessment involves the practitioner making an informed judgement about the child's learning. (Moylett, 2022: 99)

What educators base those judgements on and how they do it can have far reaching implications both for the individual child and wider society. In the nursery or classroom, measuring childhood involves educators making two types of assessment: ongoing formative (often informal) assessment, and summative (snapshot) judgements. Formative assessment is an almost inevitable consequence of interacting with children and happens both in the moment and over time. Day to day reflection on the child's play, well-being and interactions enables educators to strengthen their understanding of the child. It informs educators about how to adjust nurturing care and experiences to foster the child's motivation and relationships, as well as specific knowledge and skills. Formative assessment can be messy; it requires the practitioner to connect to the child's play and thinking, and it requires positive relationships with parents and carers.

In contrast, summative assessment requires the educator to step back, draw upon the formative professional knowledge of the child, and make an overall judgement of development. Summative assessment also requires a judgement of how a child's individual development pathway compares to a standardised model. Done well, and with inclusion at its heart, high quality summative assessment supports educators to spot emerging needs and make any adaptations to practice needed to develop learning.

Purposeful measurement of early childhood is therefore dependent on the quality of the educator's knowledge of holistic child development across different areas of learning at different ages and stages, and the accuracy and inclusiveness of the standardised development frameworks used. 'Good' measurement of childhood should focus on what children can do, but when it is centred on what they cannot do or don't know, it creates a distraction from the complex developmental journeys that are required for children to thrive and learn. Many standardised frameworks of Early Years development are limited to able-bodied and neuro-typical development only. This restricts a broad understanding of all children, creating a deficit model of thinking about children with delays and differences focused on 'fixing' the child, rather than building-on their strengths, interests and needs (Murphy, 2022). Positive measurement starts with a celebration of the unique child and family, reflecting on the experiences, adaptations and adjustments to provision, communication and interactions that help them engage and learn. Purposeful assessment captures the child's strengths on a 'good day' (Murphy, 2022) and focuses on the experiences and adjustments that support the child to succeed rather than being about problems.

As well as the implications for children with learning delays and differences, measurement of early childhood must also consider how it supports children from all backgrounds and heritages. Standardised measures of childhood do not always support equality. The benchmarks for measuring all children in the western world are often based on the knowledge and accomplishment of middle-class white children, contributing to a deficit view of children from certain groups (Hamilton, 2021). This is illustrated by recent educational policy development in America and the United Kingdom which has been informed by the popular discourses of 'powerful knowledge' (Young, 2013; Young et al., 2014) and the ideas of 'cultural literacy' (Hirsch, 1983) reflecting a white-framed view of what and how children should learn. Concepts of 'powerful knowledge' are often referenced by neoliberal governments in educational accountability policy. It is a politically charged term, not just because it's obvious corollary is that any 'other knowledge' has less value, but also because it benefits the social groups with better access and experience of it (White, 2018). To be equitable, measurement models of childhood must include all children and be manifested in culturally sustaining practices that value and uphold each child's identity and lived experiences. Reflecting on the five key considerations of culturally sustaining pedagogies (Paris & Alim, 2017) can facilitate educators to identify and implement practices to support all children.

- An understanding of systemic inequalities.
- Acknowledgement that education can perpetuate inequality.
- Understand that the deficit approaches to education and assessment support inequality and that these can be countered by strengths-based approaches.
- Recognise that standard measures of achievement are often narrow.
- Pedagogy is based in respect and a relationships-approach to care and learning. (Cheruvu, 2020: 109)

Settings that follow the pedagogical tradition of Reggio Emilia, where early childhood education mirrors the children's own cultures and experiences are often a good place to see culturally sustaining practices. In 'Reggio approaches' children are trusted as capable agents of learning, with the child and educator co-constructing a curriculum that supports children to think for themselves (Dahlberg et al., 2013), contrasting starkly with educational systems focused on the performative acquisition of standardised knowledge and expectations. Child development is nuanced and cannot be easily distilled into meaningful data. Measurement of it requires a deep understanding of child development to avoid simplistic misinterpretation in educational systems that are increasingly dominated by commodification of children as units of data in league tables and charts (Bradbury, 2021).

Reflective Questions 9.1

The Role of the Educator

How are educators in your setting afforded opportunity to:

- Uphold, celebrate and build on the full range of development journeys and the experiences they need to thrive?
- Uphold, celebrate and build on individual histories and heritages?
- Reflect critically on standardised systems and frameworks?

The Bad: The Proliferation of the Measurement Culture in Early Childhood

Some standardised frameworks of child development in England have seen an increasingly formal slant in recent decades (Biesta 2013; Moss, 2020), a change which has occurred alongside increasing accountability and an inspection system that rewards compliance and punishes providers judged not to be achieving its goals (removing funding and shutting them down). This demand for gradings and league tables in education is a product of the neoliberal politics of our times. Neoliberalism (see Chapter 2) is a free-market philosophy that creates winners and losers in units of capital from every facet of society, including young children (Moss, 2019). In England, the statutory framework for Early Years has changed several times in the last 20 years, with vocabulary like 'curriculum' and 'knowledge' emphasised over play and development (Fisher, 2024). In a relatively short space of time, the narrative of Early Years in England has shifted significantly from one about children's holistic development, to a focus on the achievement of goals that demand that 4- and 5-year-olds can automatically recall number bonds, and lists of adult-led literacy outcomes that are limited to the acquisition of phonics (Department for Education, 2024c).

The drive for measuring childhood by formal outcomes has been accelerated by the revision of England's schools inspection framework with an emphasis on young children 'knowing and remembering more' (Ofsted, 2019). Pressure on educators to comply with this new ideology of Early Years has also been exerted by Ofsted's own 'research' reports such as *Bold Beginnings* with its conclusion that Reception classes should involve more structured learning (Ofsted, 2017). This rejection of the strong evidence on the value and importance of play (Gopnik, 2009; Hirsch-Pasek et al., 2009; Whitebread, 2012) is echoed today with the inspectorate's latest research reports that suggest that play in Reception classes, 'sometimes does no more than occupy children's time' (Ofsted, 2024b). By publishing these reports, the inspectorate, as a legal arbiter of quality in schools, presents itself as an authority on childhood and pedagogy, enabling it to enforce 'conformity to standards and position children and practitioners in particular ways' (Wood, 2019: 790). The direction of educational policy in the UK and USA of the last two decades reflects wider political leanings towards positivist approaches in education (Moss, 2019). Positivism is the pursuit of exact truths through data and fact. In education this frames young children as vessels to be filled with knowledge, and a prescribed way to do it, enabling measurement frameworks to function as 'normalising technologies' (Moss, 2019), changing not only the early experiences of children in settings but also society's perceptions of what childhood should be.

The school readiness agenda which now dominates narratives of childhood across English-speaking nations is measured not by children's well-being, motivation for learning or language development, but by statutory assessments of early reading and phonics. In England, outcomes for Reception-aged children even prescribe a minimum number of digraphs that a child must memorise (Department for Education, 2024b). This new agenda of early childhood measurement is reinforced by the government-validated phonics schemes which schools must follow, with prescriptive schedules of instruction and progression. Children who fail to keep up with the pace and speed of the programme are quickly identified as in need of remediation and given catch-up interventions. The word 'Play' is now missing from state-prescribed models and measures of early literacy and although phonics is an essential competency for reading fluency, so are the developmental experiences and skills acquired through play that build visual and auditory processing, and the motivation required to become joyful fluent readers. Reducing child development and learning to a series of steps and linear trajectories simply cannot account for the complexity of early childhood development and the lived experiences of children and families and therefore relying on these systems for formative or summative assessment will inevitably be limited or 'convergent' as Carr (2001) identified.

Positivist policies, which reduce education to empirical data, are manifested through the local and national comparisons of development data, Ofsted judgements and the international league tables of early childhood performance. These measures oversimplify child development, denying value and meaning to individual lived experiences (Pence, 2016; Urban, 2019). The impact of this is illustrated in the OECD *International Early Learning and Child Well-being Study* (IELS), also known as Baby PISA due to its global rankings similar to the OECD Programme for International Student Assessment (PISA) charts. These performance leagues have fuelled a political push to do well in some countries and the abandonment of holistic practices in early childhood policy (Urban, 2017). For the USA the move away from developmental practice in favour of formal outcomes resulted in some of the lowest IELS of any participating country (OECD, 2020).

The impact of the way we measure childhood has far reaching consequences. Far from being the instruments of social mobility they are upheld to be, positivist early education measures replicate inequality at all levels, from what and how the curriculum is provided and assessed through to the way educators are trained (Giroux, 2011). Cultural Capital theory (see Chapter 3) describes the proliferation of inequality by standardised education as a 'scholastic fallacy' because far from being the route to social equity, it actually damages the well-being and education of some children, with social theorists calling it an act of 'symbolic violence' against them (Bourdieu and Passeron, 1977). Cultural Capital acts as a limiting factor to the most disadvantaged when the educational system operates under the same cultural expectations (or the Doxa) of the dominant political classes of the society. This enables children born into the communities that prescribe the Doxa to naturally acquire the modes of behaviour and culture to achieve well in the curriculum, whilst presenting barriers to those with a different cultural experience. In early education this is evidenced in the wide gaps between the outcomes of 5-year-olds qualifying for free school meals and their more affluent peers, and also between global majority groups and their white peers (Department for Education, 2024a).

It is not just children's progress that can be limited by systems of measurement, educators are affected too. Reducing and limiting the prescribed narratives on early education restricts the practitioner's agency to understand a child's learning and development through alternative lenses and evidence bases (Moss, 2019). So, instead of a focus on the unique child and child development, discussions can become distorted into numbers and spreadsheets. Educators with salaries to be earned and rent to pay, in settings dependent on pleasing government inspectors for funding, have little choice but to adapt the provision and experience for children to meet the demands of the accountability criteria. The way we measure early childhood matters because it shapes the way we view young children and learning. The narrative on measuring early childhood, changing from one in which the young child is a natural and capable agent in learning through play, to one where the child requires explicit adult direction to acquire units of knowledge. Biesta (2013) calls this the 'learnification' of education. The challenge for educators is therefore how to carve a path through the 'learnification' of early childhood to satisfy statutory accountability requirements and also enable a celebratory, evidence-informed understanding of children's development and progress.

A way forward can be forged through a curriculum model based on values that start with the child and family, and on which adult intentions for the child flex collaboratively. In this model, the intersectionality of the child's and adult's curriculum is seen as an asset, an enriching opportunity to balance respect for the child's agency and interests in learning with ambition for each child's unique development and learning journey (Fisher, 2024).

Case Study 9.1

Building on EYFS: A Local Authority Response to Supporting Children and Educators in the 2020 Pandemic

Recognising that the city's 4- and 5-year-olds had missed most of their foundational Reception Year in schools, and developmental play both in and out of school, as a result of the Covid-19 lockdown, local authority advisors in Bristol, in collaboration with a leading national Early Years expert, created an initiative to support children and their teachers with their transition to Year

One and beyond. Called *Building on EYFS*, the initiative started with an informative briefing for school leaders on child development and learning. LA advisors channelled the enthusiasm for more support and pedagogical knowledge from school leaders and teachers, and the pandemic freedoms from the grip of inspection and statutory assessment into a collaborative online community of learning, facilitating ongoing reflection on children's unique development.

Throughout the project, LA advisors encouraged and enabled teachers to consider the research on strategies and pedagogies that best supported children's needs rather than just delivering the standardised outcomes. This involved regular online clusters of practitioners coming together with advisors and experts to discuss evidence on developmental needs, play and appropriate pedagogy, mirroring a praxeological and participatory approach to evaluating quality in early learning (Pascal and Bertram, 2018). As well as impacting positively on children's transition and learning, there was a transformative impact on teachers' competence and professional well-being in responding to children's learning needs. The project was instrumental in helping teachers navigate the tension between their own philosophies of education, the science of child development and external accountability pressures (Nicholson and Wilkins, 2024) – as the advisors explain, 'you can have good child-centred practice which doesn't lose sight of the fact that good numeracy skills, good oracy skills and strong writing skills are absolutely front and centre to the journey for the children. It is not a choice of one or the other' (Nicholson and Wilkins, 2024: 9).

The Ugly: Discrimination in Measurement

Models of early education and care in the western world are almost exclusively founded on white patriarchal views of children and learning (Salazar Perez, 2020) and by default they exclude generations-worth of knowledge and ways of being and thriving that the families of the global minority bring to our settings. Measures of early childhood with pre-planned flightpaths often reflect affluent, white-centric views of child development, which creates a narrative of groups being 'at risk' or 'falling behind' that disproportionally impacts the learning experiences of children from low-income and immigrant families (Cheruvu, 2020). The gaps between the outcomes of children from minoritised and under-served communities in the EYFS Profile national statistics (Department for Education, 2024a) and the rise of 'catch-up' interventions for them are testament to this. The impact however is uglier than just achievement data. When the cultural modes and languages of minoritised communities are not supported in the same way those of the affluent white population are, young children are denied an equal sense of belonging and learning which is harmful to their self-esteem, identity and well-being (Louis and Betteridge, 2024).

Unfortunately, a deficit view of some groups of children is deeply embedded in early education systems. In recent years dominant narratives in English education and the education inspectorate have appropriated the use of cultural capital theory in a new definition as, 'the essential knowledge that children need to prepare them for their future success' and 'introducing them to the best that has been thought and said' (Ofsted, 2024a). In this statement the inspectorate upholds a particular western-based cultural view of what is the 'best' that it wants pupils to access, which in turn negates efforts to value and celebrate every child's home culture (Wilson-Thomas and Brooks, 2024). Diminishing the value of individual cultural identities is also evident in the way wording that detailed the need for respect for diversity and to challenge inappropriate values, has disappeared from the English Early Years curriculum guidance (Tembo and Bateson, 2024). A line in a report by the English education inspectorate also reflects a diminished view of some young children, 'for children with fewer opportunities and experiences in their home lives there is little to tell' (Ofsted, 2024b).

Themes of race and cultural identity are particularly relevant to the persistence of the 'word-gap' narrative in the measurement of early education, despite the term being both outdated and debunked (Cushing and Snell, 2023). The infamous Hart and Risley (1995) study on which so much early language policy and measurement systems are based, upholds a prejudiced view of children from Black and minoritised heritages (Moore, 2004; Cushing and Snell, 2023) and the idea that children can 'catch-up' by being encouraged to modify their speech and language is misguided at best (Cushing and Snell, 2023). In educational systems that prioritise standard English above all else, young children and their families quickly learn to 'code-switch', keeping their educators happy on one hand, whilst doing their best to hang onto the cultural identities that are being systematically eradicated by educational accountability (Saavedra and Esquierdo, 2020). Measures of early childhood with limited views of success inherently omit the wider aspects that matter, with serious implications for children's progress, as well as their well-being and self-identity (Biesta, 2013; Fisher, 2024). This calls for critical reflection and action on race and racism by Early Years educators if inequality is to be addressed effectively (Early Years Coalition, 2021). To avoid this negative impact, educators need to do more than not be racist, 'being non-racist is a start but being anti-racist is what makes the difference for the children in our care' (Daniel, 2023: 89).

Becoming an anti-racist educator involves confronting the ugly systemic racism in measures of education and its impact on children's emotional well-being and educational achievement. This can be an uncomfortable process for educators, myself included, who are racialised as 'white', but embracing the discomfort is essential to a pathway to honest reflection and importantly, meaningful action. How we value and celebrate diversity and difference matters, because both social theory and the gaps in standardised achievement outcomes tells us that ignoring it harms children and their education. It is important to remember that 'children are not born with self-esteem' (Betteridge et al., 2024: 70) and that as educators we have a critical role in supporting children's self-image and confidence. It is not enough to simply see all children as equal; educators have a duty to question and address how standardised practices and interpretations of policy might unthinkingly or unknowingly, impact on each child in their care. 'No intent to harm cannot excuse the actual harm being perpetuated on black and ethnic minority children' (Daniel, 2023: 49). By adopting anti-racist practice educators are encouraged to explore and develop proactive experiences that 'allow children to understand and celebrate difference and form a positive sense of self' (Louis and Betteridge, 2024: 3).

Reflective Questions 9.2

Celebrating All Children

What steps can you take as an educator to:

- Create authentic opportunities for all children to become capable agents in their own learning and development?
- Capture and celebrate the unique strengths of all children and avoid the use of measures based on white-centric notions of achievement?
- Learn more about systemic racism in education and the steps you can take to become anti-racist in your practice?

Case Study 9.2

A Nursery Reflects and Acts on the Systemic Racism in Children's Books

As part of its quality improvement self-evaluation cycle, a busy city centre nursery wanted to understand more about how to best support its children with black and minoritised cultural heritages. As well as taking steps to build better partnerships with families, the setting's leaders also took their team on a reflective journey into anti-racism through the lens of hidden racism in many of the books in popular early childhood culture.

Using resources from www.tinytravels.co.uk and supported by a local Early Years anti-racist group of likeminded practitioners, the team learned more about how popular books, particularly books about colours, often depict black and brown as scary, dirty and revolting, and the damage this does to young children's identities and well-being. As part of their anti-racist journey the team educated themselves about systemic racism and the difference between overt and covert racism, and the historical harms and ramifications of slavery which are prevalent today. Leaders were careful to use regular supervision sessions to support individuals with their own personal journeys and well-being. With a deepened understanding of the unintentional harm that some books contain, the setting undertook an audit of all its books, removing those they found to be potentially damaging and making sure that there were plenty of books with positive representation of all the children and their families available. This progressed to reviewing all the resources available, from dolls and dressing up clothes, to the role play area and even resources used for loose parts play through an anti-racist lens. Leaders from this nursery now share their learning with others in local reflective forums.

Beyond Systems and Measures

This chapter has confronted many of the assumptions about systems for measurement and accountability that are commonplace in early education. Whilst it is true that educators work within the confines of statutory frameworks and assessments and in England, a statutory inspection framework too, there is still room for educators to exercise professional responsibility for ethical and well-informed practice. The' bad' and 'ugly' consequences of early childhood measurement are not inevitable, but they are often the result of narrow interpretation. Luckily, there are many positive and practical things every educator can do to disrupt and counter them. At the time of writing, the English early education system is facing increasing challenges with higher numbers of children living in poverty and identified with additional needs, after a decade of educational policy-making that has done little to improve outcomes for children from disadvantaged and minoritised groups (National Audit Office, 2024). The NAO study warns of the limitations of relying on academic measures, highlighting, 'the importance of wider outcomes, including well-being and developing softer skills' (National Audit Office, 2024: 2.4).

A good starting point in ethical application of standardised systems is to consider the statutory frameworks themselves in more detail. The four overarching principles of the English EYFS Framework itself – The Unique Child, Positive Relationships, Enabling Environments and Learning and Development – ask educators to be reflective, well informed and to develop practice starting from the child. This legally binding framework requires educators to 'consider the individual needs, interests, and development of each child in their care' (Department for Education, 2024b: 1.12) and states that children learn best when they are healthy, safe, secure, when their individual needs are met, and when they have positive relationships with the adults caring for them (Department for Education, 2024b: 3.1). By prioritising these, implementing and articulating them through inclusive and culturally sustaining pedagogies that value and uphold the lived experiences of the children and families they serve, educators can start to resist and disrupt any reductive interpretations.

There is scope for positive interpretation in England's Early Years assessment too. The *EYFS Profile Assessment Handbook* (Department for Education, 2024a) demands that judgements of children's attainment against the goals are assessed inclusively, and for educators to consider a child's attainment with any adaptations and reasonable adjustments in place, thereby minimising a deficit view of the child. The statutory handbook also requires educators to provide the 'culturally relevant experiences' that allow children to demonstrate what they can do, and to enable children whose first language is not English, to 'engage in activities in the security of their home language' (Department for Education, 2024a). It is therefore for educators to make sure that these positive aspects of measurement are enacted and upheld.

Unless children can experience joy and fulfilment in learning, their attention, motivation and inevitably their learning, will not be as positive as it could be. So as an antidote to systems that focus on performance and data, this chapter encourages educators to reflect on the conditions needed for all children to thrive and flourish. This means taking account of relationships, identities, children's engagement and involvement in their play and learning, building trust and agency for both the child and educator alike. What if we measured childhood by the opportunities for children to develop curiosity and get deeply involved in activities and learning? Even very young children have the capacity to concentrate deeply and for sustained periods of time when the activity is of their choosing, giving rise to the conditions for deep learning to take place (Stewart, 2022, in Moylett, 2022). Deep concentration supports positive dispositions such as persevering and resilience which in turn support children to explore their own ideas in their literal and imaginary worlds and make links between facts, concepts and ideas. Autonomy in learning also supports the development of intrinsic motivation which is linked to higher academic outcomes (Gottfried, 1990; Lemos and Verissimo, 2014). Supporting such learning behaviours is not a polemic act. Indeed, these behaviours are enshrined in the English *Early Years Statutory Framework* as the Characteristics of Effective Teaching and Learning (Department for Education, 2024b: 1.18) and when implemented through inclusive and anti-racist values they create opportunities for all children to thrive. Flourishing is an essential component of a fulfilled life at every stage – 'For children it includes a life in which joy, love and trust are nurtured and there is support to develop the skills to connect to, and interact with others experiencing both autonomy and empathy' (Pascal and Bertram, 2023: 306).

Just like engagement and involvement, supporting children's well-being is crucial to development and learning. An insecure child–teacher bond can reduce children's participation in collaborative learning and not only is a poor educator-child bond linked to lower outcomes, but failure to establish such relationships is also linked to learning difficulties when these children begin primary school (Commodari, 2013). It is therefore no surprise that a curriculum focused on emotional well-being and cognitive regulation is shown to be a protective factor against under-achievement (Pascal and Bertram, 2016). As early childhood provision expands in England there are calls for reforms to early childhood education and care to be centred around children's well-being and the experiences that support them to thrive (Fawcett Society, 2024).

Navigating the tensions between what can often be polarised positions in measuring early childhood is demanding, but there is scope and hope when we consider what really matters. 'We believe our attention in ECE (early childhood education) should now turn more fully to developing the conditions for children to flourish and feel fulfilment in their lives' (Pascal and Bertram, 2023: 1), and as Early Years educators we have the unique privilege of making that happen in our settings every day.

Further Reading

Measuring Childhood

If you would like to read more about the topics touched upon in this chapter, we recommend the following:

Aynsley-Green, A. (2019) *The British Betrayal of Childhood*. Abingdon: Routledge.

Based on the insight and experiences of a previous Children's Commissioner, this book is a compelling introduction to the disconnects between politics and public policy development, and the actions that might better support children and families living with poverty and disadvantage.

Biesta, G. J. J. (2013) *The Beautiful Risk of Education*. Boulder USA: Paradigm.

A thought-provoking book which explores how what are often presented as weaknesses in education by policy-makers, are also its strengths. An absorbing read.

Carr, M. (2001) *Assessment in Early Childhood Settings*. London: Sage.

Combining perspectives from psychology, sociology and education, Carr's book has become a seminal text on Early Years assessment, as relevant today as when it was first published over 20 years ago.

Nuxmalo, F. and Brown, C.P. (2020) *Disrupting and Countering Deficits in Early Childhood*. New York, Abingdon: Routledge.

A varied collection of discourses from global researchers on early education and care, curated through the lens of minoritised and under-served groups. Each chapter robustly challenges the deficit thinking that pathologises certain children and communities with practical solutions and advocacy for ethical and democratic educational practice.

References

Aynsley-Green, A. (2019) *The British Betrayal of Childhood*. Abingdon: Routledge.

Betteridge, H., Louis, S., and Pemberton, L. (2024) 'The voice of the child', in *Let's Talk About Race in the Early Years*. Abingdon: Routledge, pp. 54–74.

Biesta, G. J. J. (2013) *The Beautiful Risk of Education*. Boulder, USA: Paradigm.

Bradbury, A. (2021) *Ability, Inequality and Post-pandemic Schools*. Bristol: Bristol University Press.

Bourdieu, P. and Passeron J. J. (1977) *Reproduction in Society, Education and Culture*. London: Sage.

Carneiro, P., Cattan, S. and Ridpath, N. (2024) *The Short- and Medium-Term Impacts of Sure Start on Educational Outcomes*. London: Institute for Fiscal Studies.

Carr, M. (2001) *Assessment in Early Childhood Settings*. London: Sage.

Cheruvu, R. (2020) 'Disrupting standardised education through culturally sustaining pedagogies with young children', in F. Nuxmalo and C. P. Brown (eds), *Disrupting and Countering Deficits in Early Childhood*. New York, Abingdon: Routledge.

Commodari, E. (2013) 'Preschool teacher attachment, school readiness and risk of learning difficulties', *Early Childhood Research Quarterly*, 28 (1), 123–33.

Cushing, I. and Snell, J. (2023) 'The (white) ears of Ofsted: A raciolinguistic perspective on the listening practices of the schools inspectorate', *Language in Society*, 52 (3), 363–86.

Dahlberg, G., Moss, P. and Pence, B. (2013) *Beyond Quality in Early Childhood Education and Care: Languages of Evaluation*, 3rd edn. London: Routledge.

Daniel, V. (2023) *Anti-Racist Practice in the Early Years*. Routledge: Abingdon.

Department for Education (2021) *The Reading Framework*. Available at: www.gov.uk/government/publications/the-reading-framework-teaching-the-foundations-of-literacy (accessed 4 March 2025).

Department for Education (2024a) *Early Years Foundation Stage Profile Handbook*. Available at www.gov.uk/government/publications/early-years-foundation-stage-profile-handbook (accessed 4 March 2025).

Department for Education (2024b) *Early Years Foundation Stage Statutory Framework*. Available at: https://assets.publishing.service.gov.uk/media/65aa5e42ed27ca001327b2c7/EYFS_statutory_framework_for_group_and_school_based_providers.pdf (accessed 4 March 2025).

Department for Education (2024c) *Development Matters*. Available at: www.gov.uk/government/publications/development-matters--2 (accessed 2 August 2024).

Early Years Coalition (2021) *Birth to Five Matters*. Available at: https://birthto5matters.org.uk/wp-content/uploads/2021/03/Birthto5Matters-download.pdf (accessed 4 March 2025).

Early Education and Childcare Education Coalition (2024) *Rescue and Reform: A Manifesto to Transform Early Education and Childcare in England*. Available at Rescue&Reform+Manifesto+FINAL.pdf (accessed 21 March 2025)

Fawcett Society (2024) *Transforming Early Education and Care*: *Part 2*. Available at: www.fawcettsociety.org.uk/transforming-early-childhood-education-and-care-part-2 (accessed 4 March 2025).

Fisher, J. (2024) *Starting from the Child*. Maidenhead: Open University Press.

Giroux, H. (2011) *On Critical Pedagogy*. London: Continuum Publishing.

Gopnik, A. (2009) 'Alison Gopnik on young children's intelligence and the role of play', *National Institute of Early Education Research*, 1 April. Available at: https://nieer.org/research-library/alison-gopnik-young-childrens-intelligence-role-play (accessed 4 March 2025).

Gottfried, A. E. (1990) 'Academic intrinsic motivation in young elementary school children', *Journal of Educational Psychology*, 82 (3), 525–38.

Hamilton, P. (2021) *Diversity and Marginalisation in Childhood: A Guide for Inclusive Thinking*. London: Sage.

Hart, B. and Risley, T. R. (1995) *Meaningful Differences in the Everyday Experience of Young American Children*. London: Paul Brookes Publishing.

Hirsch, E. D. (1983) 'Cultural literacy', *American Scholar*, 52 (2), 159–69.

Hirsh-Pasek, K., Michnick Golinkoff, R., Berk, L. and Singer, D. (2009) *A Mandate for Playful Learning in Preschool: Reading the Evidence*. Oxford: Oxford University Press.

Lemos, M. and Verissimo, L. (2014) 'The relationships between intrinsic motivation, extrinsic motivation, and achievement, along elementary school', *Procedia Social and Behavioural Sciences*, 112 (7), 930–8.

Louis, S. and Betteridge, H. (2024) *Let's Talk About Race in the Early Years*. Abingdon: Routledge.

Male, T. and Palaiologou, I. (2016) 'Historical developments in policy for early childhood education and care', in I. Palaiologou (ed.), *The Early Years Foundation Stage: Theory and Practice*. London: Sage.

Moore, R. (2004) 'Cultural capital: Objective probability and the cultural arbitrary', *British Journal of Sociology of Education*, 25 (4), 445–56.

Moss, P. (2019) *Alternative Narratives in Early Childhood*. Abingdon: Routledge.

Moss. P. (2020) *Transforming Early Childhood in England*. London: UCL Press.

Moss, P. and Cameron, C. (2020) *Transforming Early Childhood in England. Towards a Democratic Education*. London: UCL Press.

Moylett, H. (ed.) (2022) *The Characteristics of Effective Early Learning*, 2nd edn. Maidenhead: Open University Press.

Murphy, K. (2022) *A Guide to SEND in the Early Years*. Bury: Featherstone.

National Audit Office (2024) *Improving Educational Outcomes for Disadvantaged Children*. Available at: www.nao.org.uk/wp-content/uploads/2024/07/improving-educational-outcomes-for-disadvantaged-children-1.pdf

Nicholson, P. M. and Wilkins, A. W. (2024) 'Intermediaries in local schooling landscapes: Policy enactment and partnership building during times of crisis', *Journal of Education Policy*, 1–22. doi: 10.1080/02680939.2024.2346140

Nutbrown, C. and Clough, P. (2014) *Early Childhood Education*. London: Sage.

Ofsted (2017) *Bold Beginnings*. Available at: www.gov.uk/government/publications/reception-curriculum-in-good-and-outstanding-primary-schools-bold-beginnings (accessed 4 March 2025).

Ofsted (2019) Education Inspection Framework 2019: inspecting the substance of education. Available at: https://www.gov.uk/government/consultations/education-inspection-framework-2019-inspecting-the-substance-of-education

Ofsted (2024a) *Best Start in Life Part 3: The 4 specific areas of learning*. Available at: www.gov.uk/government/publications/best-start-in-life-a-research-review-for-early-years/best-start-in-life-part-3-the-4-specific-areas-of-learning (accessed 4 March 2025).

Ofsted (2024b) *Strong Foundations in the First Years of School*. Available at www.gov.uk/government/publications/strong-foundations-in-the-first-years-of-school/strong-foundations-in-the-first-years-of-school (accessed 12 October 2024).

Organisation for Economic Co-operation and Development (OECD) (2020) *International Early Learning and Child Well-being Study*. Available at: www.oecd.org/en/about/projects/international-early-learning-and-child-well-being-study.html (accessed 4 March 2025).

Paris, D., and Alim, H. S. (2017) *Culturally Sustaining Pedagogies: Teaching and Learning for Justice in a Changing World*. London: Teachers College Press.

Pascal, P. and Bertram, T. (2016) *High Achieving White Working Class Boys Project*, Centre for Research in Early Childhood. Available at: www.crec.co.uk/hawwc-boys (accessed 4 March 2025).

Pascal, C. and Bertram, T. (2018) 'Effective early learning: a praxeological and participatory approach to evaluating and improving quality in early childhood education', *Revista da FAEEBA. Educação e Contemporaneidade*, 27(51), 105–120.

Pascal, P. and Bertram, T. (2023) 'Evidencing practice: Re-focusing on children's flourishing, fulfilment and wellbeing', *European Early Childhood Education Research Journal*, 31 (3), 305–10.

Pence, A. (2016) 'Baby PISA: Dangers that can arise when foundations shift', *Journal of Childhood Studies*, 41 (3), 54–8.

Salazar Perez, M. (2020) 'Dismantling racialised discourses in early childhood education and care', in F. Nuxmalo and C. P. Brown (eds), *Disrupting and Countering Deficits in Early Childhood*. New York, Abingdon: Routledge.

Saavedra, C. M. and Esquierdo, J. J. (2020) 'Platicas on disrupting language ideologies in the Borderlands', in F. Nuxmalo and C. P. Brown (eds), *Disrupting and Countering Deficits in Early Childhood*. New York, Abingdon: Routledge

Tembo, S., Bateson, S., (2024) 'Skin Deep: A review of early childhood policy affordances for anti-racist practice in England and Scotland', *Journal of Early Childhood Research 1–13*. London: Sage.

Torrance, H. and Pryor, J. (1998). *Investigating Formative Assessment: Teaching, Learning, and Assessment in the Classroom*. Buckingham: Open University Press.

Urban, M. (2017) 'We need meaningful, systematic evaluation, not a preschool PISA', *Global Education Review*, 4 (2), 18–24.

Urban, M. (2019) 'The shape of things to come and what to do about Tom and Mia: Interrogating the OECD's International Early Learning and Child Well-Being Study from an anti-colonialist perspective', *Policy Futures in Education*, 17 (1), 87–101.

White, J. (2018) 'The weakness of powerful knowledge', *London Review of Education*, 16 (2), 325–35.

Whitebread, D. (2012) *The Importance of Play*. Cambridge University.

Wilson-Thomas, J. and Brooks, R. J. (2024) 'Investigating Ofsted's inclusion of cultural capital in early years inspections', *British Journal of Sociology of Education*, 45 (3), 381–401.

Wood, E. (2019) 'Unbalanced and unbalancing acts in the Early Years Foundation Stage: A critical discourse analysis of policy-led evidence on teaching and play from the office for standards in education in England (Ofsted)', *Education 3–13*, 47 (7), 784–95.

Young, M. (2013) 'Overcoming the crisis in curriculum theory: A knowledge-based approach', *Journal of Curriculum Studies*, 45 (2), 101–19.

Young, M., Lambert, D., Roberts, C. and Roberts, M. (2014) *Knowledge and the Future School*. London: Bloomsbury.

Chapter 10

The Unique Child

Sarah Gillie, Rhiannon Packer and Sally Spruce

Introduction

This chapter explores the arguably hard-won rights of all children to be included in the context of such rights being defined, fought for and granted by powerful adults. Building on earlier chapters, we consider definitions of inclusion, how this is reflected in policy and what this means for children as individuals across the UK nations. As well as questioning related terminology, we reflect on key debates around inclusion versus integration and equality versus equity. Employing a case study approach, we discuss how children, and their families, are constructed by society and examine the compounding implications of this for children from diverse backgrounds and cultures and/or with learning differences or disabilities. We challenge a medicalised deficit model of difference that seems somehow to prevail in and beyond educational settings and contemplate the role of reflective practice and adopting a *funds of knowledge* (Moll, 2019) approach in valuing and celebrating diversity. In doing this, we ask you to consider the extent to which children's equal rights can be determined and met in macrosystems dominated by social, cultural and policy perspectives of adult ruling classes in the global north. We explore the tensions between ensuring access to educational opportunities and enabling every child to meet their potential. The first of four overarching principles of England's Early Years Foundation Stage (EYFS) (DfE, 2024: 7) appears to recognise children as successful rights-holders, discussed already in previous chapters:

> Every child is a **unique child**, who is constantly learning and can be resilient, capable, confident and self-assured.

From this EYFS guiding principle, it may seem reasonable to assume that within their respective and overlapping microsystems, all children are constructed as agentic individuals. However, as noted by Rix and Parry (2014), it is important to acknowledge tensions between the idea of each child as the focal point in their ecosystem and the risk of othering individual children through what might be considered supplemental, rather than inclusive, practice. To align with the principle of the Unique Child, policy expectations such as the EYFS (DfE, 2024) and SEND code of practice (DfE/DoH, 2015) significantly reflect the results of work developed nationally and internationally over decades, where professionals consult and collaborate (see, e.g., Moll, 2019; Messiou and Ainscow, 2020). This highlights the importance of gathering a full and respectful picture of interests, experiences, culture and priorities from children, and their families, to ensure inclusion.

Defining Inclusion in Education

Equal rights to education have been agreed internationally for over 75 years (UN, 1947) and for children specifically since the undersigning of the UNCRC (UN, 1989). Nevertheless, it is important to acknowledge how inclusion in education has been interpreted. In the UK context, use of the term often seems to reflect the long-established 'special' education focus of the Warnock Report (1978). Booth and Ainscow (1998: 2) contend that:

> Inclusion or exclusion are as much about participation and marginalisation in relation to race, class, gender, sexuality, poverty and unemployment as they are about traditional educational concerns with students categorised as low in attainment, disabled or deviant in behaviour.

A danger of the prevailing approach is that educational practices intended to guarantee *certain* children equal access may instead emphasise differences, unintentionally othering, rather than including. This reflects a deficit model of diversity, focusing on what children have not yet experienced or attained. This might be avoided through adopting a *funds of knowledge* (Moll, 2019) approach to practice, whereby settings and professionals work with families to build trust and develop a holistic understanding of individual children, as discussed in previous chapters. The *funds of knowledge* concept is derived from a recognition that a family's culture and practices develop from their daily lives. When educators are conscious of the rich experiences of children beyond the classroom, practice and provision can respect and build on existing knowledge and skills (Moll, 2019).

To align with Global Goal 4, Quality Education (UN, 2015), perspectives on inclusion need to 'ensure inclusive and equitable quality education and promote lifelong learning opportunities for all'. This builds on UNESCO's (2005: 15–16) position of inclusion in education as a process that identifies and works to remove barriers to ensure 'presence, participation and achievement' for *all* learners, with regard for individuals and groups at risk of 'marginalization, exclusion or underachievement'. This phrasing reflects the requirements of educators' professional standards across the UK's four nations to meet all children's needs (e.g. DfE, 2021) and arguably goes beyond requirements of the Equality Act 2010 to protect the rights of children with protected characteristics.

Knight et al. (2023) consider how educational inclusion is conceptualised in the policies of the four UK nations and they highlight requirements to remove barriers to learning juxtaposed with supplementary practices. Inclusion in these parallel but distinct systems is underpinned by the UNCRC – part of Wales's and Scotland's domestic laws – and, as noted, in mainland Britain by the Equality Act 2010. As discussed by Bešić (2020) from an international perspective, UK education-specific policy on inclusion is often limited to consideration of special educational needs and disability. In each case, terminology used implies that the provision some children need is *other* than 'ordinary' (DoE, 2020: 2) and 'additional to or different from' (DfE/DoH, 2015: 16). This perspective has been reported from educators. Rutherford (2016: 32) describes a 'dysconscious' ideology that inclusion is beyond the scope of 'regular' teachers, debatably an attitude that in itself leads to exclusion. Pratt (2016) additionally considers that the neoliberal practice of evaluating schools based on standardised assessment scores can result in a deficit model of pupil appraisal and cause teachers to value higher attaining children. Arguably, the decontextualised rating of 'academic' attainment as measured by standardised testing rejects the EYFS (DfE, 2024) construction of children as competent and confident individuals. A collaborative *funds of knowledge* and intersectional approach to education could avoid such discrimination. However, the above evidence indicates that there are still challenges for inclusive education in the UK.

Key Terminology

Beyond exploring the definition of inclusion, it is necessary to reflect on how inclusion is interpreted in relation to integration. Whilst both approaches aim for all children to learn and belong in mainstream provision, the expectation in integration is that the individual must adapt to the pre-existing composition of the classroom. This might apply equally across clubs and activities beyond schools. An inclusive approach, on the other hand, requires the environment to adapt and be flexible to meet the needs of the individual. Figure 10.1 is a visual illustration of what this might look like.

Figure 10.1 ▪ Inclusion vs Integration

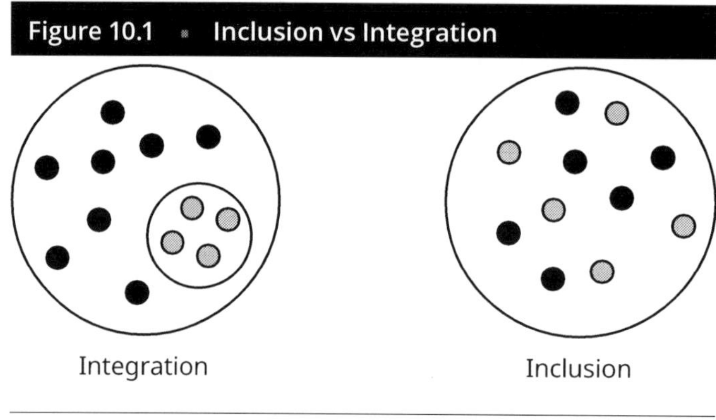

Source: adapted from Hehir et al., 2016

While both approaches can accommodate learners with different needs, integration can emphasise difference by providing additional, overt support to the learner. This highlights the additional needs of individuals within the educational environment. In adopting an inclusive approach, it is important to start with the belief that all children belong; they are different, will learn differently and should be able to engage fully with the curriculum. Educators are often expected to adapt an environment to meet the needs of learners with identified SEND, including in policy, for example England's SEND code of practice (DfE/DoH, 2015). Yet, from an inclusive perspective, the learning environment should be designed to enable *all* children. Working in this way expects and respects diversity, and recognises that individuals have different experiences, strengths and challenges. Often, schools' efforts to celebrate diversity include cultural events and supporting awareness raising, which provides a starting point for inclusion that can develop mutual respect and understanding. However, this arguably is simplistic and fails to recognise the nuances involved in being inclusive, the need to be reflective, and the need for ongoing consideration and dialogue with the learners involved.

Messiou and Ainscow (2020) highlight the value of co-construction where teachers discuss with children about how their lessons can be developed to respond positively to diversity. As with *funds of knowledge*, this *inclusive inquiry* requires a cultural change within the educational setting, with a reframing of perceived problems by identifying the barriers to participation and learning. It also requires a detailed analysis of practice to facilitate mutual reflection and sharing of ideas. However, there are challenges to effective implementation. At the local level these include the allocation of time and the acceptance of challenging views that may be difficult to implement. At a wider level there is a need for ongoing reflection to challenge preconceptions and ensure shared professional values and understanding. Such coherent implementation will promote a consistent and systematic approach to inclusive practice.

Questioning how the learning environment is organised to support all children requires an exploration of whether we are working in an equal or an equitable way. Debating issues of equality versus equity can lead to different outcomes for disadvantaged children. Ensuring equality for learners means that all children within a setting are given the same resources or opportunities. While this is beneficial, it often fails to address the specific needs of individuals. For example, providing all children with laptops to complete homework is not equitable if Wi-Fi access is not available to all learners. Ensuring equity recognises the differences in learners within a setting by providing the resources and opportunities so that all learners have the tools to achieve the same outcome. As noted, professional standards arguably require equitable practices of educators and other professionals working with children. However, the challenge is how best these values are aligned by practitioners in the interests of the learners and embedded in practice to authentically meet the needs of the 'unique child'.

Inclusion in Practice

Case study 10.1 illustrates the type of early support that may be available for learners across the UK, depending on the approach of the local authority or academy trust (England). Consider the extent to which the experiences of Amir and his parents reflect the co-productive multi-disciplinary approach and foregrounding of children's voice expected by international goals and national policy. While reading the case study consider what could have been done differently, and how your changes would affect Amir.

Case Study 10.1

Amir's Story

Amir's early years were during the Covid lockdown, and so he and his parents had little contact with family and friends. Both parents were concerned about his gross motor skills and speech development and raised this at his 2-year development review but were reassured when the health visitor suggested this was a result of limited opportunities to interact with other children and a wider social circle. Amir started at a local nursery but did not seem to settle or develop meaningful relationships with other children or adults, despite efforts to facilitate this. Growing concern about Amir's social and communication difficulties and meetings with Amir's parents led to the implementation of strategies at the nursery to support Amir. However, there was no change in Amir's progress and teachers at the nursery were at a loss as to how to provide the best support. Later consultation with the Local Authority's SEN advisory team agreed that Amir might benefit from attending the Early Intervention Base (EIB), linked to another local mainstream school. Practitioners made additional, detailed observations at nursery, and Amir's GP referred him to a clinical geneticist, who diagnosed DiGeorge syndrome.

Amir was invited to the EIB, which was established to provide initial early support on a temporary wraparound basis for young learners with diagnosed learning needs or whose parents and key workers have noticed communication delays. Teachers at the base work with the child and their keyworker to identify specific targets that are barriers to learning. Amir was assessed and observed by EIB staff in his mainstream nursery classroom and at the base to build a full picture of his support needs. His keyworker received training at the EIB, then set up and coordinated ongoing communication between the settings and parents to share Amir's strengths, interests, relevant support strategies and progress. This helped to ensure understanding and consistency. Because it serves schools across the local authority, the base has not been given a name, and there is no requirement to wear uniform. Pupils can choose to wear their own clothes or the uniform of their mainstream school. Children who would like to wear a specific colour on days they attend the base are invited to wear purple.

Amir was prescribed supportive footwear and could choose between purple boots from a shoe shop or NHS black boots. Although they were less supportive than the NHS boots, Amir's parents selected the purple boots because they were his favourite colour and would blend in at the EIB. They wanted to avoid him being regarded as 'special'. To help Amir become confident in his new boots, his keyworker drew on information from home that he loved squirrels and flying insects. Activities were planned at both settings for him to go into the playground and hunt for these, giving him opportunities to build muscle strength.

Analysis

To consider potential benefits or challenges of focusing on individual characteristics in cases such as Amir's, it can be helpful to apply a conceptual framework. Our discussion uses the familiar bioecological systems model (Bronfenbrenner and Morris, 2007) as a lens to recognise perspectives in practice, with Amir at the centre. Visualising the relationships in this way enables an evaluation of the extent to which practitioners and professionals engage, communicate and reflect a *funds of knowledge* approach in practice.

Figure 10.2 ■ Bronfenbrenner As Applied to Amir's Story

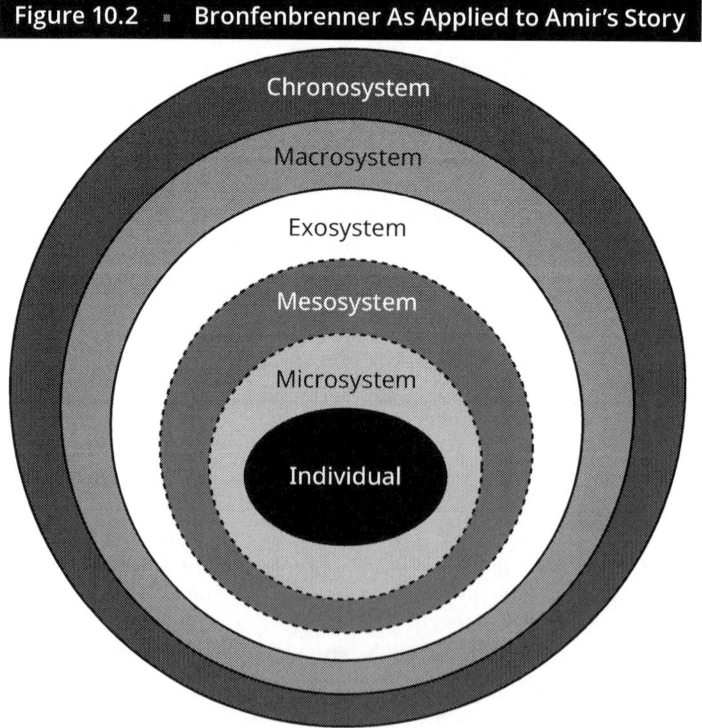

As can be seen in Figure 10.2, Bronfenbrenner's systems model can be applied to Amir at each different level:

- *Chronosystem* – changes over time for Amir, his family, practitioners, allied professional and settings
- *Macrosystem* – cultural values and societal norms related to inclusion and education
- *Exosystem* – e.g., external funding and staff training affecting implementation of policy in practice; factors impacting families' educational experiences, including parental employment
- *Mesosytem* – interactions between systems on Amir's behalf
- *Microsystem* – proximal processes – professional/practitioner interactions with Amir and his family at setting/service level
- *The individual* – Amir, the processes that affect him as a person and his changing contexts over time

Relationships

Amir's parents first raised concerns before he began nursery, at his 2-year health and development review. In this case, microsystemic interactions between his parents and the health visitor served to reassure the family. As discussed, policy assumes a model of co-production, where parents' knowledge and understanding of their children are valued. Amir's parents might have requested onward referral at this stage. Yet, as Vincent (2017) notes, intersecting factors such as class and/or ethnicity can heighten a power imbalance that means certain families may be reluctant to question professional judgement. Professionals have busy caseloads and may not have time to fully appreciate information shared by families or recognise potential reserve on the part of parents to push their point. You might question whether sufficient assessment of Amir as an individual was completed before attributing both speech and motor delays to the Covid lockdown, and what criteria may have prevented referral to investigate either at that stage. Perhaps, in this instance, Amir would have benefited from being perceived a unique child, rather than an assumption being made that, in common with many children at the time, any delays resulted from a lack of socialisation. Arguably, the construction of children as unique individuals can prevent uninformed suppositions that might result in setbacks.

Collaboration

The case study raises several questions related to inclusion and co-production. For example, recognising that a child may require additional educational support and ensuring the most appropriate means of providing it can be a challenge. In some instances, several professionals might be called upon to work together to advise and give guidance, known as interprofessional or multi-agency working. Promotion of effective collaboration by different agencies in agreeing the most appropriate support for the child has been at the forefront of government policy in the UK (see Knight et al., 2023) working on the premise that high-quality inclusive care and best outcomes come from a considered joined-up approach. However, central for such collaboration between professionals to work effectively is the need for clear communication between all parties involved (including parents and, where appropriate, the child) to ensure shared decision-making and opportunities for open reflections as a team. The case study highlights the importance of effective communication between the nursery setting, Amir's parents and the Local Authority's SEN advisory team in requesting support and guidance on how to best provide for Amir at the setting. Using the framework highlighted above, we can see interactions in Amir's microsystems, influenced by interprofessional agencies at the mesosystem level, have a direct impact upon Amir. For example, discussions between Amir's parents and the nursery setting, and subsequent collaborations with the EIB.

Children with a variety of needs require co-ordinated collaboration from a range of professionals to address developmental issues effectively (Castro-Kemp and Samuels, 2022). There are advantages to a cohesive multi-agency approach in addressing the needs of young children which include a holistic assessment of the child and an individualised response. In addition, continued multi-agency working can enable professionals to learn from each other, while recognising expertise and experience. Developing communities of practice and a systematic approach to educational provision for children with needs can enable early support and intervention, thus mitigating later difficulties. However, there are challenges in achieving this and tensions between what is considered in the best interest of the individual involved and what can be actioned in practice.

Challenges

Barriers to effective multi-agency working and collaboration include: initiating and maintaining relationships between professionals; a lack of information about what services are available; a lack of knowledge about the individual roles of multi-agency professionals and how they can interact and support each other; issues around confidentiality across practices/institutions; differences in terminology and a lack of a common language between practitioners; and the absence of effective liaison structures and guidelines (Van Dongen et al., 2019). Recognising each other's perspectives and establishing the context of support for the child can also present differences of opinion. Fundamental to ensuring effective collaboration is time. Professionals need time to begin working together to ensure that they have a common understanding of the context in which they are working and a shared language of communication. Bringing a keyworker from the nursery to work with Amir in the EIB gave an opportunity for practitioners at the nursery to tailor support while also upskilling the individual. Developing partnership working in this way allows for information to be cascaded to the setting while also setting up networks for professionals to communicate and share information with each other. However, it could also be argued that by moving Amir to the EIB, there is a sense of 'othering', in that the mainstream setting is unable to provide for Amir's needs and include him. This can be viewed from several perspectives, including his social and emotional development, with potential for longer term consequences.

Authentic Inclusion?

The case study evidences how agencies can interact and work together in partnership to support a child. However, consideration has not been given to hearing Amir's voice in the decisions that are being made for him. Person-centred planning is an approach adopted from health and social care professions designed to empower individuals with intellectual and developmental disabilities to co-construct and plan for their futures with key stakeholders. In an education context this can include working with learners (and their families) using resources such as one-page profiles, person-centred reviews and individualised education or learning plans and can be a powerful tool in ensuring that children are at the heart of decision-making. Developing these *funds of knowledge* allows for a more holistic presentation of the individual, with a greater understanding of the essential cultural practices and routines that are embedded in the daily practices and routines of families. Eliciting the voice or opinions of some children may be a challenge due to age or current communication skills, as outlined by Palikara et al. (2018). Indeed, they note that there is a lack of research on how the voices of learners are captured in a way that consistently informs a holistic, multi-disciplinary overview of a child's strengths and needs.

As well as addressing Amir's short-term needs, attention to what the future might hold also needs consideration. Longer term planning might occur as a result of the time spent at the EIB where practitioners consider what is best for Amir in terms of his educational journey. This should be done with Amir and his family and include all agencies involved in supporting Amir. While it is clear from the case study that Amir will need long term support, it is worth considering how this can be achieved inclusively, in a way that systems are structured to provide support without the requirement of additional or extra provision that is ordinarily available.

In reflecting on Amir's case study, we invite you to question whether it represents the 'unique child' approach, and if so, how. Using *inclusive inquiry* to question practice with the aim of strengthening approaches focuses on finding ways of including all children and involves a process of a three-phased action research process of planning, teaching and evaluating. Each phase requires dialogue between both practitioners and children. Drawing upon this approach facilitates consideration of whether the approach taken in the case study is truly inclusive and always in the individual's best interests, and any reasons for challenging the perspective. It is important to continually reflect on decisions that have been made to ensure that approaches are inclusive, involve both the learner and their family and are equitable. As the learner grows and develops, decisions that have been made need to be revisited, questioning whether they remain appropriate.

Reflective Questions 10.1

Addressing Inclusion

- What are some possible issues around the construction of a 'unique child'?
- What are some benefits and challenges of specialist provision?
- Can the child's voice be captured authentically?
- What might be the tensions between parental and professional perspectives, and how is this affected by constructing the child as a competent, agentic individual?

Conclusion

Practices such as *inclusive inquiry* or *funds of knowledge* arguably embody the expectations of legislation, national policy and professional guidelines, including the EYFS. Such practice also reflects the aims of the Sustainable Development Goals to address inequalities at local and system levels and provide quality education for all. However, as noted in the case study, at times, a family's concerns about their unique child's individual development may not be properly acted on, or heard, by busy professionals. This inconsistency in communication can also be seen between professionals who should be collaborating in each child's best interests (Van Dongen et al., 2019). If children as individuals are not directly involved when consultation occurs, resulting planning and provision can tend to focus on their needs as perceived by parents/carers and educators or other professionals. Such practice might not fully regard the welfare of individual children and could be enhanced by consulting and – importantly – authentically listening to children when considering targeted provision. Pressures on time and other resources can mean that professionals' decisions may be informed by overly generalised assumptions, such as attributing Amir's delays to Covid lockdowns.

On the other hand, viewing a child as 'unique' can problematise their learning and development in ways perhaps not anticipated by those involved in drafting guidance documents such as the EYFS. Issues of staffing and funding can lead to few opportunities for whole staff development, and/or limit the cascading of information from courses attended by individual staff members. There is a risk that such training is seen as targeted to specific key workers for particular children, or for distinct roles in inclusion and/or management. This can result in a notion that others employed in settings do not possess the knowledge or skills to work meaningfully with certain individuals or groups. Consider this in the context of supplemental rather than universal practice, discussed at the start of this chapter. We invite you to reflect on how such potential othering in children's earliest years might impact their feeling of belonging throughout, and beyond, their education. Including and celebrating children's diverse views, interests, experiences and culture might instead promote resilience, capability, confidence and self-assurance for lifelong learning.

Further Reading

The Unique Child

If you would like to read more about the topics touched upon in this chapter, we recommend the following:

Knight, C., Conn, C., Crick, T. and Brooks, S. (2023) 'Divergences in the framing of inclusive education across the UK: A four nations critical policy analysis', *Educational Review*, 77 (2), 495–511. https://doi.org/10.1080/00131911.2023.2222235.

This article explains how inclusion is viewed in the four UK nations, analysing the national legislation, policy documents and associated key resources. It's a useful way to begin to explore differences in perspectives and how this translates into practice.

MESH: Mapping Educational Specialist KnowHow. Available at: www.new.meshguides.org/what-is-mesh/.

This website offers a series of 'guides' and collates evidence-based research, useful information and resources to inform practitioners.

European Agency for Special Needs and Inclusive Education. Available at: www.european-agency.org.

This is a useful website for exploring how countries in Europe approach inclusive education. It includes qualitative and quantitative reports from different countries and comparative research.

Inclusive Education Resources and Toolkit. Available at: https://resourcecentre.savethechildren.net/pdf/IE-Resources-and-Tookit-final.pdf/.

This educator toolkit from Save the Children contains sections relevant to the topics covered in this chapter, along with related resources and activities.

References

Bešić, E. (2020) 'Intersectionality: A pathway towards inclusive education?', *Prospects*, 49, 111–122. https://doi.org/10.1007/s11125-020-09461-6

Booth, T. and Ainscow, M. (1998) *From Them to Us: An International Study of Inclusion in Education*. London: Routledge.

Bronfenbrenner, U. and Morris, P. (2007) 'The bioecological model of human development', in D. Kuhn and R. Siegler (eds), *Handbook of Child Psychology*, 6th edn. Hoboken: John Wiley & Sons, Inc, pp. 793–828.

Castro-Kemp, S. and Samuels, A. (2022) 'Working together: A review of cross-sector collaborative practices in provision for children with special educational needs and disabilities', *Research in Developmental Disabilities*, 120. https://doi.org/10.1016/j.ridd.2021.104127

Central Advisory Council for Education (1967) *Children and their Primary Schools: A Report of the Central Advisory Council for Education (England)*. London: Her Majesty's Stationery Office.

Department of Education (DfE) (2020) *Draft SEN Code of Practice*. Available at: www.education-ni.gov.uk/consultations/consultation-draft-sen-code-practice (accessed 10 March 2025).

Department for Education (DfE) (2021) *Teachers' Standards: Guidance for School Leaders, School Staff and Governing Bodies*. (July 2011, introduction updated June 2013, latest terminology update December 2021.) London: Department for Education.

Department for Education (DfE) (2024) *Early Years Foundation Stage Statutory Framework for Group and School-Based Providers*. Available at: www.gov.uk/government/publications/early-years-foundation-stage-framework--2 (accessed 10 March 2025).

Department for Education/Department of Health (DfE/DoH) (2015) *SEND Code of Practice: 0 to 25 Years Effective from 1 September 2014* (updated January 2015). London: Department for Education and Department of Health.

Hehir, T., Grindal, T., Freeman, B., Lamoreau, R., Borquaye, Y., and Burke, S. (2016) *A Summary of the Evidence on Inclusive Education*. Abt Associates. Available at: https://files.eric.ed.gov/fulltext/ED596134.pdf

Knight, C., Conn, C., Crick, T. and Brooks, S. (2023) 'Divergences in the framing of inclusive education across the UK: A four nations critical policy analysis', *Educational Review*, 77 (2), 495–511. https://doi.org/10.1080/00131911.2023.2222235

Messiou, K. and Ainscow, M. (2020) 'Inclusive inquiry: Student–teacher dialogue as a means of promoting inclusion in schools', *British Educational Research Journal*, 46 (3), 670–87. https://doi.org/10.1002/berj.3602

Moll, L. C. (2019) 'Elaborating funds of knowledge: Community-oriented practices in international contexts', *Literacy Research*, 68 (1), 130–8. https://doi.org/10.1177/2381336919870805

Palikara, O., Castro, S., Gaona, C. and Eirinaki, V. (2018) 'Capturing the voices of children in the education health and care plans: Are we there yet?', *Frontiers in Education*, 3. https://doi.org/10.3389/feduc.2018.00024

Pratt, N. (2016) 'Neoliberalism and the (internal) marketisation of primary school assessment in England', *British Educational Research Journal*, 45 (5), 890–905. https://doi.org/10.1002/berj.3233

Rix, J. and Parry, J. (2014) 'Without foundation: The EYFS framework and its creation of needs', in J. Moyles, J. Payler and J. Georgeson (eds), *Early Years Foundations: Meeting the Challenge*, 2nd edn. Maidenhead: Open University Press, pp. 203–14.

Rutherford, G. (2016) 'Questioning special needs-ism: Supporting student teachers in troubling and transforming understandings of human worth', *Teaching and Teacher Education*, 56, 127–37. https://doi.org/10.1016/j.tate.2016.02.009

United Nations (UN) (1947) *Universal Declaration of Human Rights*. Available at: www.un.org/en/about-us/universal-declaration-of-human-rights

United Nations (UN) (2015). *Transforming our world: the 2030 Agenda for Sustainable Development*. Available at https://www.refworld.org/legal/resolution/unga/2015/en/111816

United Nations Educational, Scientific and Cultural Organisation (UNESC) (2005) *Ensuring Access to Education for All*. Available at: https://unesdoc.unesco.org/ark:/48223/pf0000140224 (accessed 10 March 2025).

UN General Assembly (1989) *Convention on the Rights of the Child, 20 November 1989, United Nations, Treaty Series, vol. 1577*. Available at: www.unicef.org.uk/what-we-do/un-convention-child-rights/ (accessed 10 March 2025).

Van Dongen, T., Sabbe, B. and Glazemakers, I. (2019) 'Collaboration for children with complex needs: What adolescents, parents and practitioners tell us', *Journal of Child Health Care*, 24 (1), 19–32. https://doi.org/10.1177/1367493518823906

Vincent, C. (2017) '"The children have only got one education and you have to make sure it's a good one": Parenting and parent–school relations in a neoliberal age', *Gender and Education*, 29 (5), 541–57. https://doi.org/10.1080/09540253.2016.1274387

Warnock, H.M. (1978) *Report of the Committee of Enquiry into the Education of Handicapped Children and Young People (Cmnd. 7212)*. Available at: https://webarchive.nationalarchives.gov.uk/ukgwa/20101007182820/http:/sen.ttrb.ac.uk/attachments/21739b8e-5245-4709-b433-c14b08365634.pdf

Chapter 11

Taking Childhood Seriously: Listening, Agency and Advocacy

Timothy Clark and Rebecca Kingsley-Jones

Introduction

As many of the chapters in this collection have illustrated, constructions of childhood in the 21st century are frequently dominated by powerful adult voices including politicians, policy-makers and the media, who often frame children as under-developed, passive and in need of adult intervention (e.g. Ofsted, 2024). In response, some authors have highlighted concerns that this framing contributes to the 'marginalisation' of children in society (Wall, 2022) and creates a growing need for a response from adults who work with, and for, children. These competing perspectives frame an important debate regarding what it might mean for adults to prioritise taking children, and childhood, 'seriously' (Brooker, 2011). Dominant narratives in media and policy often reflect this seriousness through paternalistic developmental models where an uneven balance of power and agency is assumed to be an inevitable, and perhaps necessary, feature of society. This understanding indicates that adults should be 'in charge' because children need to be controlled and managed, to become well-mannered and productive adults. Conversely, some academics and professionals argue that the role of adults in taking childhood seriously should perhaps have more commonality with forms of activism, focusing on advocating for social justice, particularly in relation to children's rights and agency (Alanen, 2016). This understanding asserts that first and foremost adults should seek to empower, listen to and advocate for children.

With consideration of these competing understandings, and their related constructions of childhood, this chapter seeks to conclude this collection by exploring the potential role of adults in terms of agency and advocacy. The chapter begins by outlining and expanding on the idea of childism (Wall, 2022) as a lens for reflecting on the, seemingly taken for granted, positioning of children as subordinate to adults. It then seeks to explore listening, agency and advocacy as key terms in the context of discussions regarding contested notions of equality, rights and purpose. Finally, the chapter progresses to offer some reflections on the practical implications of these understandings for the role of adults in young children's lives.

Childism – Considering Context and Theory

Taking some time to reflect on the values and constructions of childhood highlighted throughout this book as a whole, will support you to begin to explore the nature and importance of the role of adults in young children's lives. The previous chapters have outlined childhood as being a socio-cultural construction (Chapter 1) increasingly framed in the global north by a wider neoliberal ideology (Chapter 2) which in turn shapes and defines dominant ideas of success and purpose (Chapter 3 and 5). As a result, important questions are posed about the status of children's rights in society (Chapter 4) and the rationale which underpins policy and practice, particularly in the education sector (Chapters 8 and 9). In her recent work framing the notion of 'slow pedagogy', Alison Clark captures these ideas particularly well, highlighting the increasingly rushed nature of a childhood driven by 'economic concern, rather than pedagogical or social' (2022: 9) and the growing need to pause to consider questions of purpose and destination.

When thinking about the role of the adult in early childhood, we might typically begin with influential pedagogical theorists such as Vygotsky and Bruner. The ideas of these key thinkers are important in understanding how young children learn, and highlight the significance of social context; however we could question whether they are often framed in a relatively reductionist or mechanistic fashion. Accompanied by the adoption of a construction of children as *becomings*, who need to be supported by a 'more knowledgeable' other to meet economically driven outcomes and ideas of 'readiness', there is often little space for questions about the nature of, and aspirations for, this social context itself. In short, to consider to what extent the role of adults in early childhood should be to get children 'ready' for society and to what extent it should be to model and influence a more inclusive and empowering society which acknowledges children first and foremost as social *beings*. As with many of the debates introduced throughout this book, thinking about this is not necessarily a case of needing to identify or argue one 'right' answer. Rather, through academic study we may seek to use theory to support critical consideration of an issue, and to unpick and explore dominant, unquestioned and 'hidden' assumptions. This process can have a powerful impact in terms of individual, and collective, thinking, reflection and practice.

In relation to the role of the adult, we propose here that Wall's (2022) conceptualisation of 'childism' offers a provocative, although potentially complex, starting point for thinking. Wall seeks to introduce the idea of childism as part of an argument that in western society our cultures, rights and relationships are built on a 'powerful', and seemingly unquestioned, 'bedrock of adultism' (Wall, 2022: 258). Constructed chiefly as 'developing adults', children are frequently positioned as passive objects of research, study and policy which, on a societal level, results in them being both disempowered and marginalised. In short, he argues that there is lots of important work and dialogue about children, which influences and shapes their lives, but too little of this actually prioritises children's views or children's rights. Yet, Wall suggests that whilst increasingly other social dimensions such as gender, class and race are recognised as significant in understanding social structures and social injustice, childhood is rarely considered in the same way. In research, and everyday practice, he argues that we do not generally question aspects of society in terms of their potential to limit or support children's rights and agency. So, in drawing parallels with the value of other advocacy movements including feminism and environmentalism, Wall proposes that the notion of 'childism' has the potential to offer a powerful lens for critical study of, and positive responses to, the 'marginalisation' of children across society. The idea of childism is outlined as requiring adults to begin by questioning the hidden 'social and political foundations' (Wall, 2022: 260) which children's lives are informed by – some of which have been illustrated by the examples explored in the chapters throughout this collection.

For childism then, taking childhood seriously is an important role, which requires adults to take positive action to reflect on and challenge the assumptions underpinning their normalised practices. As a result, the role of adults is potentially seen primarily through the lens of activism, advocacy and relationships, rather than education. This is not to devalue the importance of adults as educators but, amongst other things, to provoke consideration of the dominant ideas and structures which frame this.

That is to say, to question to what extent aspects of things like teaching practices, social policy and curriculum frameworks, may be premised on constructions of children as essentially being underdeveloped adults. However, as a potentially wide-reaching critique of society as a whole, the idea of childism also has the potential to seem complex, overwhelming and possibly even disheartening – this perhaps echoes concerns about anxiety relating to complex challenges in other movements such as environmentalism. For example, we might question the extent to which we can meaningfully challenge aspects of a national policy or statutory requirement. This may be particularly true for practitioners and students in the early childhood education and care (ECEC) sector who are often already directly impacted by the related limitations in value and status placed on their work with young children (Fairchild and Mikuska, 2021). The idea of childism may be a useful tool for analysing the impact of wider macrosystems, including politics and mass media, on young children's lives then, but in personal interactions, professional practice and academic study there may be a need to think about the smaller steps we can take. Illustrating this within the ECEC sector, Archer's (2022) research captures some powerful examples of what he frames as 'micro resistance', local acts of resistance in response to conflicts between pedagogical and ethical values and potentially problematic aspects of policies and requirements. In this vein, the next sections will draw on work, including Archer's, to provoke consideration of the relevance, and nature, of acts of listening, agency and advocacy as potentially positive responses to debates regarding the role of the adult and the marginalisation of children.

Reflective Questions 11.1

Thinking About 'Childism'

- What are your initial reactions to the argument that children are 'marginalised' in society? Does this argument seem helpful, overwhelming, provocative, sensationalising?
- Considering the idea of childism, can you identify any policies which might illustrate this marginalisation? For example, is it 'adultist' to require children to obtain adult permission to use the toilet at school? (Or to deny this permission.)
- Where does the section above begin to offer critical analysis in relation to this idea and debate by considering the merits and challenges associated with the viewpoints?

Beginning with Listening

In relation to the role of the adult, the act of listening is often cited as being one of the most important, but potentially misunderstood, actions that adults can take to value and empower children. Dictionary definitions of listening outline it as simply an act of 'hearing' and 'giving attention to', yet many argue that the intent and attitude of adults to this act is highly important. Brooker (2011: 140) outlines the difference between the 'somewhat benevolent gesture' of 'letting children have their say despite their assumed immaturity and ignorance' and the act of genuinely providing environments which value the child's voice. Similarly, Hart's (1992) relatively well-known 'ladder of participation' traces the steps from listening to children as 'tokenism' and 'decoration', through to listening as being participatory and informing 'shared decision making'. In many ways, this reflects the competing constructions of childhood and outlines the significance of adult attitudes in framing acts and interactions. In the act of listening, do we perceive that it is our role to 'allow' children to speak within an adult managed framework or are we genuinely interested in, and open to engaging with, the viewpoints we hear? From the perspective of childism, we might also reflect on how, and why, we differentiate between the nature of conversations with children and with other adults in the first place. These considerations frame interpretations of Articles 12 and 13 of the United Nations Conventions on the Rights of the Child (UNCRC, 1989), which set out children's rights to be heard and to have freedom of expression.

To expand on this understanding, we can also draw on the powerful and influential words of Carlina Rinaldi (2021), which are supported by her work in Reggio Emilia. Positioning listening as part of a participatory pedagogy, Rinaldi outlines eight thought provoking definitions of listening which draw on terms including 'sensitivity', 'curiosity', 'interest', 'emotion', 'relationships', 'enrichment' and perhaps most interestingly 'doubt'. For Rinaldi, genuine listening involves the suspension of judgements and prejudices which, through the lens of childism, we may argue should include our preconceived notions of the relative capability, authority and status of children and adults. Alongside this, Rinaldi draws on the idea of the 'hundred languages of children' to outline the importance of an understanding of listening as being about more than just spoken words. This point is particularly significant to debates about the role of the adult, for two reasons. Firstly, the use of spoken language itself may represent a societal barrier for children. One key challenge highlighted in relation to the notion of childism is that, unlike some other marginalised groups, it is not necessarily straightforward to empower very young children by facilitating for them to speak for themselves in existing public structures and forums (Wall, 2022). And secondly, it is important to note that marginalisation is also intersectional (as highlighted in Chapter 3), and as a result, a commitment to listening only to spoken language will still fail to fully include and represent all groups of children. For example, how do our approaches to listening include babies, children with special educational needs and disabilities, or children with English as an additional language?

In response to these concerns and the call for an inclusive, participatory and meaningful approach to listening to young children, the most prominent and accessible guide for adults arguably comes from Alison Clark and Peter Moss's development of the 'Mosaic Approach', which was introduced over 20 years ago (Clark and Moss, 2001). Conceptualised as a 'framework for listening' (Clark, 2017), the Mosaic Approach was developed as a participatory approach to conducting research *with* (rather than on) young children, to create an image and understanding of their lives and worlds. In doing so, it offers an insight for adults into key principles for listening, including adopting a multimodal approach and therefore seeking to value the 'hundred languages'. The approach offers clear and practical examples of how we might achieve this, including drawing on aspects of arts-based research to create opportunities for expression through acts including photography, map making and drawing. Seeking to position children as experts in their own lives, it could therefore be argued that the Mosaic Approach is a pioneering example of the type of practice Wall (2022) seeks to advocate through the application of the lens of childism.

Promoting Agency

Within the context of these understandings of listening, consideration of children's agency is particularly significant. As prominent voices in relation to the sociological study of childhood, James and Prout (2015: 4) have previously outlined the emergence of a 'new sociology of childhood', which increasingly recognises the construction of children as active social agents. The concept of agency itself centres on notions of intentionality, choice and free will and has long been the subject of significant philosophical debate. This debate reflects the potentially complex entanglement between social structures and individual choice (Varpanen, 2019), which leads some to question to what extent any of our decisions can ever be independent of the social structures and systems of meaning around us. In the context of listening, and of children's position in society however, perhaps the most important consideration within these structures is the relative difference between perceptions of children's and adults' agency. Tracing a historical shift in viewpoints on children's agency, James and Prout (2015: 154) cite a particularly extreme example of a piece of research in the 1980s which was criticised for 'anthropomorphising' children. In other words, 'naively' treating children as fully human, possessing agency, rights and an ability to contribute to understanding! However, Sirkko et al. (2019) argue that, despite progressions in understanding, children's position as social agents remains a complex matter, which calls for critical and contextual consideration. Whilst some may argue that 'common sense' indicates that the relative levels of maturity and vulnerability mean that children will inevitably have fewer opportunities than adults to make choices which impact on their lives, others highlight that this rationale often leads to this position becoming the status quo, regardless of the context. For example, does this argument mean that adults must impose behavioural 'rules' in educational contexts, without genuinely consulting with children? And might an alternative co-constructed approach to this offer enhanced social, educational and ethical value?

If agency has the potential for significant value for children but exists within the context of social structures where dominant understandings assume an inequality of power, then reflecting on, and responding to this imbalance should therefore be seen as our second key aspect for taking childhood seriously. Baker and Le Courtois (2022) argue that this is about adults seeking to enhance opportunities for children's sense of control, participation and the potential for deliberate, rather than automatic, action. However, they explain that this does not mean that adults simply need to take a laissez-faire approach and avoid any interference at all, but rather that they should view agency as relational and part of a wider ecosystem. They offer the interesting argument that the complexity of children's agency means that it is not necessarily something which should be seen as binary (i.e. either present or absent), but rather as something which is dynamic and can be 'thickened or thinned' through the nature of adult judgements, interventions and support. Accordingly, we might suggest that active, critical consideration of interactions with children through the understanding of childism, may support the kind of reflective practice which enables this 'thickening' of children's agency.

Case Study 11.1

Children's Participation in Schools Project

The Children's Participation in Schools Project is an Economic and Social Research Council (ESRC) funded research project, taking place across four universities. In keeping with the ideas about listening to children, supporting children's agency and reflecting on adults' responsibilities which are introduced in this chapter, the project aims to identify and establish teaching practices which embed young children's participative rights in classrooms and schools. This work focuses on pedagogy in Wales, with specific consideration of the experiences of 5–7-year-olds. It is significant in seeking to engage with the views of both children and adults, and to directly influence key structural aspects relating to agency and participation, including teacher training and educational policy. In doing so, it represents an example which aims to take these aspects of childhood seriously at both a micro and macro level. The project's website (https://childrens-participation.org/) provides some useful resources for further consideration. In particular, it may be useful to reflect on how the resources here aspire to value children's voices in academic publications and reports aimed at adults, but also offer a research vlog designed for children, which utilises Makaton to enhance its accessibility. The overarching aim of this project is to support the development of environments where 'children's voices are not only valued, but actively integrated'.

Advocating for Children

The final key consideration for this chapter is the idea of advocacy. Whilst agency may be understood as enabling and supporting children's opportunities for participation, voice and decision-making, advocacy is about seeking to champion and promote change across wider contexts. In relation to early childhood Mevawalla and Archer (2022: 1) conceptualise this as 'the proactive promotion or awareness-raising of a cause or barriers'. They highlight its relationship to, and overlap with, ideas of activism, but differentiate it on the basis that advocacy seeks to influence change from within systems and structures, whilst activism is characterised by resistance, for example through acts such as protest. Arguably, in relation to the ideas introduced here, both terms may be considered to have relevance and there are many examples in recent literature which outline the significance and role of resistance and activism in challenging dominant neoliberal narratives relating to early childhood, perhaps most notably the work of Peter Moss (see 2017, 2018). As highlighted earlier in the chapter Archer's (2022) research also captures understandings of early childhood education professionals who advocate for children by enacting aspects of 'micro-resistance' in their practice, to resist and challenge structures which conflict with professional and ethical values, in relation to aspects such as children's agency.

The act of advocacy has significance in relation to the ideas introduced in this chapter, as a process of proactive response to the marginalisation of children's voices and participation rights. Indeed, we might argue that this chapter, and this collection as a whole, seeks in part to engage in acts of advocacy by aiming to raise awareness of, and reflection on, 'alternative narratives' (Moss, 2018) in these areas. However, whilst predominantly framed as a positive act, it may be the case that in seeking to challenge and further a cause, advocacy will also involve elements of discomfort and conflict. Richardson et al. (2023: 7) reflect on experiences of advocacy in an ECEC context, framing this discomfort as 'necessary for transformative change' and echo our earlier suggestion of the risk of this feeling overwhelming. Challenging policies, practices or dominant understandings grounded in the 'bedrock of adultism' (Wall, 2022) to advocate for children's rights and agency inevitably carries potential for disagreement and also risks exposing the limitations in our own impact and influence. A final key point we would therefore add to this understanding, is that effective advocacy is entangled with ideas of effective leadership and acting as an agent for change. Firstly, this means seeing leadership as a process and practice, rather than a role, and seeking to influence and inspire others in relation to a common vision (Northouse, 2021). And secondly, in keeping with O'Sullivan and Sakr's (2022) helpful conceptualisation of 'social leadership in ECEC', it means aspiring to place social justice at the heart of our vision for settings, communities and ultimately society. Clearly this remains a significant task; however as a starting point it offers us a provocation for thinking about meaningful actions which may support the act of taking childhood seriously from a social justice, as opposed to purely developmental, perspective. Thus advocacy, as our final proposed aspect of taking childhood seriously, involves raising awareness, challenging and speaking out against inequality in relation to children's agency and voice.

Implications for Practice

This section aims to conclude this collection by offering some provocations and ideas relating to the role of adults in responding to the issues and debates which have been highlighted, and in taking childhood seriously. Considering the ideas of listening, agency and advocacy, it acknowledges that readers may be considering childhood from a wide range of contexts.

Honest Reflection of Our Own Assumptions

The idea of childism, it has been noted, invites us to challenge the assumptions underpinning our normalised practices. Given that these assumptions are likely to be firmly embedded throughout our entire lives, it can be challenging to identify them in our own behaviours. However, this should be our first step in recognising how we are 'positioning' children. Exactly what this looks like will vary depending on the nature of our interactions and roles, but some common areas of practice will be recognised below. In supporting children's agency, we will need to reflect on the purpose and quality of our practice and how we are achieving our role(s).

Interactions

Interactions where all parties work together to co-construct their understanding are recognised as valuable to quality of engagement and development of understanding. Pedagogies of playful engagement and child-led activity can support such interactions, with both children and adults taking the lead depending on the activity. However, the quality of this interaction may be difficult to maintain, unless we reflect on the implicit verbal and non-verbal messages that we are sending as adults. For example, we might recognise the value of open-ended questions, but is it always necessary to question at all? The practice of 'confirm, repeat, validate' is a common adult practice ['Yes, Jane, its red, well done'] and whilst it has a role when teaching specific subject knowledge, do we need to assert our dominance in this way in all interactions? If this seems a little overstated, imagine if the children responded to your ideas in this format!

Consider some of the questions below in the context of your interactions with children and reflect on how your practice positions the child and gives them agency over their own activity, learning and achievements:

- Are your interactions conversations or a set of queries?
- Do you share the same kind of information with the child as they do with you?
- Do you ask questions of a child that you would be happy for them to ask you? (e.g., how old are you?)
- In your interactions does the child have as much time to listen and think as they need? How do you know?

- Are there quiet times for thoughtfulness and consolidation? Sometimes words are not required.
- Do children set the topic of conversation as much as you do?
- At the end of your time with the child whose voice was heard most and whose ideas were most discussed?

Observations and Other Data Collection

We are likely to observe and collect data about children constantly as part of our professional role. This is an important part of developing our understanding and providing appropriate support. However, in gathering data we are changing our relationship with the child, positioning ourselves as 'more than' as we are holders of what constitutes a positive outcome to any activity.

As adults we would feel very uncomfortable if someone had notes and observations on us, especially if it was kept out of our reach and written in a language we could not understand, but in practice do we recognise that this is equally true whatever age people are?

Consider some of the questions below in the context of observation and other data collection with children and reflect on how your practice positions the child and gives them agency over their own learning and achievements:

- Do you take the time to explain all data collection to the child?
- Do you give the child opportunity to hear or comment on observations or other data collected?
- Do you record children's own choice of data?
- Do you show them all visual evidence and ask if it can be kept or shared with others (including friends and parents)?
- Is this data kept where children can access it, or are they able to access it when they ask?
- Do you erase a video/photo/ comment if a child asks you to?
- Can you identify ways to collect observations and data to include children and value their voice as part of that data?

Environments

How do our environments reflect the needs and interests of the children in our care? Children generally see spaces differently to adults. The way a chair tips, or a beanbag makes a noise, or the exciting patterns on the underside of a table are all learning opportunities. As adults we may struggle to see these. We have to 'hear' from the children to 'see' the environment they are in so that we can understand how we might achieve our role.

Consider how you can see the spaces from a child's point of view. Physically we can make ourselves shorter, but not smaller, so may fail to see the potential of a space. Watching how the children negotiate and use their spaces, asking them directly or using photos may offer more insight. In an Early Years setting children were asked to photograph their favourite places, and whilst the mud pit and climbing space were recognised, one of the most popular were the arms of a practitioner who 'gave the best cuddles'. Adults at the setting had not anticipated how children would value a person as a space!

Consider some of the questions below in the context of the environment you work in and reflect on how your practice positions the child and gives them agency over their own space:

- Do children have voice in decisions about colours/textures/furniture in the space?
- Does the way in which adults use the space differently implicitly imply a lack of agency for the child? (e.g., certain resources are kept out of reach of children, or adults have chairs and children sit on the floor. There may be reasons for these, but are these explained to the child?)
- Can children move furniture such as chairs or resources around the room as they require? (If they cannot, is this explained?)
- Can children choose what displays and spaces should look like?
- Are children involved in discussions about the admin of the day such as timetabling?

Leadership and Advocacy

Reflecting on our own assumptions and considering some of the key questions above will support the development of our own practice in relation to listening and agency. As highlighted in this chapter, moving beyond this, and seeking to advocate and initiate wider change will also require reflection on approaches to leading and influencing others. Consider some of the questions below in relation to creating opportunities to inform a wider culture which seeks to take childhood seriously:

- How can you create opportunities to model and demonstrate approaches which illustrate genuine listening and supports children's agency?
- What opportunities are there for constructive and in-depth reflection and debate within your communities of practice? Are meetings dominated by discussions about rotas or about children's rights?
- What opportunities are there for sharing provocations relating to listening and agency, including readings and research?
- How might engaging in the practice of research *with* children be used to inspire and provoke others to consider these topics?

Conclusion

Intending to act as provocation for reflection on the role of adults in early childhood, this chapter has introduced an exploration of some key considerations relating to the call to take childhood seriously (Brooker, 2011). It has argued that whilst dominant understandings of the role of the adult take a developmental perspective, exploration of this from a social justice perspective is also important. Framed by the introduction of Wall's (2022) concept of childism as promoting consideration of the marginalisation of children in society, the chapter has introduced understandings of listening, agency and advocacy as being particularly important in relation to informing the role of the adult. In doing so, it has introduced some ideas and possible implications for practice, which will have particular relevance if you are a student, graduate, practitioner and/or leader involved in early childhood. As part of this group of adults you have the potential to play a key role in informing future scholarship, policy and practice which will influence the lives of young children in our society. However, it is worth reiterating that in offering provocations relating to a range of debates, this chapter and this book as a whole, does not suggest that there will ever be one straightforward answer in relation to the issues raised. Its aim is to provoke reflection and to encourage you to continue to engage with a range of theoretical perspectives, to support the development of a critical mindset and well-informed approach when thinking about key issues relating to the lives of young children.

Further Reading

Listening, Agency and Advocacy

The following readings will support you to consider some of the key ideas which have been introduced in this chapter in further detail.

Clark, A. (2017) *Listening to Young Children: A Guide to Understanding and Using the Mosaic Approach*. London: Jessica Kingsley Publishers.

This popular title provides a comprehensive introduction to researching with, and listening to, children. It includes clear examples and illustrations of practical approaches to these practices.

Wall, J. (2022) 'From childhood studies to childism: Reconstructing the scholarly and social imaginations', *Children's Geographies*, 20 (3), 257–70.

Whilst this is a relatively complex journal article, given its central role in this chapter we have included it here with a view to encouraging engagement with 'primary' sources. It may be useful to look at it in the context of the introduction we've provided and to consider how key ideas are shared, particularly in the abstract, introduction and conclusion.

Chicken, S., Tur Porres, G., Mannay, D., Parnell, J. and Tyrie, J. (2024) 'Questioning "voice" and silen ce: Exploring creative and participatory approaches to researching with children through a Reggio Em ilian lens', *Qualitative Research*, 25 (1), 3–20.

This article links to the case study project in this chapter 'Children's Participation in Schools' and offers an exploration of a participatory approach to research with children.

References

Alanen, L. (2016) '"Intersectionality" and other challenges to theorizing childhood', *Childhood*, 23 (2), 157–61.

Archer, N. (2022) '"I have this subversive curriculum underneath": Narratives of micro resistance in early childhood education', *Journal of Early Childhood Research*, 20 (3), 431–45.

Baker, S. and Le Courtois, S. (2022) 'Agency, children's voice and adults' responsibility', *Education 3-13*, 50 (4), 435–8. doi: 10.1080/03004279.2022.2052234

Brooker, L. (2011) 'Taking children seriously: An alternative agenda for research?', *Journal of Early Childhood Research*, 9 (2), 137–49.

Clark, A. (2017) *Listening to Young Children: A Guide to Understanding and Using the Mosaic Approach*. London: Jessica Kingsley Publishers.

Clark, A. (2022) *Slow Knowledge and the Unhurried Child: Time for Slow Pedagogies in Early Childhood Education*. Abingdon: Taylor & Francis.

Clark, A. and Moss, P. (2001) *Listening to Young Children: The Mosaic Approach*. London: National Children's Bureau Enterprises.

Fairchild, N. and Mikuska, E. (2021) 'Emotional labor, ordinary affects, and the early childhood education and care worker', *Gender, Work & Organization*, 28 (3), 1177–90.

Hart, R. A. (1992) 'Children's participation: From tokenism to citizenship', *Innocenti Essay*, 4, 1–38.

James, A. and Prout, A. (eds) (2015) *Constructing and Reconstructing Childhood Contemporary Issues in the Sociological Study of Childhood*, 3rd edn. London: Routledge.

Mevawalla, Z. and Archer, N. (2022) *Advocacy and Activism in Early Childhood*. Oxford: Oxford University Press.

Moss, P. (2017) 'Power and resistance in early childhood education: From dominant discourse to democratic experimentalism', *Journal of Pedagogy*, 8 (1), 11–32.

Moss, P. (2018) *Alternative Narratives in Early Childhood: An Introduction for Students and Practitioners*. Abingdon: Routledge.

Northouse, P. G. (2021) *Leadership: Theory and Practice*. Thousand Oaks, CA: Sage Publications.

Ofsted (2024) *Early Years Inspection Handbook for Ofsted Registered Provision*. London: Crown Copyright.

O'Sullivan, J. and Sakr, M. (2022) *Social Leadership in Early Childhood Education and Care: An Introduction*. London: Bloomsbury Publishing.

Richardson, B., Powell, A., Johnston, L. and Langford, R. (2023) 'Reconceptualizing activism through a feminist care ethics in the Ontario (Canada) early childhood education context: Enacting caring activism', *Social Sciences*, 12 (2), 89.

Rinaldi, C. (2021) *In dialogue with Reggio Emilia: Listening, Researching and Learning*. New York: Routledge.

Sirkko, R., Kyrönlampi, T. and Puroila, A. M. (2019) 'Children's agency: Opportunities and constraints', *International Journal of Early Childhood*, 51, 283–300.

United Nations (1989) *Convention on the Rights of the Child*. Available at: www.unicef.org.uk/what-we-do/un-convention-child-rights

Varpanen, J. (2019) 'What is children's agency? A review of conceptualizations used in early childhood education research', *Educational Research Review*, 28 (2), 100288. doi:10.1016/j.edurev.2019.100288

Wall, J. (2022) 'From childhood studies to childism: Reconstructing the scholarly and social imaginations', *Children's Geographies*, 20 (3), 257–70.

INDEX

P

R

S

Zeitfracht Medien GmbH
Ferdinand-Jühlke-Straße 7
99095 Erfurt, Deutschland
produktsicherheit@kolibri360.de